GRAMMAR FOR LANGUAGE LEARNING

ELEMENTS of SUCCESS

ANNE M. EDIGER

LINDA LEE

2 B

OXFORD

UNIVERSITY PRESS

SHAPING learning TOGETHER

We would like to thank the following classes for piloting *Elements of Success*:

University of Delaware English Language Institute
Teacher: Kathleen Vodvarka
Students: Ahmad Alenzi, Bandar Manei Algahmdi, Fadi Mohammed Alhazmi, Abdel Rahman Atallah, Anna Kuzmina, Muhanna Sayer Aljuaid, Coulibaly Sita

ABC Adult School, Cerritos, CA
Teacher: Jenni Santamaria
Students: Gabriela A. Marquez Aguilar, Yijung Chen, Laura Gomez, Terry Hahn, EunKyung Lee, Subin Lee, Sunmin Lee, Jane Leelachat, Lilia Nunezuribe, Gina Olivar, Young Park, Seol Hee Seok, Kwang Mi Song

---

During the development of *Elements of Success*, we spoke with teachers and professionals who are passionate about teaching grammar. Their feedback led us to create *Elements of Success: Grammar for Language Learning*, a course that solves teaching challenges by presenting grammar clearly, simply, and completely. We would like to acknowledge the advice of teachers from
**USA • BRAZIL • CANADA • COSTA RICA • GUATEMALA • IRAN • JAPAN • MEXICO • OMAN • RUSSIA
SAUDI ARABIA • SOUTH KOREA • TUNISIA • TURKEY • UKRAINE • THE UNITED ARAB EMIRATES**

Mehmet Abi, Mentese Anatolian High School, Turkey; **Anna-Marie Aldaz**, Doña Ana Community College, NM; **Diana Allen**, Oakton Community College, IL; **Marjorie Allen**, Harper College, IL; **Mark Alves**, Montgomery College, Rockville, MD; **Kelly Arce**, College of Lake County, IL; **Irma Arencibia**, Union City Adult Learning Center, NJ; **Arlys Arnold**, University of Minnesota, MN; **Marcia Arthur**, Renton Technical College, WA; **Alexander Astor**, Hostos Community College, NY; **Chris Atkins**, CHICLE Language Institute, NC; **Karin Avila-John**, University of Dayton, OH; **Ümmet Aydan**, Karabuk University, Iran; **Fabiana Azurmendi**; **John Baker**, Wayne State University, MI; **Sepehr Bamdadnia**; **Terry Barakat**, Missouri State University, MO; **Marie Bareille**, Borough of Manhattan Community College, NY; **Eileen Barlow**, SUNY Albany, NY; **Denise Barnes**, Madison English as a Second Language School, WI; **Kitty Barrera**, University of Houston, TX; **Denise Barsotti**, EID Training Solutions, FL; **Maria Bauer**, El Camino College; **Christine Bauer-Ramazani**, Saint Michael's College, VT; **Jamie Beaton**, Boston University, MA; **Gena Bennett**, Cornerstone University, NE; **Linda Berendsen**, Oakton Community College, IL; **Carol Berteotti**; **Grace Bishop**, Houston Community College, TX; **Perrin Blackman**, University of Kansas, KS; **Mara Blake-Ward**, Drexel University English Language Center, PA; **Melissa Bloom**, ELS; **Alexander Bochkov**, ELS, WA; **Marcel Bolintiam**, University of Colorado, CO; **Nancy Boyer**, Golden West College, CA; **T. Bredl**, The New School, NY; **Rosemarie Brefeld**, University of Missouri, MO; **Leticia Brereton**, Kingsborough Community College, NY; **Deborah Brooks**, Laney College, CA; **Kevin Brown**, Irvine Community College, CA; **Rachel Brown**, Center for Literacy, NY; **Tracey Brown**, Parkland College, IL; **Crystal Brunelli**, Tokyo Jogakkan Middle and High School, Japan; **Tom Burger**, Harris County Department of Education, TX; **Thom Burns**, Tokyo English Specialists College, Japan; **Caralyn Bushey**, Maryland English Institute, MD; **Gül Büyü**, Ankara University, Turkey; **Scott Callaway**, Community Family Centers, TX; **Adele Camus**, George Mason University, VA; **Nigel Caplan**, University of Delaware, DE; **Nathan Carr**, California State University, CA; **Christina Cavage**, Savannah College of Art and Design,

GA; **Neslihan Çelik**, Özdemir Sabancı Emirgan Anatolian High School, Turkey; **Shelley Cetin**, Kansas City Kansas Community College, KS; **Hoi Yuen Chan**, University of Wyoming, WY; **Esther Chase**, Berwyn Public Library, IL; **Suzidilara Çınar**, Yıldırım Beyazıt University, Turkey; **Diane Cirino**, SUNY Suffolk, NY; **Cara Codney**, Emporia State University, KS; **Catherine Coleman**, Irvine Valley College, CA; **Jenelle Collins**, Washington High School, AZ; **Greg Conner**, Orange Coast Community College, CA; **Ewelina Cope**, The Language Company, PA; **Jorge Cordon**, Colegio Montessori, Guatemala; **Kathy Cornman**, University of Michigan, MI; **Barry Costa**, Castro Valley Adult and Career Education, CA; **Cathy Costa**, Edmonds Community College, WA; **Julia Cote**, Houston Community College NE, TX; **Eileen Cotter**, Montgomery College, MD; **Winnie Cragg**, Mukogawa Fort Wright Institute, WA; **Douglas Craig**, Diplomatic Language Services, VA; **Elizabeth Craig**, Savannah College of Art and Design, GA; **Ann Telfair Cramer**, Florida State College at Jacksonville, FL; **R. M. Crocker**, Plano Independent School District, TX; **Virginia Cu**, Queens Adult Learning Center, CT; **Marc L. Cummings**, Jefferson Community and Technical College, KY; **Roberta Cummings**, Trinidad Correctional Facility, CO; **David Dahnke**, Lone Star College-North Harris, TX; **Debra Daise**, University of Denver, CO; **L. Dalgish**, Concordia College, NY; **Kristen Danek**, North Carolina State University, NC; **April Darnell**, University of Dayton, OH; **Heather Davis**, OISE Boston, MA; **Megan Davis**, Embassy English, NY; **Jeanne de Simon**, University of West Florida, FL; **Renee Delatizky**, Boston University, MA; **Sonia Delgadillo**, Sierra Community College, NY; **Gözde Burcu Demirkul**, Orkunoglu College, Turkey; **Stella L. Dennis**, Longfellow Middle School, NY; **Mary Diamond**, Auburn University, AL; **Emily Dibala**, Bucks County Community College, PA; **Cynthia Dieckmann**, West Chester East High School, PA; **Michelle DiGiorno**, Richland College, TX; **Luciana Diniz**, Portland Community College, OR; **Özgür Dirik**, Yıldız Technical University, Turkey; **Marta O. Dmytrenko-Arab**, Wayne State University, MI; **Margie Domingo**, Intergenerational Learning Community, CO; **Kellie Draheim**, Hongik University, South Korea; **Ilke Buyuk Duman**, Sehir University, Turkey; **Jennifer Eick-Magan**, Prairie State College, IL;

Juliet Emanuel, Borough of Manhattan Community College, NY; **David Emery**, Kaplan International Center, CA; **Patricia Emery**, Jefferson County Literacy Council, WI; **Eva Engelhard**, Kaplan International Center, WA; **Nancey Epperson**, Harry S. Truman College, IL; **Ken Estep**, Mentor Language Institute, CA; **Cindy Etter**, University of Washington, WA; **Rhoda Fagerland**, St. Cloud State University, MN; **Anrisa Fannin**, Diablo Valley College, CA; **Marie Farnsworth**, Union Public Schools, OK; **Jim Fenton**, Bluegrass Community Technical College, KY; **Lynn Filazzola**, Nassau BOCES Adult Learning Center, NY; **Christine Finck**, Stennis Language Lab; **Mary Fischer**, Texas Intensive English Program, TX; **Mark Fisher**, Lone Star College, TX; **Celeste Flowers**, University of Central Arkansas, AR; **Elizabeth Foss**, Washtenaw Community College, MI; **Jacqueline Fredericks**, West Contra Costa Adult Education, CA; **Patricia Gairaud**, San Jose City College, CA; **Patricia Gallo**, Delaware Technical Community College, DE; **Beverly Gandall**, Coastline Community College, CA; **Alberto Garrido**, The Community College of Baltimore County, MD; **Debbie Garza**, Park University, MO; **Karen Gelender**, Castro Valley Adult and Career Education, CA; **Ronald Gentry**, Suenos Compartidos, Mexico; **Kathie Madden Gerecke**, North Shore Community College, MA; **Jeanne Gibson**, Colorado State University, CO; **A. Elizabeth Gilfillan**, Houston Community College, TX; **Melanie Gobert**, The Higher Colleges of Technology, UAE; **Ellen Goldman**, West Valley College, CA; **Jo Golub**, Houston Community College, TX; **Maria Renata Gonzalez**, Colegio Montessori, Guatemala; **Elisabeth Goodwin**, Pima Community College, AZ; **John Graney**, Santa Fe College, FL; **Karina Greene**, CUNY in the Heights, NY; **Katherine Gregorio**, CASA de Maryland, MD; **Claudia Gronsbell**, La Escuelita, NY; **Yvonne Groseil**, Hunter College, NY; **Alejandra Gutierrez**, Hartnell College, CA; **Eugene Guza**, North Orange County Community College District, CA; **Mary Beth Haan**, El Paso Community College, TX; **Elizabeth Haga**, State College of Florida, FL; **Saeede Haghi**, Ozyegin University, Turkey; **Laura Halvorson**, Lorain County Community College, OH; **Nancy Hamadou**, Pima Community College, AZ; **Kerri Hamberg**, Brookline Community and Adult Education, MA;

ii

Katia Hameg, L'Envol Des Langues, Québec, Canada; **Sunsook Han**, King Abdulaziz University, Saudi Arabia; **Aniko Harrier**, Valencia College, FL; **James M. Harris**, University of Texas-Pan American, TX; **Susan Haskins-Doloff**, Pratt Institute, NY; **Olcay Havalan**, Bursa Anadolu Erkek Lisesi, Turkey; **Marla Heath**, Sacred Heart University, CT; **Jean Hendrickson**, SUNY Stony Brook, NY; **Tracy Henninger-Willey**, Lane Community College, OR; **Emily Herrick**, University of Nebraska, NE; **Jan Hinson**, Carson Newman University, TN; **Lisa Hockstein**, SUNY Westchester, NY; **Sarah Hodge**, Defense Language Institute, TX; **Kristie Hofelich**, Brown Mackie College, KY; **Harry Holden**, North Lake Community College, TX; **Elke Holtz**, Escuela Sierra Nevada, Mexico; **Hirofumi Hosokawa**, Fukuoka Jo Gakuin University, Japan; **Elisa Hunt**, North Dakota State University, ND; **Lutfi Hussein**, Mesa Community College, AZ; **Curt Hutchison**, Leeward Community College, HI; **Elizabeth Iannotti**, LaGuardia Community College, NY; **Barbara Inerfeld**, Rutgers University, NJ; **Julie Ingber**, Columbia University, NY; **Debbie Janysek**, Victoria College, TX; **Joan Jarrett**, Feather River College, CA; **Shawn Jarvis**, St. Cloud State University, MN; **Justin Jernigan**, Georgia Gwinnett College, GA; **Melanie Jipping**, Tokyo International University of America, OR; **Catherine Jones**, Excellent Interpreting, CO; **Jackie Jones**, Wayne State University, MI; **Irene Juzkiw**, University of Missouri, MO; **Aysegul Liman Kaban**, Gedik University, Turkey; **Vivian Kahn**, Long Island University, NY; **Eleanor Kamataris**, Harris Middle School, TX; **Gursharan Kandola**, University of Houston, TX; **Emily Kaney**, Northern Michigan University, MI; **Krystal Kaplan**, Pace University, NY; **Linda Karlen**, Oakton Community College, IL; **Katherine Katsenis**, Lyceum Tutorial Services, LLC, CA; **Martha Kehl**, Ohlone College, CA; **Scott Keller**, Literacy Volunteers of Leon County, FL; **Robert Kelso**, Miami Dade College, FL; **Alicia N. Kenter**, City College of San Francisco, CA; **Paul Kern**, Green River Community College, WA; **Mignon Kery**, H-B Woodlawn Secondary Program, VA; **Candace Khanna**, Laney College, CA; **Joy Kidstry**, University of Phoenix, AZ; **Cynthia Kilpatrick**, The University of Texas at Arlington, TX; **Doe-Hyung Kim**, Georgia Gwinnett College, GA; **Kindra Kinyon**, Los Angeles Trade-Technical College, CA; **James Kirchner**, Macomb Community College, MI; **Renee La Rue**, Lone Star College-Montgomery, TX; **Marjorie Labe**, Montgomery County Community College, PA; **Peter LaFontaine**, Alexandria Adult Learning Center, VA; **Katie Land**, St. Giles International, Canada; **Renee Lane**, Oxnard Adult School, CA; **Alan Lanes**, The Higher Colleges of Technology, UAE; **Stephanie Lange**, Cuyamaca College, CA; **T. Jonathan Lathers**, Macomb Community College, MI; **Margaret Vera Layton**, University of Nevada, NV; **Susan Leckart**, Middlesex County College, NJ; **Suzanne Leduc**, The New America College, CO; **Judy Lee**, Central Connecticut State University, CT; **Joy Leventhal**, Cuyahoga Community College, OH; **Helen Lin**, University of Florida, FL; **Amy Lindstrom**, University of New Mexico, NM; **Gytis Liulevicius**, Wellstone International High School, MN; **Robyn Lockwood**, Stanford University, CA; **Victoria Loeb**, Houston Community College, TX; **Janet Long**, University of Missouri, MO; **Roland Lopez**, Santa Monica College, CA; **Alexandra Lowe**, Westchester Community College (SUNY), NY; **Mary Lozano**, Pierce College, CA; **Gail Lugo**, Trine University, IN; **Joanna Luper**, Liberty University, VA; **Jaime Lyon**, University of Northern Iowa, IA; **Doris Macdonald**, Northern Illinois University, IL; **Bridgette MacFarlane**, Brewster Technical Center, FL; **Kevin Mackie**, Austin Community College, TX; **Mercedes Martinez**, Global Language Institute, MN; **Tetiana Maslova**, Kyiv Polytechnic Institute, Ukraine; **Terry Masters**, American School for Women and Children, OH; **Maryann Matheny**, Campbellsville University, KY; **Jennifer Maxwell**, Daytona State College, FL; **Halina Mazurak**, Cleveland State University, OH; **Susan McAlister**, University of Houston, TX; **Luke McCarthy**, Norwalk Community College, CT; **Marlo McClurg**, Cosumnes River College, CA; **Deb McCormick**, Doña Ana Community College, NM; **Chris McDaniel**, Yale University, CT; **Bridget McDonald**, Independent Learning Services, MA; **Deborah McGraw**, Syracuse University, NY; **Lisa McHenry**, GEOS Languages Plus, CA; **Deirdre McMurtry**, University of Nebraska at Omaha, NE; **Aziah McNamara**, Kansas State University, KS; **Ellen Measday**, Middlesex County College, NJ; **Nancy Megarity**, Collin College, TX; **Diane Mehegan**, Harvard University, MA; **Michelle Merritt**, Harmony School of Innovation, TX; **Nila Middleton**, Lone Star College-Cypress, TX; **Brandon Mills**, ELS Language Center, ND; **Malgorzata Moll**, St. Louis Community College, MO; **Kathleen Molzan**, Cuyahoga Community College, OH; **Adrienne Monaco**, Erie 1 BOCES, NY; **Beth Montag**, University of Nebraska at Kearney, NE; **Elisabete Montero**, Val Hala escola de idiomas, Brazil; **Do Sik Moon**, Hanyang Cyber University, South Korea; **Diane Mora**, Johnson County Community College, KS; **Micheline Morena**, College of the Desert, CA; **Gloria Munson**, University of Texas, TX; **Gino Muzzatti**, Santa Rosa Junior College, CA; **Myo Myint**, Mission College, CA; **Kathy Najafi**, Houston Community College, TX; **Patricia Nation**, Miami Dade College, FL; **Elizabeth Neblett**, Union County College, NJ; **Karen Nelson**, Pittsburgh State University, PA; **Marley Nelson**, English Center USA, IL; **Anastasia Nizamova**, New York University, NY; **Sharon Nunn**, Englishdom; **Karla Odenwald**, Boston University, MA; **Tina O'Donnell**, Language Center International, MI; **Ann O'Driscoll**, Southern Oregon University, OR; **Donna Ogle**, Arkansas Tech University, AR; **Nastaran Ohadi**, Ganjineh Danesh, Iran; **Iris Oriaro**, Arkansas State University, AR; **Fernanda Ortiz**, University of Arizona, AZ; **Susan Osuch**, Englishworks, Inc., TX; **Kris Oswald**, Kansas State University, KS; **Stephanie Owens**, ELS, CT; **Gorkem Oztur**, Özel Manavgat Bahcesehir Anadolu Lisesi, Turkey; **Ümit Öztürk**, İzmir-Torbalı Anatolian Teacher Training High School, Turkey; **Murat Ozudogru**, Maltepe University, Turkey; **Marilyn Padgett**, Calhoun Middle School, NY; **Bilsev Pastakkaya**, Yalova University, Turkey; **Angela Pastore-Nikitenko**, Embassy English, CA; **Wendy Patriquin**, Parkland College, IL; **Irina Patten**, Lone Star College, TX; **Jennifer Paz**, Auburn University, AL; **Mary Peacock**, Richland College, TX; **Randi Lynn Peerlman**, Texas A&M University, TX; **Jeanne Peine**, University of Houston, TX; **Nuran Peker**, Nazilli High School, Turkey; **Susan Pelley**, Doña Ana Community College, NM; **Jorge Perez**, Southwestern College, CA; **Kim Perkins**, Boston University, MA; **William Phelps**, Southern Illinois University, IL; **Tom Pierce**, Central New Mexico Community College, NM; **Jennifer Piotrowski**, Language Center International, MI; **Carole Poppleton-Schrading**, Johns Hopkins University, MD; **Valentina Portnov**, Kingsborough Community College, NY; **Nancy Price**, University of Missouri, MO; **Catherine Ramberg**, Albany Adult School, CA; **Brian Ramey**, Sehir University, Turkey; **Steven Rashba**, University of Bridgeport, CT; **Victoria Reis**, Language Studies International, NY; **Amy Renehan**, University of Washington, WA; **Elizabeth Reyes**, Elgin Community College, IL; **Kathleen Reynolds**, Harper College, IL; **Tom Riedmiller**, University of Northern Iowa, IA; **Dzidra Rodins**, DePaul University, IL; **Ana Rodriguez**, Elliston School of Languages, FL; **Ann Roemer**, Utah State University, UT; **Margot Rose**, Pierce College, WA; **David Ross**, Houston Community College, TX; **Robert Ruddy**, Northeastern University, MA; **Peter Ruggiero**, Boston University, MA; **Phil Ruggiero**, The University of Missouri, MO; **Anne Sadberry**, The Language Company, OK; **Jessica Saigh**, University of Missouri-St. Louis, MO; **Irene Sakk**, Northwestern University, IL; **Kamila Salimova**, TGT, Russia; **Chari Sanchinelli**, Colegio Valle Verde, Guatemala; **Christen Savage**, University of Houston, TX; **Boutheina Sayadi**, Virtual University of Tunis, Tunisia; **Rosemary Schmid**, University of North Carolina, NC; **Diana Schoolman**, St. John's University, NY; **Myrna Schwarz**, La Roche College, PA; **Karen Schwenke**, Biola University, CA; **Dilek Batur Secer**, Toros University, Turkey; **Diana Sefchik**, Raritan Valley Community College, NJ; **Ertan Selimoglu**, Yildiz Technical University, Turkey; **Rene Serrano**, Universidad Nacional Autónoma de México, Mexico; **Gul Shamim; Amir Sharifi**, California State University, CA; **Caroline Sharp**, University of Maryland, MD; **Shixian Sheng**, Boston Chinatown Neighborhood Center, MA; **Oksana Shevchenko**, Horlivka Language School, Ukraine; **A. Shipley**, Academy of Art University, CA; **D. H. Shreve**, University of North Texas, TX; **Meire Silva**, Celebration Language Institute, FL; **Fiore Sireci**, Hunter College, NY; **Anita Teresa Smith**, Majan College, Oman; **Jacqueline Smith**, The New School, NY; **Jeff Smith**, Ohio Northern University, OH; **Lorraine Smith**, Queens College, NY; **Barbara Smith-Palinkas**, Hillsborough Community College, FL; **Kimberly Spallinger**, Bowling Green State University, OH; **James Stakenburg**, Rennert International, NY; **Katrina Tamura**, Palomar College, CA; **Dan Tannacito**, Indiana University of Pennsylvania, PA; **Jamie Tanzman**, Northern Kentucky University, KY; **Tara Tarpey**, New York University, NY; **Amy Tate**, Houston Community College, TX; **Rose Tauscher**, Skyline High School, TX; **Tamara Taylor**, University of North Texas-IELI, TX; **Cihan Tekin**, İMKB 24 Kasım Anadolu Lisesi, Turkey; **Kelly Tennison**, Roseville Area High School, MN; **Abby Thomas**, Northern Essex Community College, MA; **Brett Thomas**, Sacramento City College, CA; **Linda Thomas**, Lone Star College-Montgomery, TX; **Edith Thompson**, Purdy R-II School District, MO; **Sylwia Thorne**, Kent State University, OH; **Donna Tooker**, Miramar College, CA; **Beth Topping**, Auburn University, AL; **Carolyn Trachtova**, Webster University, MO; **William Trudeau**, Ohio Northern University, OH; **Kathy Truman**, Haverford High School, PA; **Karen Tucker**, Georgia Institute of Technology, GA; **Gretchen Twohig**, ASC English, MA; **Blanca Ugraskan**, Del Mar Community College, TX; **Serkan Ülgü**, Air Force Academy, Turkey; **Mecit Uzun**, Gaziosmanpaşa, Turkey; **Cynthia Valdez**, Palisade High, CO; **Kanako Valencia Suda**, De Anza College, CA; **Michelle Van de Sande**, Arapahoe Community College, CO; **Sharon Van Houte**, Lorain County Community College, OH; **Sara Vandenberg**, University of Colorado, CO; **Lillian Vargas**, University of Florida, FL; **Tara Vassallo**, Pace University, NY; **Stephanie Viol**, Palm House; **Kathleen Vodvarka**, University of Delaware, DE; **Kerry Vrabel**, GateWay Community College, AZ; **Carol Wachana**, ELS Language School; **Christine Waddail**, Johns Hopkins University, MD; **Christina Wade**, Liberty University, VA; **Wendy Walsh**, College of Marin, CA; **Colin Ward**, Lone Star College-North Harris, TX; **Mary Kay Wedum**, Colorado State University, CO; **Linda Wesley**, Pennsylvania State University, PA; **Lynne Wilkins**, The English Center, CA; **Betty Williams; Jeff Wilson**, Irvine Community College, CA; **Lori Wilson-Patterson**, Ivy Tech Community College, IN; **Kirsten Windahl**, Cuyahoga Community College, OH; **Aleasha Winters**, Lingo TEFL Language Institute, Costa Rica; **Jing Zhou**, Defense Language Institute, CA; **Yelena Zimon**, Fremont Adult School, CA; **Koraljka Zunic**, Grossmont College, CA

Contents

10|Adjectives and Other Forms That Describe Nouns

11|Adverbs and Prepositional Phrases

12|Adverb Clauses

8 Present Perfect and Past Perfect

Two roads diverged in a wood, and I—
I took the one less traveled by,
And that has made all the difference.

—ROBERT FROST, POET

(1874–1963)

Talk about It What does the quotation above mean to you?

WARM-UP

A | Check (✓) the sentences that describe you. Then compare with a partner. Who is the most adventurous person in the class?

How Adventurous Are You?

☐ 1. I **have given** one or more speeches in my life.

☐ 2. I **have traveled** to a place where I couldn't speak the language.

☐ 3. I **have tried** a somewhat[1] dangerous sport such as surfing.

☐ 4. I **have done** something even though I was afraid.

☐ 5. I **have eaten** unusual foods from other countries.

☐ 6. I **have** always **enjoyed** trying new things.

☐ 7. I **have tried** to do something difficult and failed.

☐ 8. I **have taken** a trip alone.

- If you checked 7 to 8 boxes, you are extremely adventurous.
- If you checked 5 to 6 boxes, you are very adventurous.
- If you checked 2 to 4 boxes, you are somewhat adventurous.
- If you checked 0 to 1 box, you might need a little more adventure in your life.

B | The verbs in blue above are present perfect verbs. Based on these examples, what can you say about the present perfect? Check (✓) *True* or *False*.

	TRUE	FALSE
1. We usually form the present perfect with the helping verb *have* + the *-ed/-en* form of the main verb (the past participle).	☐	☐
2. The past participle is always the same as the simple past form.	☐	☐
3. We use the present perfect to talk about a specific time in the past (such as *last year* or *yesterday*).	☐	☐

C | Look back at the quotation on page 250. Identify any present perfect verb forms.

[1] **somewhat:** a little bit

8.1 Using the Present Perfect (I); Statements

A

1 I've lived here **all my life**.
(= I've lived here from the time I was born up until now.)

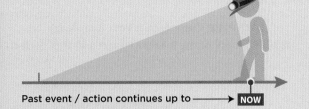

Past event / action continues up to ⟶ **NOW**

2 A: Nice car! Is it new?
B: No, **I've had** it **since 2010**.
(= I've had the car from 2010 up until now.)

3 Carl **has always been** a good friend. (= Carl was a good friend in the past, and he is a good friend now.)

When we want to show that something started in the past and continues up to the present (the moment of speaking), we often use the **present perfect** form of a verb, as in **1 – 3**.

Some common verbs for this use of the present perfect are:

be	have	live
feel	know	work

Notice: We sometimes use a **time expression** in a sentence with a present perfect verb, as in **1 – 3**.

B

POSITIVE AND NEGATIVE STATEMENTS

have (+ *not*)   past participle

4	I You We They	**have** **'ve** **have not** **haven't**	**lived**	there	for years.

has (+ *not*)   past participle

5	He She It	**has** **'s** **has not** **hasn't**	always	**lived**	there.

We form the present perfect with *have / has* (+ **not**) + the **past participle of a main verb**, as in **4 – 5**. In conversation, we often use contractions.

Notice: We use the verb *have* as a helping verb in the present perfect form.

C

The past participle of regular verbs looks the same as the simple past form, as in **6**. We add -(e)d to the base form. The past participle of many (but not all) irregular verbs is different from the simple past, as in **7**.

REGULAR VERBS		
base form	simple past	past participle
like	like**d**	like**d**
live	live**d**	live**d**
want	want**ed**	want**ed**
work	work**ed**	work**ed**

6

IRREGULAR VERBS		
base form	simple past	past participle
be	was/were	**been**
feel	felt	**felt**
have	had	**had**
know	knew	**known**

7

For spelling rules of -*ed* endings, see the Resources, page R-5.

For a list of past participles of irregular verbs, see the Resources, page R-3.

1 | Noticing the Present Perfect Underline the present perfect verb forms in these conversations. Then practice with a partner. `8.1 A`

1. A: Are you OK?
   B: I'm not sure. I've had a headache all day.
2. A: You look tired.
   B: I am. I've worked hard all week.
3. A: Is Amanda a good cook?
   B: She should be. She's worked in restaurants all her life.
4. A: Do you know David?
   B: Sure. I've known him all my life.
5. A: I'm sleepy.
   B: Me too. I've been up since 3 this morning.
6. A: Nice coat. Is it new?
   B: No, I've had it since November.
7. A: Where should I stay in San Francisco?
   B: Email James Bailey and ask him. He's lived there for years.
8. A: What's the matter?
   B: I don't know. I haven't felt good all day.
9. A: We're going to Chicago next weekend. Do you want to come?
   B: Sure. I've always wanted to go there.
10. A: You're a good student.
    B: Thanks. I like to study. I've always liked to study.

Are you OK?

Is Amanda a good cook?

Think about It Make a list of the time expressions in sentences with the present perfect above.

all day, all week,

Think about It Circle the other verb forms in the conversations above. What other verb forms often appear together with the present perfect?

2 | Usage Note: *For and Since* Read the note. Then do Activity 3.

> We can use the time expressions *for* and *since* in sentences with the present perfect.
>
> **1** To show "for how long," we use *for* + **a length of time**.
>
> We haven't lived there for **5 years**. (= for the past 5 years / from 5 years ago until now)
> I've known him for **23 years**. (= for the past 23 years / from 23 years ago until now)
>
> **2** To show "from when," we use *since* + **a specific time in the past**.
>
> We've lived here since **1995**. (= from 1995 to now)
> She hasn't felt good since **the picnic**. (= from the day of the picnic until now)
>
> **3** We can also use *since* in a **time clause** (with a subject and a verb). We usually use the simple past in the time clause.
>
> I've known him since **we were children**. (= from the time we were children to now)

3 | Using For and Since Underline the present perfect verbs in these sentences. Then complete the sentences with *for* or *since*. 8.1 A–B

DESCRIBING RELATIVES

My sister Anna

1. She <u>has lived</u> in Vancouver _____*since*_____ she graduated from college in 2001.

2. She has been married _____ a few years.

3. She has been an art teacher _____ 12 years.

4. She has taught at an elementary school _____ the past 4 years. Before that she taught at a private school.

5. She and her husband have lived in their present apartment _____ 2010.

My grandfather John

6. He has lived in California _____ he was a child.

7. He has lived in the same house _____ most of his life.

8. He has lived alone _____ his wife died.

9. He hasn't worked full-time _____ he was 70 years old.

10. He has been a chess player _____ most of his adulthood.

Write about It What do you know about these two people now (in the present)? Use present verb forms to write as many sentences as you can about the two people above.

Anna lives in Canada.
She has a college degree.

4 | Forming Present Perfect Statements Choose verbs from these charts to complete the sentences on page 255. (More than one verb may be possible.) Use the present perfect and contractions where possible. Then check (✓) *True* or *False*. 8.1 B–C

REGULAR VERBS		
Base form	**Simple past**	**Past participle**
enjoy	enjoyed	**enjoyed**
like	liked	**liked**
live	lived	**lived**
own	owned	**owned**
want	wanted	**wanted**
work	worked	**worked**

IRREGULAR VERBS		
Base form	**Simple past**	**Past participle**
be	was / were	**been**
feel	felt	**felt**
have	had	**had**
know	knew	**known**
make	made	**made**
say	said	**said**
teach	taught	**taught**

MY FAMILY	TRUE	FALSE
1. My parents ____*have*____ always ____*lived*____ in the same city.	☐	☐
2. My parents _____ married for a long time.	☐	☐
3. They _____ a car since they got married.	☐	☐
4. They _____ each other since they were children.	☐	☐
5. My father _____ always _____ at the same place.	☐	☐
6. My father _____ at a high school for many years.	☐	☐
7. My mother _____ many different jobs.	☐	☐
8. My mother _____ always _____ me laugh.	☐	☐
9. My aunts and uncles _____ never _____ to this country.	☐	☐
10. No one in my family _____ in a movie.	☐	☐
11. My relatives _____ always _____ important in my life.	☐	☐
12. People in my family _____ always _____ that I have a talent for sports.	☐	☐
13. My parents _____ always _____ me to become a doctor.	☐	☐
14. My mother and her mother-in-law _____ always _____ each other.	☐	☐
15. The people in my family _____ always _____ getting together.	☐	☐

Write about It Write six sentences about your family. Use *always, since,* or *for* and the present perfect form of a verb from the charts in Activity 4.

My parents have always lived in Barcelona.

5 | Error Correction Correct any errors in these sentences. (Some sentences may not have any errors.)

1. He hasn't in this country eight years.
2. I has been here only since last week.
3. My sister been in the United States from the last seven months.
4. She hasn't lived here for very long.
5. My father has worked for the same company since ten years.
6. I loved scary movies since I was a child.
7. We have only knew him since we moved here.
8. Football haven't always been my favorite sport.
9. This city has changed a lot since I came here.
10. A: Is that a new computer?
    B: No, I had it for almost a year.
11. A: Do you know Sam Davidson?
    B: Of course. I've known him since a year.
12. A: Did you talk to Anne?
    B: Not yet. She been on the phone.

> **F Y I**
>
> Sometimes we use an expression for a finished time (*yesterday, last week,* etc.) after *since.* The main clause still uses the present perfect.
>
> I haven't seen him **since I talked to him** yesterday.
>
> We haven't gone anywhere **since last week**.

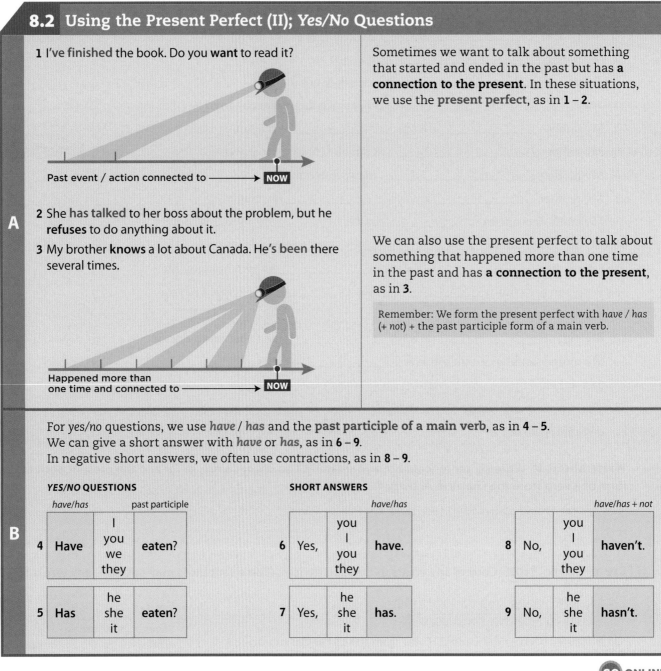

8.2 Using the Present Perfect (II); Yes/No Questions

A

1 **I've finished** the book. Do you **want** to read it?

Past event / action connected to ⟶ **NOW**

2 She **has talked** to her boss about the problem, but he **refuses** to do anything about it.

3 My brother **knows** a lot about Canada. He's **been** there several times.

Happened more than one time and connected to ⟶ **NOW**

Sometimes we want to talk about something that started and ended in the past but has **a connection to the present**. In these situations, we use the **present perfect**, as in **1 – 2**.

We can also use the present perfect to talk about something that happened more than one time in the past and has **a connection to the present**, as in **3**.

Remember: We form the present perfect with *have / has* (+ *not*) + the past participle form of a main verb.

B

For yes/no questions, we use *have / has* and the **past participle of a main verb**, as in **4 – 5**.
We can give a short answer with *have* or *has*, as in **6 – 9**.
In negative short answers, we often use contractions, as in **8 – 9**.

YES/NO QUESTIONS

	have/has		past participle
4	Have	I you we they	eaten?
5	Has	he she it	eaten?

SHORT ANSWERS

			have/has
6	Yes,	you I you they	have.
7	Yes,	he she it	has.

			have/has + not
8	No,	you I you they	haven't.
9	No,	he she it	hasn't.

GO ONLINE

6 | Connecting to the Present Match each past event with a connection to the present. [8.2 A]

PAST ACTIONS OR EVENTS

1. I've lost Ahmad's phone number. ___d___

2. We have never eaten Japanese food. ____

3. My brother has had a few accidents with his car. ____

4. Matt has missed a lot of classes. ____

5. I've stopped caring about football. ____

6. I haven't found my keys. ____

7. Mr. Jones has already gone. ____

8. I've studied this subject before. ____

CONNECTIONS TO THE PRESENT (NOW)

a. I don't think he's a very good driver.

b. I can't open the door.

c. I don't want to watch the game.

d. I can't call him.

e. He's not here now.

f. I know a lot about it.

g. He's in trouble with his teacher.

h. I don't know what it tastes like.

Think about It Underline the present perfect verb in the sentences in Activity 6. Does the verb describe something that happened one time or more than one time in the past? Share ideas with your classmates.

Write about It Choose three past actions or events in Activity 6. Write another sentence showing a connection to the present.

7 | Usage Note: Irregular Past Participles Study the chart. Then answer the questions below.

GROUP 1		
base form	simple past	past participle
cut	cut	cut
put	put	put

GROUP 2		
base form	simple past	past participle
become	became	become

GROUP 3		
base form	simple past	past participle
eat	ate	eaten
fall	fell	fallen
see	saw	seen
show	showed	shown
write	wrote	written

GROUP 4		
base form	simple past	past participle
find	found	found
leave	left	left
lose	lost	lost
say	said	said

GROUP 5		
base form	simple past	past participle
break	broke	broken
forget	forgot	forgotten

GROUP 6 (OTHER)		
base form	simple past	past participle
begin	began	begun
fly	flew	flown

QUESTIONS

1. What is similar about the form of the verbs in each group? Use the colors to help you identify a pattern. Then share ideas with your classmates.

   "In group 1, the base form, the simple past, and the past participle are the same."

2. Add these verbs to the correct groups in the chart above. Then think of six other verbs to add to the chart.

buy/bought/bought	go/went/gone	speak/spoke/spoken
do/did/done	hurt/hurt/hurt	take/took/taken
get/got/gotten	make/made/made	think/thought/thought
give/gave/given	run/ran/run	throw/threw/thrown

8 | Using the Present Perfect Complete these conversations with the present perfect form of a verb from Activity 7. Use contractions where possible. Then practice with a partner. **8.2 A**

1. A: Do you still have Emma's phone number?

   B: No, I ___*'ve lost*___ it.

2. A: I _____ some coffee. Do you want some?

   B: Sure. Thanks.

3. A: Are the children doing their homework?

   B: No, they _____ already _____ it.

4. A: Are you hungry?

   B: No, I _____ already _____.

5. A: Why don't we go to Art Café anymore?

   B: It _____ too popular. It's always crowded.

6. A: Do you want to go to the science museum with me today?

   B: I don't think so. I _____ several times this year. That's enough for me.

7. A: Where is Carlos?

   B: They _____ him to the hospital. He fainted!

8. A: Who's the new student in your class?

   B: I _____ her name. Ask Mary. She'll know it.

9. A: Nice jacket. Is it new?

   B: You _____ it before. I wore it last week.

10. A: Don't forget to take your lunch. I _____ your name on the bag.

    B: OK. Thanks, Mom.

RESEARCH SAYS...

Common verbs used with the present perfect in speaking and writing include:

be	give	say
become	go	see
call	have	show
come	lose	take
do	make	think
get	put	win

CORPUS

Think about It Why do you think the speakers chose to use the present perfect in each conversation above?

Talk about It Choose one of the conversations in Activity 8. Add three or four more lines. Try to use other present forms. Then present it to your classmates.

9 | Usage Note: *Just, Recently,* and *Finally* Read the note. Then do Activity 10.

We sometimes use *just, recently,* and *finally* with the present perfect. We often do this when we are talking about something that started and ended in the past but has a connection to the present.

1 *Just* means "a very short time ago." We use *have/has + just +* the past participle.

   I think somebody's **just knocked** on the door. Can you get it?

2 *Recently* means "not long ago." We can use *recently* in different places in a sentence.

   She **has recently completed** a degree in architecture, and now she is looking for a job in New York.

   Recently, she **has completed** a degree in architecture, and now she is looking for a job in New York.

   She **has completed** a degree in architecture **recently,** and now she is looking for a job in New York.

3 *Finally* means "after a long time." We can use *finally* in different places in a sentence.

   My brother **has finally found** a new job. He's really excited about it.

   Finally, my brother **has found** a new job. He's really excited about it.

   My brother **has found** a new job **finally.** He's really excited about it.

10 | Using the Present Perfect with *Just, Recently,* and *Finally* Complete these sentences with the words in parentheses. Use the present perfect form of the **bold** verb and contractions where possible. `8.2 A`

1. We _'ve recently gotten_____ a new cell phone, and I'm having trouble using it. (**get**/recently)

2. The snow _____. Let's go outside. (**stop**/finally)

3. I don't want to go jogging now. I _____. (**eat**/just)

4. My father has a lot more free time now because he _____. (**retire**²/finally)

5. Our school _____ a new program for foreign students. (**begin**/recently)

6. I'm tired of winter. I'm glad that warmer weather _____. (**arrive**/finally)

7. Sarah is pretty angry because Rob _____ her new laptop. (**lose**/just)

8. Everyone is celebrating because peace _____ to the country. (**come**/finally)

9. The college _____ a handbook with study tips. (**publish**/recently)

10. Hurry up. The movie _____. I don't want to miss the beginning. (**start**/just)

Write about It Which sentences above can you rewrite and put the time word in a different place?

1. Recently, we've gotten a new cell phone. OR *We've gotten a new cell phone recently.*

11 | Asking *Yes/No* Questions Ask a *yes/no* question with the present perfect and write an answer with *yes* or *no* and more information. Then compare and practice with a partner. `8.2 B`

1. A: I can't find my laptop. _Have you seen it?_____ (you/**see**/it)

   B: _Yes, I have. It's on the kitchen table._____ (yes)

2. A: _____ (anyone/**call**/today)

   B: _____ (yes)

3. A: _____ (Sam/**leave**)

   B: _____ (no)

4. A: _____ (the movie/**begin**)

   B: _____ (no)

5. A: _____ (you/**take** your medicine)

   B: _____ (yes)

6. A: _____ (the plane/**land**)

   B: _____ (no)

7. A: _____ (you/**talk** to your parents/recently)

   B: _____ (yes)

8. A: _____ (the rain/**stop**)

   B: _____ (no)

9. A: I'm going to Costa Rica next year. _____ there before? (you/**be**)

   B: _____ (no)

10. A: _____ (you/**have** lunch)

    B: _____ (yes)

²**retire:** stop working because you are a certain age

12 | Usage Note: *Ever* and *Never* Read the note. Then do Activity 13.

We sometimes use *ever* and *never* with the present perfect.

1 We can use *ever* in questions to ask: Has something happened "at some time before now"?

A: **Have** you **ever been** to Spain?	A: I need a good book to read.
B: No, I haven't. Why do you ask?	B: **Have** you **ever read** *The Road*? It's great.

2 We use *ever* in negative statements. It means something has not happened "before now."

I **haven't ever visited** Hawaii. I want to go.   Nobody **has ever called** me lazy.

3 We can use *never* in positive statements. It also means something has not happened "before now."

I**'ve never visited** Hawaii. I want to go.	A: Do you like Vietnamese food?
	B: I don't know. I**'ve never tried** it.

WARNING! We don't usually use *ever* in a statement without a negative word (*not*, *nobody*, etc.).
NOT: ~~I have ever been to Hawaii.~~

13 | Using *Ever* and *Never* Complete these conversations with the words in parentheses. Use the present perfect form of the **bold** verb and contractions where possible. Then practice with a partner. `8.2 A–B`

1. A: What does a cheetah look like?

    B: I don't know. I _____*haven't ever seen*_____ one. (**see**/not/ever)

2. A: You're a really good football player.

    B: Really? You _____ that before. (**say**/never)

3. A: _____ the band Snow Patrol?

    (you/**hear**/ever)

    B: Sure. Why do you ask?

    A: Because they're playing at the university tonight. Do you want to go?

4. A: Do you like Indian food?

    B: I don't know. I _____ it. (**have**/never)

5. A: Look at the water. _____ a blue like that? (you/**see**/ever)

    B: No, it's beautiful.

6. A: You're a really good cook. _____ opening a restaurant?

    (you/**think of**/ever)

    B: I have, but it's a lot of work.

7. A: Tom and I are going skateboarding this afternoon. Want to join us?

    B: I don't know. I _____ it. (**try**/not/ever)

    A: Oh, come on. I think you'll like it.

8. A: What do you do when you get a parking ticket?

    B: I don't know. I _____ one. (**get**/never)

a cheetah

Think about It Look at the sentences you completed above. Which ones could you rewrite using *ever* instead of *never* or *never* instead of *ever*?

1. I've never seen one.

14 | Usage Note: *Yet* and *Already* Read the note. Then do Activity 15.

We sometimes use *yet* and *already* with the present perfect to talk about our expectations.

1 We use *yet* and *already* in questions when we expected something to happen.
   We ask: Has it happened?

   A: **Have you finished your essay yet?**
   B: No, I'm still working on it.

   A: **Have you eaten already?**
   B: Actually, I haven't.
   A: Good. Then let's eat out.

2 We use *yet* in negative statements. It means something we expected has not happened.

   Sit down. **I haven't excused you yet.**

   A: Where's Nick?
   B: I don't know. **I haven't seen him yet.**

3 We use *already* in positive statements. It means something has happened earlier than we expected.

   A: Do you want to pay for that now?
   B: **I've already paid** for it.

   A: Don't forget to do your homework.
   B: **I've already done** it.

15 | Using *Yet* and *Already* Complete these conversations with the words in parentheses. Use the present perfect form of the **bold** verb and contractions where possible. 〔8.2 A–B〕

1. A: We're going to the National Museum this weekend. Do you want to come?

   B: Thanks, but I ___*'ve already been*___ there. (**be**/already)

2. A: Where's Isabel?

   B: She _____ . (**arrive**/not/yet)

3. A: _____ ? (you/**eat**/already)

   B: Sorry. I was really hungry.

4. A: What's the score?

   B: There is no score. The game _____ . (**start**/not/yet)

5. A: Where do you want to go for dinner?

   B: I _____ . (**decide**/not/yet)

6. A: Do you like that new software?

   B: Yeah. It _____ very useful. (**be**/already)

7. A: Toshi isn't going to be here tomorrow.

   B: Yeah, he _____ me. (**tell**/already)

8. A: _____ ? (anything/**happen**/yet)

   B: No, we are still waiting.

9. A: Do you need any help with the picnic?

   B: No, Amanda _____ everything. (**take care of**/already)

10. A: Come on. Let's go.

    B: Wait. We _____ . (**finish**/not/yet)

11. A: Why don't you want to watch this movie with us?

    B: Because I _____ it. (**see**/already)

8.3 *Wh-* Questions with the Present Perfect

When we ask *wh-* questions with the present perfect, we use a **wh- word** + *have / has* and the **past participle of a main verb**, as in **1 – 10**.

A

WH- QUESTIONS

	wh- word	have	subject	past participle
1	What		I	done?
2	Why		you	called?
3	Where	have	we	been?
4	Who		the people	elected?
5	How		they	changed?

	wh- word	has	subject	past participle
6	What		he	done?
7	Where		she	gone?
8	How	has	it	changed?
9	Who		your sister	invited?
10	Why		the store	closed?

WH- QUESTIONS ABOUT THE SUBJECT

	subject	has	past participle	
11	Who		been	there?
12	What	has	happened?	

Sometimes the *wh-* word is the subject of the sentence, as in **11 – 12**.

B

13	How long	have you been here?
14	How far	have the children gone?
15	How many times	has he called you today?
16	How many cups	of coffee have you had today?
17	How much coffee	have you had today?

We sometimes ask questions with:

- *how* + an adjective, as in **13 – 14**
- *how* + *many* + a plural noun, as in **15 – 16**
- *how* + *much* + a noncount noun, as in **17**

16 | Forming *Wh-* Questions with the Present Perfect Complete these questions with the words in parentheses. Use the present perfect form of the **bold** verb. **8.3 A**

QUESTIONS FROM INTERVIEWS WITH FAMOUS PEOPLE

1. How _____*has the president done*_____ so far?
   (the president / **do**)

2. What _____ from this experience?
   (you / **learn**)

3. What _____ your biggest frustration³?
   (**be**)

4. Who _____ the most fun with on a movie set?
   (you / **have**)

5. Why _____ to make this change and why now?
   (you / **decide**)

6. How _____ to keep your positive attitude?
   (you / **manage**)

7. How _____ your family life?
   (your success / **affect**)

8. What _____ since you lost weight?
   (**change**)

9. What _____ to prepare for this movie?
   (you / **do**)

10. Where _____ ?
    (the money / **go**)

FYI

We often use the present perfect to describe experiences that we bring to present situations, such as interviews.

³**frustration:** a feeling of anger because you cannot do what you want to do

262

11. Why _____ ?
    (unemployment / **go down**)
12. Why _____ a comedy?
    (you / **make**)

Talk about It For each question in Activity 16, do you think the interviewer is talking to a politician, an entertainer (actor, comedian, etc.), and/or an athlete? Why? Share ideas with your classmates.

17 | Asking Questions with *How* and the Present Perfect Complete the conversations below with words from the box. Then practice with a partner. 8.3 B

| how far | how long | how many | how much |

1. A: Do we have enough money to go out tonight?

   B: I don't know. _____*How much*_____ have we spent this week?

   A: Not much. About $50.

2. A: Mika wants another aspirin. Can I give her one?

   B: _____ has she had so far today?

   A: Only one.

   B: OK then. Let her have another one.

3. A: Are we there yet?

   B: No, not yet.

   A: _____ have we gone?

   B: About 300 miles.

4. A: I hear you're going back home this summer.

   B: Yeah, I'm really excited.

   A: _____ has it been since you were there?

   B: Just three years.

5. A: I can't work on this paper anymore.

   B: _____ hours have you spent on it?

   A: Seems like a million.

6. A: Hey, Carlos, are you still asleep? It's ten o'clock.

   B: No, I'm reading.

   A: _____ have you been awake?

   B: About an hour. I've already had two cups of tea.

7. A: Do you want to go out?

   B: I can't. I'm still doing today's reading assignment.

   A: _____ have you gotten?

   B: I'm only up to page 32.

8. A: Have you finished your homework yet?

   B: No, not yet.

   A: Well, _____ have you done?

   B: About half of it.

> **RESEARCH SAYS...**
>
> When we ask a present perfect question with *when*, we are often making a complaint. (These questions are not common.)
>
> **When have** you ever **done** the dishes?
>
> **When have** you **been** on time to class?
>
> CORPUS

8.4 The Simple Past vs. the Present Perfect

A

THE SIMPLE PAST

We often use the **simple past** to describe something that began and ended in the past. It is *no longer connected to now* (the moment of speaking), as in **1a – 3a**.

1a Nobody lived here in 1990. It was very quiet then.

2a I saw Linda at the theater last night.

3a We read that book several times in high school. It was one of my favorite books.

THE PRESENT PERFECT

We usually use the **present perfect** to describe something that started or happened in the past but is *still connected to now*, as in **1b – 3b**.

1b Nobody has lived here since 1990. I wonder why.

2b I've seen Linda today, but I don't know where she is now.

3b We've read that book several times. It's great.

B

TIME EXPRESSIONS WITH THE SIMPLE PAST

We use the simple past with time expressions that identify a *finished time*, including:

in	+	1990 / the past / the 1980s
during	+	the 1990s / the past few weeks
from	+	1980 to 1990
last	+	week / month / year / December
until	+	2009 / last year / last week
when	+	I was a child / I got there

a day / a month / a year / soon	+	**after that**
two days / a week / a few years	+	**ago**
several days / a month / a year	+	**later**

TIME EXPRESSIONS WITH THE PRESENT PERFECT

We use the present perfect with time expressions that identify a time period *up until now*, including:

all my life	**my whole life**	**until now**	**yet**

over	+	the past year / the last month / the years
since	+	then / yesterday / I was a child / I arrived

C

THE SIMPLE PAST

4a I **always** did well in school. My parents were very proud of me.

5a I was in Spain **for a week**. I didn't want to leave.

THE PRESENT PERFECT

4b I have **always** done well in school. My parents are very proud of me.

5b I have been in Spain **for a week**. I don't want to leave.

We can use some time expressions with either the simple past or the present perfect, including:

already	before	never	today
always	ever	recently	

this	+	week / month / year
for	+	an hour / a day / five years / a long time

The choice of verb form depends on how we interpret the event and when it happened, as in **4 – 5**.

 ONLINE

18 | Choosing the Correct Time Expressions Underline the verbs in these sentences. Then circle the correct time expression in bold. `8.4 A–B`

Sports

1. Gymnastics <u>is</u> a very popular sport. It <u>has been</u> in every Olympic Games
   in 1896 / (**since 1896**).

2. Brazil has won five World Cups **several years ago / over the past 60 years**.

3. Professional tennis players started using yellow balls **in 1986 / since 1986**
   so that TV viewers could see the ball.

gymnastics

4. **Over the years / In 2012**, the Korean archery team has won many Olympic medals.

archery

5. In 1954, Roger Bannister became the first person to run a mile in less than four minutes. **During the 1990s / Since then**, many runners have broken his record.

6. Tennis became an Olympic sport **more than 20 years ago / over the past 20 years**.

7. **A long time ago / Over the years**, there have been many football-like games.

8. The astronaut Alan Shepard hit a golf ball **when he was on the moon / since he was on the moon**.

9. Golf has become a popular sport in Denmark **a year ago / recently**. It is especially popular among people over age 24.

10. **In the early 1900s / Since the early 1900s**, baseball players wore leather helmets[4]. Head injuries were common.

tug of war

11. Queenie Newall was 53 years old **when she won an Olympic gold medal / since she won an Olympic gold medal** in 1908.

12. Tug of war was an Olympic event **from 1900 to 1920 / since 1920**.

13. Runners didn't use a crouching[5] position at the start of a race **since 1908 / until 1908**. This change helped them to finish a race much faster.

14. Since the first World Cup in 1930, European teams have reached the final **every year / last year** except 1930 and 1950.

Think about It Choose five sentences in Activity 18. Change the verb form in each sentence so that you can use the other time expression in **bold**. You may also need to make other changes.

Gymnastics was in the Olympic Games in 1896.

19 | Simple Past or Present Perfect? Complete these sentences with the simple past or present perfect form of the verb in the box. `8.4 A–C`

ACCOMPLISHMENTS

win

1. I think Taylor Swift is an accomplished[6] musician. She _____ *has won* _____ many awards this year, and she continues to make hit songs.

2. The actress Meryl Streep _____ an Academy Award in 2012. She got the award for playing British Prime Minister Margaret Thatcher in *The Iron Lady*.

3. Lawrence Bragg was just 25 years old when he _____ the Nobel Prize in Physics.

[4] **helmet:** a hard hat that keeps your head safe
[5] **crouching:** bending low or close to the ground

[6] **accomplished:** skillful; very good

> travel

4. On her flight around the world, Amelia Earhart _____ about 23,000 miles before her plane disappeared.

5. Dr. Helen Caldicott is a famous anti-nuclear activist[7]. She _____ around the world many times on lecture tours.

6. Karen Bass _____ to every continent to make films. She has recently finished a TV series on the natural history of North, South, and Central America.

> be

7. Will Smith _____ an actor for a long time. His most recent film is *After Earth*.

8. William Shakespeare _____ an actor before he started writing plays.

9. The inventor Thomas Edison _____ a very creative person. During his lifetime, he invented 1,093 different things.

10. Brenda Brathwaite _____ an important figure in the field of game design for the past decade.

> write

11. Naguib Mahfouz _____ many good books during his lifetime. His best book was probably *Midaq Alley*.

12. Toni Morrison _____ many good books. Her most famous book is probably *Beloved*.

13. Cameron Crowe _____ his first movie script in the early 1980s. Since then, he _____ the stories for many famous movies.

14. Rodney Mullen is one of the most famous skateboarders in the world. In 2003, he _____ an autobiography titled *The Mutt: How to Skateboard and Not Kill Yourself*.

Toni Morrison

Talk about It Choose three of the people from the sentences in Activity 19. Look online to find more information about them, and share information about their other accomplishments with your classmates.

[7] **activist:** a person who works to make changes in the world

20 | Error Correction Correct any errors in these sentences. (Some sentences may not have any errors.)

1. On that day we celebrated my father's birthday. We've invited more than 40 people to our house for dinner.
2. I have ever been to England. I learned that it is a very interesting place.
3. When I came here, I have studied the language and gotten a job.
4. Did you ever feel that life is very difficult?
5. I really miss my friend Erica. I haven't seen her since one year ago.
6. Recently this profession became more popular among young people.
7. When we arrived here, we have known we were lucky.
8. Lee is my new best friend. I met him last year when I started this class.

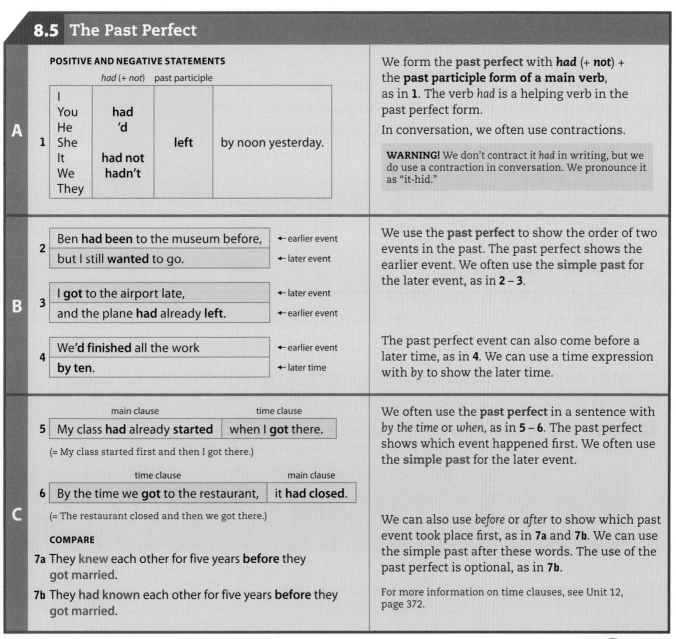

8.5 The Past Perfect

A

POSITIVE AND NEGATIVE STATEMENTS

	had (+ *not*)	past participle	
I You He She It We They	had 'd had not hadn't	left	by noon yesterday.

We form the **past perfect** with **had** (+ **not**) + the **past participle form of a main verb**, as in **1**. The verb *had* is a helping verb in the past perfect form.

In conversation, we often use contractions.

WARNING! We don't contract *it had* in writing, but we do use a contraction in conversation. We pronounce it as "it-hid."

B

2 Ben **had been** to the museum before, ← earlier event
but I still **wanted** to go. ← later event

3 I **got** to the airport late, ← later event
and the plane **had** already **left**. ← earlier event

4 We**'d finished** all the work ← earlier event
by ten. ← later time

We use the **past perfect** to show the order of two events in the past. The past perfect shows the earlier event. We often use the **simple past** for the later event, as in **2 – 3**.

The past perfect event can also come before a later time, as in **4**. We can use a time expression with *by* to show the later time.

C

main clause	time clause
5 My class **had** already **started**	when I **got** there.

(= My class started first and then I got there.)

time clause	main clause
6 By the time we **got** to the restaurant,	it **had closed**.

(= The restaurant closed and then we got there.)

COMPARE

7a They **knew** each other for five years **before** they got married.

7b They **had known** each other for five years **before** they got married.

We often use the **past perfect** in a sentence with *by the time* or *when*, as in **5 – 6**. The past perfect shows which event happened first. We often use the **simple past** for the later event.

We can also use *before* or *after* to show which past event took place first, as in **7a** and **7b**. We can use the simple past after these words. The use of the past perfect is optional, as in **7b**.

For more information on time clauses, see Unit 12, page 372.

21 | Forming the Past Perfect Complete these sentences with the past perfect. Then read each sentence again and check (✓) *That's surprising!* or *That's not surprising.* 8.5 A

GREAT ACCOMPLISHMENTS?	THAT'S SURPRISING!	THAT'S NOT SURPRISING.
1. By age 8, the Bangladeshi artist Sunny Sanwar _____*had learned*_____ six languages. (learn)	☐	☐
2. By age 8, I _____ a few words in another language. (memorize)	☐	☐
3. By age 23, Facebook CEO Mark Zuckerberg _____ a billionaire. (become)	☐	☐
4. By age 23, I _____ a lot of money to pay for my education. (borrow)	☐	☐
5. By age 9, March Tian Boedihardjo _____ his studies at a Hong Kong university. (start)	☐	☐
6. By age 17, I _____ my university studies. (begin)	☐	☐
7. The actress Shirley Temple began her career in movies at the age of 3. By age 20, she _____ more than 25 films. (make)	☐	☐
8. By age 3, I _____ a few movies, but I don't remember them. (watch)	☐	☐
9. By the age of 12, Lope de Vega _____ his first play. (write)	☐	☐
10. By the age of 12, I _____ in several school plays. (be)	☐	☐
11. The Australian artist Aelita Andre _____ paintings worth over $30,000 by age 4. (sell)	☐	☐
12. By age 4, I _____ some pictures that my mother liked. (make)	☐	☐

Write about It What had you done by the age of 5? By the age of 15? Write several sentences.

22 | Simple Past or Past Perfect? Complete these sentences with the verbs in parentheses. Use the simple past or the past perfect form and contractions where possible. 8.5 B

I Can't Believe I Did It!

1. I _____*mailed*_____ the letter but I _____*hadn't put*_____ any stamps on it.
   (mail)   (not put)

2. I _____ the washing machine but I _____ in the clothes.
   (turn on)   (not put)

3. Dinner _____ in the oven for an hour, but I _____ to turn the oven on.
   (be)   (forget)

4. I _____ to the airport in time but I _____ my passport.
       (get)   (not bring)

5. My phone _____ yesterday because I _____ it.
              (not work)   (not recharge)

6. My computer _____ and I _____ anything.
                 (crash)   (not back up)

7. I _____ to the store to buy some things, but I _____ my wallet at home.
      (go)   (leave)

8. I _____ a message to my brother, but I _____ an old email address, so
     (send)   (use)

he _____ it.
    (not receive)

Think about It Which action or event happened first in each sentence in Activity 22? Write the number *1* over it.

23 | Combining Sentences with the Past Perfect
Underline the time expressions in the sentences. Then connect each pair of sentences using the words in parentheses. Change one of the verbs to the past perfect, and leave out the underlined time expressions. 8.5 C

WHAT HAPPENED FIRST?

1. I got to school <u>at 9:10</u>. My class started <u>at 9</u>. (already/by the time)

    By the time I got to school, my class had already started.

2. She finished the report at 9:30 on Monday. The meeting started at 10. (just/when)

3. It started to rain at 6:45. The football game began at 7. (just/when)

4. The big sale took place in August. I spent all my savings in July. (already/by the time)

5. My friends ate breakfast at 7. I woke up at 8. (already/by the time)

6. The movie started at 7. I got to the movie theater at 7:15. (already/when)

7. Hassan didn't finish his work on Friday. He went on vacation on Saturday. (still/when)

8. On Wednesday afternoon, I decided to go to the concert. On Wednesday morning, they sold out of tickets. (by the time)

9. David's mother ate dinner at 8. She made dinner for her kids at 7. (before)

10. I ate dinner at 7. I was still hungry at 8. (after)

> **FYI**
> We often use time words (*already, always, finally, just, never,* etc.) with the past perfect form of a verb.

A BATTLE FOR NO REASON

Fast and clear communication has always been very important. Without the correct information, people can lose money, time, or even their lives. One clear example of this happened during the War of 1812 when Britain and the U.S. were fighting. During the Battle of New Orleans, hundreds of people died.

Soon after the battle, the British and the Americans discovered some shocking news—they had not needed to fight at all. Two weeks before the battle, the U.S. and Britain had signed a peace treaty[8] in Ghent, Belgium. However, this information had not reached the U.S. when the Battle of New Orleans began. Because information about the peace treaty had not arrived quickly enough, many people had died unnecessarily.

General Andrew Jackson at the Battle of New Orleans

QUESTIONS

1. What verb forms did this writer use? List them.
2. List any time words (time expressions, frequency expressions, or time clauses).

VERB FORMS	*TIME WORDS*
has been (present perfect)	*always*

3. Why do you think the writer used the past perfect instead of some other verb form?
4. Why do you think the news of the treaty didn't reach the U.S. in time?

25 | Error Correction Correct any errors in these sentences. (Some sentences may not have any errors.)

1. She had had a difficult life, but she never gives up.
2. After the accident, we thought my brother died.
3. When I was in high school, I had been a poor student.
4. It started to rain and then the game had begun.
5. This past weekend, my brothers had opened their new business.
6. By the time I had made that decision, I had already started high school.
7. When I got to work, I realized I didn't bring my keys with me.
8. Because of the bad weather, our class had started at 10 yesterday.

[8] **treaty:** a written agreement between countries

8.6 Using the Present Perfect in Speaking

A

EXPANDING AN ANSWER TO A *YES/NO* QUESTION

1 A: Do you know Jack Browne?
B: Of course. We**'ve been** friends for years.

2 A: Do you speak Arabic?
B: Well, I**'ve studied** it for a few years, but I **don't speak** it very well.

3 A: Have you seen Jack today?
B: No, he **didn't come** in today.

When we answer a *yes/no* question, we often say *yes* or *no* (or use a similar expression). Then we expand our answer to give more information. We can use:

- the **present perfect**—for past events connected to the present, as in **1 – 2**
- the **simple present**—for generally true statements, as in **2**
- the **simple past**—for finished events in the past, as in **3**

B

USING CONTRACTIONS IN SPEAKING

4 A: Do you like the new volunteers?
B: Yeah. They**'ve** already **been** really helpful.

5 A: Hi, Mom. I'm home.
B: It's late. Where[**'ve**] you **been**?

6 A: What's the matter?
B: I have bad news. There**'s been** an accident.

7 A: How is your sister in Canada doing?
B: Great. My parents[**'ve**] **visited** her twice already.

8 A: You did a great job today.
B: Really? No one**'s said** that to me before.

When we use the present perfect in speaking, we often contract *have / has*, as in **4 – 8**.

WARNING! We can write the contractions *'s* and *'ve* with pronouns. With nouns and question words, however, we usually write the full forms.

WRITTEN FORM	SPOKEN FORM
no one's	no one's
they've	they've
my sister has	my sister['s]
where have	where['ve]

Contractions are harder to hear when the main verb begins with the same or a similar sound, as in **7 – 8**.

26 | Expanding Your Answer Work with a partner. Take turns asking these questions. Answer *yes* or *no* and then add more information. (Many different answers are possible.) **8.6 A**

1. Do you live here?

   A: Do you live here?
   B: Yes, I do. I've lived here for about two years.

2. Do you play a musical instrument?
3. Have you ever tried Thai food?
4. Do you know how to cook any dishes from your country?
5. Have you seen any good movies recently?
6. Do you like to travel?
7. Do you watch much television?
8. Have you lived in any other cities?
9. Have you already graduated from college?
10. Do you like to surf?

RESEARCH SAYS...

The most common verbs used with the present perfect in conversation are *be, do, get, go,* and *have.*

Talk about It How many different ways can you answer each question above? Share ideas with your classmates.

◀)) 27 | Listening for Contractions Listen and repeat the sentences. Then write the full, written form of each sentence. [8.6 B]

CONTRACTED, SPOKEN FORM	FULL, WRITTEN FORM
1. Where['s] she gone?	*Where has she gone?*
2. What['s] happened here?	
3. Somebody's taken my book.	
4. How long['s] she been there?	
5. Nobody's heard from him.	
6. The snow['s] stopped.	
7. The weather['s] been nice lately.	
8. Everyone's heard of Einstein.	
9. Where['ve] the kids been?	
10. Why['ve] you come?	
11. Why['s] he left?	
12. My family['s] been through a lot.	
13. The president['s] made a decision on that.	
14. This country['s] been good to me.	
15. Things['ve] changed.	

◀)) 28 | Listening for Contractions Listen to the conversations and check (✓) the sentence you hear in each pair. [8.6 B]

1. ☑ a. I've voted in every election.
   ☐ b. I voted in every election.

2. ☐ a. He's lost a lot of weight.
   ☐ b. He lost a lot of weight.

3. ☐ a. She's set herself a difficult goal.
   ☐ b. She set herself a difficult goal.

4. ☐ a. They've decided to go on a trip.
   ☐ b. They decided to go on a trip.

5. ☐ a. I've paid for it already.
   ☐ b. I paid for it already.

6. ☐ a. She's studied Chinese for several years.
   ☐ b. She studied Chinese for several years.

7. ☐ a. We've visited them several times.
   ☐ b. We visited them several times.

8. ☐ a. What['s] he done?
   ☐ b. What['d] he do?

9. ☐ a. Where['s] everyone gone?
   ☐ b. Where['d] everyone go?

10. ☐ a. How long['s] she studied there?
    ☐ b. How long['d] she study there?

11. ☐ a. Mika['s] told me already.
    ☐ b. Mika told me already.

12. ☐ a. Well, John['s] heard all about it.
    ☐ b. Well, John heard all about it.

13. ☐ a. Sure. It's stopped snowing.
    ☐ b. Sure. It stopped snowing.

14. ☐ a. Yes, but he's always hated it.
    ☐ b. Yes, but he always hated it.

Think about It Which contractions above were especially difficult to hear? Why?

Talk about It Work with a partner. Read a sentence in each pair above. Ask your partner to say "Sentence A" or "Sentence B."

8.7 Using the Present Perfect and Past Perfect in Writing

A

MAKING GENERAL STATEMENTS

1 The basic design of a bicycle **hasn't changed** very much since the 1880s. Every bike still **uses** a foot-powered cog-and-chain system. . . .

2 A dance-fitness program called Zumba **has become** popular in recent years. Zumba **combines** salsa, merengue, and other forms of Latin American music. Alberto "Beto" Perez of Colombia **created** Zumba in the 1990s. Since then, it **has spread** around the world. . . .

We sometimes use the **present perfect** to make a general statement about something that has changed from a past time up until now. We then give more information using the **simple present** or the **simple past**, as in **1 – 2**.

Common verbs for this use of the present perfect include:

become	get better	increase	improve
change	get worse	decrease	grow

Remember: We use the simple present to describe things that are generally true. We usually use the simple past to describe specific past events.

B

SUPPORTING GENERAL STATEMENTS

3 Béatrice Coron **is** an artist with an interesting background. She **has been** a truck driver, factory worker, cleaning lady, and New York City tour guide. She **has lived** in France, Egypt, Mexico, and China.

When we describe someone or something in the present, we sometimes begin with a general statement, as in **3**. We then use the present perfect to show how actions and events in the past support our general statement.

C

GIVING BACKGROUND INFORMATION

4 In 1932, Robert Fulton **was** 24 years old. He **had** already **graduated** from Harvard University. He **had** recently **completed** advanced studies in Austria. He **was planning** to return to the U.S. . . .

When we write about someone or something in the past, we sometimes use the **past perfect** to give background information, as in **4**.

29 | Writing about Change Complete these sentences with the simple present, simple past, or present perfect form of the verb in parentheses. [8.7 A]

HOW HAS IT CHANGED?

1. Tennis _____*has changed*_____ a lot over the past 50 years. For many
   (change)
   years, players _____ heavy wooden tennis rackets.
   (use)
   Then, in the 1980s, very light metal rackets _____
   (become)
   available.

2. Computers _____ a lot smaller in the past 50 years.
   (become)
   The first computer _____ bigger than a small
   (be)
   house and _____ 33 metric tons. Computers today
   (weigh)
   _____ tiny and easy to carry around.
   (be)

3. Families _____ much smaller in the past 50 years.
   (get)
   Large families _____ common years ago, but today
   (be)
   many people only _____ one or two children.
   (have)

The Wimbledon Championships, 1924

4. Bicycles _____ over the years. The first bicycles _____ pedals.
   (improve)   (not have)
   Instead, riders _____ the ground with their feet.
   (push)

5. The number of cars on the road _____ dramatically over the past 30 years. In 1986,
   (increase)
   there _____ 500 million cars in the world. By 2010, there _____ more
   (be)   (be)
   than a billion.

Write about It Think of something else that has changed, gotten better, or gotten worse over the years. Write several sentences about it like the ones in Activity 29.

30 | Connecting the Past to the Present Complete each description with the words in parentheses. Use the simple present or the present perfect. **8.7 B**

Describing People

1. Amy Tan is a very talented writer. She _____ *has written* _____
   (write)
   a number of well-known novels, and one of her books, *The Joy*
   Luck Club, _____ a successful movie.
   (become)

2. My oldest brother is the most hard-working person I know.

   He _____ a demanding job, and he
   (always / have)
   _____ a day of work. Sometimes I worry
   (never / miss)
   that he works too hard.

Amy Tan

3. My youngest brother is only 14 years old, but he is already

   very spoiled. My parents _____ him everything he wants. He
   (always / give)
   _____ work for anything.
   (never / have to)

4. My cousin Matt is a very good athlete. He _____ a star basketball player,
   (be)
   and he _____ in several 10-kilometer races. He still runs several times a
   (also / compete)
   week, and now he is learning to ski.

5. My sister is an excellent student. She _____ good grades and she
   (always / get)
   _____ many academic awards. I'm sure she will do well in college.
   (win)

Write about It Choose three people you know well. Write a general statement about each person. Then give more information to support your statement.

31 | Using the Past Perfect to Give Background Information
Complete these paragraphs with the words in parentheses. Use the simple past or the past perfect. **8.7 C**

PAST EVENTS

1. One of the most important events in my life was when I moved to Costa Rica. Even though I was 26 years old, I _____*had never lived*_____ outside of my small town,
(never / live)
and I _____ communicate in a second
(never / have to)
language. That year my life _____ forever.
(change)

2. One of the most exciting days in my life was when I graduated from university. No one else in my family _____ to college. Both of my parents _____ to work
(ever / go)   (start)
at a young age, and my older sister _____ married right after high school. All
(get)
of my relatives _____ to my graduation ceremony, and I know my parents were
(come)
very proud of me.

3. One of my best memories was when my father took me to a baseball game. I
_____ only ten years old at the time, and I _____
(be)   (never / see)
a real baseball game. My father and I _____ early that day and
(get up)
_____ a bus into the city. I was so excited just to spend a whole day with
(take)
my father.

4. One of my worst memories took place when I was in elementary school. My family
_____ to a new city, and I _____ at a new school. This
(just / move)   (just / start)
new school _____ ahead of my old school in math. The students at my new
(be)
school _____ to multiply numbers, but this was new to me. On my first day,
(already / learn)
the teacher _____ me to go to the board to multiply some numbers in front of
(ask)
the whole class. I just _____ at the board because I didn't know what to do.
(stand)
I _____ so embarrassed!
(be)

Think about It Which sentences in each paragraph above give background information?

Write about It Choose one of these topics and write several sentences about it. Give some background information in your writing.
- One of the most important events in my life was when . . .
- One of the most exciting days in my life was when . . .
- One of my best memories was when . . .

A | INTERVIEW Work with a partner. Ask your partner each question. Ask follow-up questions to get more information, and take notes on your partner's answers. Then tell the class about your partner.

QUESTIONS

1. Do you play a musical instrument?
2. What sports do you play?
3. What languages do you speak?

A: Do you play a musical instrument?
B: No, I don't.
A: Does anyone in your family?
B: My father plays the piano.
A: How long has he played the piano?

A: Do you play a musical instrument?
B: Yes, I do. I play the guitar.
A: How long have you played the guitar?
B: Since high school.

B | WEB SEARCH Do an online search for the phrase "has gotten better" or "has gotten worse." Copy the five most interesting sentences you find, and then share them with your classmates.

C | TIC-TAC-TOE Follow these instructions:

1. Work with a partner. Student A is X. Student B is O.
2. Student A: Choose a square. On another piece of paper, answer the question in a complete sentence.
3. Students A and B: Check the sentence together. If the sentence has no errors, write an X in the square. If the sentence is not correct, do not write an X in the square.
4. Student B: Take your turn. Write an O for each correct answer.
5. The first person to get 3 Xs or 3 Os in a line is the winner.

What is the nicest city you have ever visited?	What is something that you have had since you were a child?	Who has been your good friend over the years?
What sports have you tried?	What's the scariest thing you have ever done?	What is something that you have always wanted to buy?
How many schools have you attended?	What are three things you had done by 9 this morning?	Where had you studied English before you started this course?

8.8 Summary of the Present Perfect and Past Perfect

PRESENT PERFECT

STATEMENTS

I You We They My friends	have 've have not haven't	been	there before.
He She It My sister	has 's has not 's not hasn't		

YES/NO QUESTIONS WITH THE PRESENT PERFECT

Have	I / you / we / they	left?
Has	he / she / it	

WH- QUESTIONS WITH THE PRESENT PERFECT

Where	have	I / you / we / they	gone?
	has	he / she / it	

What	has happened?

USES We use the **present perfect** to describe something in the past that is connected to now. This could be something that:
- started in the past and continues to now
- started and ended in the past but has a connection to now
- happened more than one time in the past but has a connection to now

PAST PERFECT

STATEMENTS

I You We They My friends He She It My brother	had 'd had not hadn't	arrived	by noon.

YES/NO QUESTIONS WITH THE PAST PERFECT

Had	I / you / we / they	left?
	he / she / it	

WH- QUESTIONS WITH THE PAST PERFECT

Where	had	I / you / we / they	gone?
		he / she / it	

What	had happened?

USES We use the **past perfect** to show that one event in the past took place before another event or time in the past.

Modals II

Knowledge can be
communicated, but
wisdom cannot.

—HERMAN HESSE, GERMAN-BORN
SWISS NOVELIST AND POET
(1877–1962)

Talk about It What does the quotation above mean? Do you agree or disagree?

WARM-UP

A | Match the beginnings and endings of these quotations. What does each quotation mean? Share your ideas with the class.

Famous Quotations

1. Failure is not fatal[1], but ____

2. If you **can** find a path with no obstacles[2], ____

3. **Perhaps** too much of everything ____

4. By the time a man realizes that **maybe** his father was right, he usually has a son ____

5. Whenever people agree with me, I always feel ____

6. When I was a boy I was told that anybody **could** become President. ____

a. I'm beginning to believe it. *(Clarence Darrow, lawyer)*

b. is as bad as too little. *(Edna Ferber, writer)*

c. who thinks he's wrong. *(Charles Wadsworth, classical pianist)*

d. I **must** be wrong. *(Oscar Wilde, writer and poet)*

e. failure to change **might** be. *(John Wooden, basketball player and coach)*

f. it **probably** doesn't lead anywhere. *(Frank A. Clark, cartoonist)*

B | Answer these questions about the sentences above.

1. Circle the words in blue that are modals. How do you know they are modals?

2. What kinds of words come before the modals? What kind of words come after them?

3. The other blue words are adverbs. Are these words followed directly by a verb?

C | Look back at the quotation on page 278. Identify any modal forms.

[1] **fatal:** causing death

[2] **obstacles:** things that make it difficult for you to do something

9.1 Present and Future Ability with *Can*

A

CAN FOR PRESENT ABILITY

1 Emma **can speak** three languages.

2 I **can't cook**. No one ever taught me.

3 A: **Can** Rob **run** a mile in eight minutes?
   B: I don't think so.

4 Excuse me, Professor. I **can't see** the board.

5 A newborn baby **cannot see** very far.

We often use **can** to talk about abilities in the present. It may have a meaning similar to:

- "know how to," as in **1 – 2**
- "have the ability," as in **3 – 5**

Notice: The contracted form *can't* is more common in conversation, as in **4**. The full form *cannot* usually appears in writing, as in **5**.

CAN WITH THINKING AND FEELING VERBS

6 You're not happy. I **can see** it in your face.

7 I **can't hear** the announcer. It's too noisy.

8 I **can understand** what you mean. I feel the same way.

We often use *can* with thinking and feeling verbs, as in **6 – 8**. Some common thinking/feeling verbs we use with *can* include:

believe	hear	see
guess	imagine	understand

B

CAN FOR FUTURE ABILITY

9 Mika works in the evenings, so she **can't study** with us tonight.

10 I'm going to the library tomorrow, so I **can pick up** that book for you.

In some situations, we also use *can* to talk about abilities in the future, as in **9** and **10**.

It is possible to use *can* in this way when a specific situation or decision leads to the future ability. These situations are often related to planned events.

 GO ONLINE

🔊 **1 | Pronunciation Note: *Can* and *Can't*** Listen to the note. Then do Activity 2.

Remember: In positive statements, **can** is not usually stressed. In negative statements, however, we usually stress **can't**.

POSITIVE STATEMENTS

1 Emma **can** SPEAK three languages.

2 I **can** UNDERSTAND what you mean.

NEGATIVE STATEMENTS

3 She **CAN'T** speak Spanish.

4 We **CAN'T** understand the homework.

🔊 **2 | Listening for *Can* and *Can't*** Listen and circle the modal you hear—*can* or *can't*. Then listen again and repeat the sentences. **9.1 A**

1. I **can** / **can't** understand that.

2. I **can** / **can't** see why.

3. She **can** / **can't** believe it.

4. They **can** / **can't** hear you.

5. We **can** / **can't** talk about it later.

6. He **can** / **can't** leave at 3:00.

7. They **can** / **can't** hear the TV.

8. She **can** / **can't** come tomorrow.

9. You **can** / **can't** believe him.

10. I **can** / **can't** tell you now.

Talk about It Take turns reading the sentences in Activity 2 to a partner. Use *can* or *can't*. Your partner listens and says yes if you used *can* and no if you used *can't*.

A: *I can't understand that.*
B: *No.*

3 | Statements with *Can* and *Can't* Complete each fact below with *can* or *can't* and a verb from the box. 9.1 A

breathe	eat	live	see	swim
climb	fly	run	sting[3]	walk

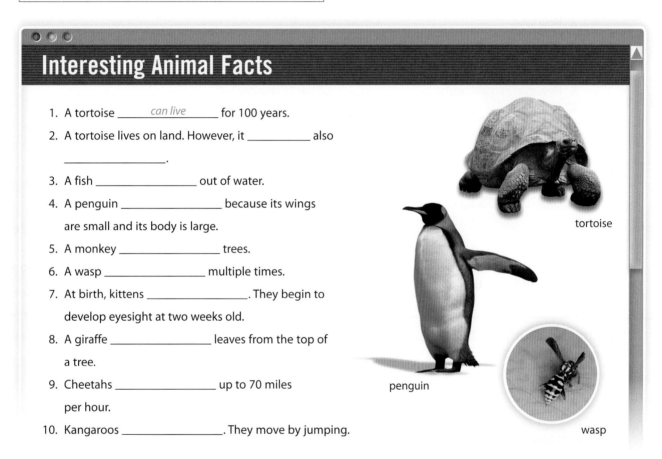

Interesting Animal Facts

1. A tortoise _____can live_____ for 100 years.

2. A tortoise lives on land. However, it _____ also _____.

3. A fish _____ out of water.

4. A penguin _____ because its wings are small and its body is large.

5. A monkey _____ trees.

6. A wasp _____ multiple times.

7. At birth, kittens _____. They begin to develop eyesight at two weeks old.

8. A giraffe _____ leaves from the top of a tree.

9. Cheetahs _____ up to 70 miles per hour.

10. Kangaroos _____. They move by jumping.

tortoise

penguin

wasp

Write about It Write four more sentences about the animals in this box with *can* or *can't*. Look for the information online if necessary.

bee	horse	shark
cow	monkey	snake
elephant	ostrich	wolf

---

[3] **sting:** to hurt (someone) by pushing a sharp, pointed part into the skin

4 | Questions with *Can* Complete the survey questions below. Use *can*, the subject *you*, and a verb from the box. (More than one answer may be possible.) Then guess your own answer for each question. **9.1 A**

add	keep	reach	run	stand
jump	name	read	spell	write

MAKE A GUESS   **YOUR ANSWER**

1. How high _____*can you reach*_____ with your arms outstretched?   _____

2. How high _____?   _____

3. How long _____ without stopping?   _____

4. How many countries _____ in 30 seconds?   _____

5. How long _____ on one leg?   _____

6. How many English verbs _____ in 15 seconds?   _____

7. How fast _____ 1,364, 267, and 4,897?   _____

8. From how far away _____ the title of this book?   _____

9. How long _____ your eyes open without blinking?   _____

10. How many names of vegetables _____   _____
   correctly in 30 seconds?

Talk about It Ask a partner the survey questions above. Then "test" one or two of your answers to see if you guessed correctly.

5 | *Can* and *Can't* with Thinking/Feeling Verbs Complete the sentences below with *can* or *can't* and a verb from the box. Add a subject if necessary. Then practice with a partner. **9.1 A**

believe	guess	hear	imagine	see	understand

1. A: Where's the dictionary?

   B: I'm sorry. I _____*can't hear*_____ you. Could you say that a little louder?

   A: I said, "Where's the dictionary?"

2. A: Is that an *A* or an *E*? I _____ it. It's too small!

   B: I think that's an *E*.

3. A: Do you think it's going to rain?

   B: Yeah, I do. I _____ storm clouds in the distance.

4. A: What is he saying? _____ him?

   B: Not a word. I don't think he's speaking English.

5. A: That guy is really rich. What do you think that's like?

   B: I have no idea. I can't even pay my rent. I _____ having that much money.

6. A: I've read this three times, but I _____ it. Can you explain it to me?

   B: Sure.

7. A: Hello? Hello? _____ me?

   B: Not very well. We have a bad connection.

8. A: I think that's the house. _____ the address?

   B: No, I _____ anything.

9. A: What do you think I have in this bag?

   B: I don't know.

   A: No idea?

   B: No! I _____. Just tell me!

10. A: Did you hear that Ramon quit yesterday?

    B: Wow, I _____ that. I thought he loved this job.

Write about It Work with a partner. Write a short conversation using *can* or *can't* with a thinking or feeling verb. Present your conversation to another pair.

6 | Can or Can't for Future Ability Look at Paula's to-do list. Complete the sentences below about the things she can and can't do tomorrow. `9.1 B`

To Do:
make dentist appointment
buy gift for Tony
call cable company
pick up coffee
do laundry
finish chemistry homework
get books

1. She _____ the laundry because she has class all day.

2. She has a long break, so she _____ her chemistry homework in the library between classes.

3. She has about an hour free in the afternoon, so she _____ the dentist appointment then.

4. She _____ the cable company because that might take a long time.

5. The store is open until 11 p.m., so she _____ some coffee on the way home.

6. She _____ Tony's gift until she gets paid.

7. She _____ her books until her check comes, either.

Talk about It Make a list of things you need to do soon. Show it to a partner, and explain which things you can and can't do tomorrow. Explain why.

A

CAN VS. *BE ABLE TO*

1a Robert **can speak** several languages.
(simple modal)

1b Robert **is able to speak** several languages.
(phrasal modal)

BE ABLE TO FOR PRESENT ABILITY

	subject	be able to	main verb	
2	I	'm (not) able to / 'm unable to		
3	He	's (not) able to / 's unable to	run	very fast.
4	They	're (not) able to / 're unable to		

Like **can**, we use the phrasal modal **be able to** to talk about abilities in the present, as in **1a – 1b**. However, **can** is more common.

Unlike simple modals, phrasal modals include a verb like *be*. The verb must agree with the subject, as in **2 – 4**.

Notice: *Unable is another way to say not . . . able.*

Remember these contractions:

am = 'm   **are** = 're   **is** = 's

B

BE ABLE TO FOR FUTURE ABILITY

5 My parents **are going to be able to come** to the wedding.

6 I **won't be able to leave** early.

7 Students **will be unable to use** the computer without a password.

8 I'm **not going to be able to give** you an answer.

9 Prediction: In the future, we **will be able to power** whole cities with solar energy.
(NOT: ~~In the future, we can power . . .~~)

We can also use **be able to** after a future form, as in **5 – 9**. In this case, the verb *be* does not change forms. Notice:

will (not)	be (un)able to	main verb
am/is/are (not) going to		

WARNING! We use *not* or *unable*, not both.

When we make a prediction about a future ability, we usually use *be able to*, as in **9**. We do not use **can** for predictions.

C

QUESTIONS ABOUT THE PRESENT

10 **Is** Lisa **able to take** time off work in the mornings?

11 How often **are** you **able to see** your family?

QUESTIONS ABOUT THE FUTURE

12 **Will** you **be able to come** tomorrow?

13 **Are** you **going to be able to make** the deadline?

14 When **will** you **be able to retire**?

We can ask questions about the present with **be able to**, as in **10 – 11**. Notice:

am/is/are	subject	able to	main verb

We can also ask questions about the future with **be able to**, as in **12 – 14**. Notice:

will	subject	—	be able to	main verb
am/is/are		going to		

---

7 | *Be Able To* for Present Ability Rewrite these sentences with *be (not) able to* or *be unable to* and frequency adverbs. **9.2 A**

ABILITIES AT DIFFERENT AGES

1. A 16-year-old can drive safely.

   A 16-year-old is often able to drive safely.

2. Eighty-year-olds can be good employees.

3. An 80-year-old can't learn a new language.

4. A 1-year-old can't walk.

5. Four-year-olds can read.

> **F Y I**
>
> You can use *never, rarely, sometimes, often, usually,* and *always* with *be able to*. We usually put them after *am/is/are* or after *not*.
>
> Young children **are sometimes able to follow** directions quite well.
>
> A 40-year-old **is not usually able to run** as fast as a teenager.

6. A 60-year-old can understand the problems of a 16-year-old.

7. A 16-year-old can understand the problems of a 60-year-old.

8. A young person without a college degree can find a good job.

9. A full-time college student can work a full-time job.

10. Teenagers can't control their emotions.

Talk about It Read the sentences you wrote in Activity 7 to a partner. See if your partner agrees or disagrees and why.

A: A 16-year-old is often able to drive safely. I was a good driver when I was 16.
B: I don't know. I think 16-year-olds get in a lot of accidents. They aren't able to make good decisions.

8 | *Be Able To* for Future Ability Complete these statements. Use a future form with *be able to* and the verb in parentheses. **9.2 B**

1. I'm sorry, but we ____*aren't going to be able to attend*____ your wedding.
   (attend)

2. I _____ early tomorrow.
   (come in)

3. I'm afraid I _____ you next weekend.
   (help)

4. I hope that you _____ us.
   (assist)

5. I _____ working on Monday.
   (start)

6. We're sorry that we _____ you the job.
   (offer)

7. You _____ that after you open it.
   (return)

8. I'm sorry. You _____ that item.
   (exchange)

9. I _____ that information for you.
   (provide)

10. I _____ the job on time.
    (finish)

Michelle
&
Steven

PLEASE REPLY
BEFORE MAY 8

Linda Lee
NAME

☐ will be attending
☑ not able to attend

Talk about It Where might you hear the sentences above? Who would say them? Share your ideas with a partner.

9 | *Can* vs. *Be Able To* Can these sentences be rewritten with *can* instead of *be able to*? Check (✓) *Yes* or *No*. Then rewrite the sentences you checked *Yes*. **9.2 B**

IN THE FUTURE	YES	NO
1. Next year we'll be able to take English 3.	☐	☐
2. We're going to be able to go home early on Friday.	☐	☐
3. Someday we'll be able to travel to other solar systems.	☐	☐
4. We won't be able to study tonight.	☐	☐
5. Our grandchildren won't be able to see many of the animals that are alive today.	☐	☐
6. In the future, more people are going to be able to work at home.	☐	☐
7. It's going to be sunny on Saturday. We're going to be able to go swimming.	☐	☐
8. The ocean levels are rising. Someday people won't be able to live along the coast.	☐	☐

Write about It Write three of your own predictions with *be able to*. Read your predictions to a partner. See if your partner agrees or disagrees and why.

10 | Asking Questions with *Be Able To* Complete these conversations with questions. Use a present or future form with *be able to*, a subject, and a verb from the box. Then practice with a partner. `9.2 C`

buy
come
concentrate
cook
go
see
sleep
stay
take
win

1. A: The Crows are playing hard today!

   B: *Will they be able to win?* _____

   A: I don't know. We'll see.

2. A: Thanks for the invitation!

   B: _____

   A: I'm not sure. I'll tell you tomorrow.

3. A: My cousins are coming to visit me.

   B: That's nice. How long _____?

   A: I'm not sure. I think about a week.

4. A: _____ home every weekend?

   B: No, I live too far away for that. I only go home on vacations.

5. A: I'm saving up for a new car.

   B: When _____ one?

   A: This summer, I think.

6. A: So, you have three roommates? How _____

   on your studying?

   B: I don't study at home. I go to the library.

7. A: I'm so tired of working.

   B: When _____ a vacation?

   A: Not until March.

8. A: I'm going back to my hometown for a few days.

   B: Nice! _____ your brother?

   A: No, unfortunately. He's away at school.

9. A: They're painting our building. It smells terrible.

   B: Oh, no! How _____ tonight?

   A: They're moving us out for a couple of days.

10. A: How often _____ dinner at home?

    B: Not often. I'm just too busy.

9.3 Past Ability with *Could* and *Was / Were Able To*

A

GENERAL ABILITY IN THE PAST

1 When I was young, I **could stay up** all night and still have energy the next day.

2 My brother **couldn't speak** until he was five.

3 Mike **was able to run** a mile in ten minutes.

4 **Could** you **hear** the speaker? It was really loud in that room.

5 **Were** you **able to speak** to the professor?

We use **could** (**not**) or **was / were** (**not**) **able to** to talk about a past ability in general, as in **1 – 5**.

B

SPECIFIC ACTION WE HAD THE ABILITY TO DO

6 Yesterday, Tom **was able to attend** the meeting.
(NOT: ~~Yesterday, Tom could attend . . .~~)

7 We **were able to improve** our sales last year.
(NOT: ~~We could improve . . .~~)

8 I pushed and pushed, but I **couldn't open** the door.

9 Mike **was unable to** participate in sports last year.

To talk about a specific past action that we had the ability to do, we don't usually use *could*. We use *was / were able to*, as in **6 – 7**.

In negative sentences, we may use *couldn't* or *was / were not able to*, as in **8 – 9**.

C

USING ADVERBS WITH *COULD*

10a I **could only get** three tickets to the game, so one of us will have to stay home.

10b I **was only able to get** three tickets.

11a He was so tired that he **could barely walk**.

11b He **was barely able to walk**.

We also use *could* with adverbs like **only** and **barely**, as in **10a – 11b**. Notice that we put *only* and *barely* after the first helping verb (*could* or *was / were*).

• *Only* means "and nothing else."

• *Barely* means "almost not."

WARNING! We don't usually use *only* and *barely* in this way in negative sentences. (NOT: ~~I couldn't barely walk.~~)

11 | General Ability in the Past and Present Use phrases from this box to write sentences about your past abilities and present abilities. 9.3 A

IN THE PAST

climb a tree	play a sport well
cook my own dinner	see without glasses
do complicated math problems	speak English
drive a car	stand on my hands
focus on my studies	stay up all night

When I was a kid, I could stand on my hands. I still can!
When I was a teenager, I wasn't able to focus on my studies.
Now I'm a much better student.

Talk about It Compare the sentences you wrote above with a partner. Discuss which things have changed and why.

stand on my hands

12 | General Ability vs. Specific Action in the Past Does each sentence describe a past ability in general or a specific action that someone did in the past? Check (✓) your answers. 9.3 A-B

School opportunities	General ability	Specific action
1. a. At my high school, students were able to take college courses in the summer before senior year.	☐	☐
b. I was able to take a college biology course before my senior year. I got four units of credit.	☐	☐
2. a. We were also able to get college credit by passing Advanced Placement tests[4].	☐	☐
b. I was able to get 15 credits this way.	☐	☐
3. a. Because of my extra credits, I was able to enter college as a sophomore.	☐	☐
b. This was great for me because sophomores were able to take more interesting classes.	☐	☐
4. a. Students were able to use the job placement service to search for internships[5].	☐	☐
b. I was able to find a paying internship in my senior year. I was very lucky.	☐	☐
5. a. Interns[6] were able to apply for full-time jobs after graduation.	☐	☐
b. I didn't get hired at first, but I was able to get a job three months later.	☐	☐

Think about It Which sentences above can you rewrite using *could*? Rewrite them. What happens to the meaning in the other sentences if you try to rewrite them?

13 | Understanding When to Use *Could* and *Couldn't* Read this text. Underline all the examples of (*not*) *be able to*. Rewrite the sentences using *could* or *couldn't* if possible. 9.3 A-B

The Amazing Ancients

1. The ancient Egyptians did not have the wheel, but they had thousands of workers who were able to move large stones. They also had advanced mathematical knowledge. Because of this, they were able to build the Pyramids of Giza.

Pyramids of Giza

2. The ancient Polynesians didn't have compasses[7], but they were able to navigate[8] using the stars. Many scientists believe that they were able to travel from Taiwan to Micronesia over 3,000 years ago.
3. Using the abacus, the ancient Chinese were able to add, subtract, multiply, and divide with amazing speed.

ancient Chinese abacus

4. There were no cows or horses in ancient America, so the Aztecs were not able to use these animals for farming. However, the Aztecs had advanced farming technology, and they were able to grow enough food for their large population.
5. The ancient Mayans had excellent astronomers and were able to develop an accurate[9] calendar.

Mayan calendar

[4] **Advanced Placement tests:** tests that secondary students can take to earn college credit
[5] **internships:** on-the-job training
[6] **interns:** people working at internships
[7] **compasses:** devices for finding directions
[8] **navigate:** to plan a route
[9] **accurate:** correct

6. The ancient Greeks had indoor plumbing. They were able to bathe inside the house.
7. The ancient Romans built thousands of miles of roads across Europe, so their army was able to travel long distances quickly. The longest and most famous road was the Appian Way. The Romans were able to build it in less than a year.
8. The Babylonians had very advanced astronomy and mathematics. They were able to predict lunar eclipses[10] with great accuracy.

Write about It Work with a partner. Write four more sentences about things ancient people could or couldn't do. Look for information online if necessary.

14 | Questions for Present, Future, and Past Ability Complete these conversations. Use *can, could,* or a form of *be able to* and a verb from the box. (More than one answer may be possible.) If necessary, look back at Charts 9.1–9.2 for information on the present and future uses. `9.3 A–B`

1. A: _Can you feel_ _____ that?

   B: Yes! That hurts! That's my sore tooth.

2. A: _____ last night?

   B: No, I was awake all night. Now I'm exhausted.

3. A: I'm confused. _____ that lecture?

   B: No, the teacher speaks too fast.

4. A: _____ the sales report?

   B: No, I'm sorry. But I'll finish it this afternoon.

5. A: _____ this dish without onions?

   B: Yes, of course. We can prepare it any way you'd like.

6. A: _____ it by tomorrow?

   B: No, there's too much damage. But I think I can fix it by Saturday.

7. A: _____ this if I don't like it?

   B: Certainly. Just keep the receipt.

feel
finish
make
repair
return
sleep
understand

Think about It Which questions above are about the past, the present, or the future?

Talk about It Practice the conversations above with a partner.

15 | Using *Only/Barely* with *Could* Complete each sentence with *could* and *only* or *barely*. Make sure that the sentences are logical and meaningful. `9.3 C`

HEALTH COMPLAINTS

1. My head hurt so much that I _____ _could barely_ _____ think.
2. My eyes were so sore. I _____ open them.
3. My tooth hurt so badly that I _____ eat very soft food.
4. My back hurt so much that I _____ walk.

My tooth hurt so badly!

[10] **lunar eclipses:** occasions when the moon passes into the earth's shadow

5. I wanted to sleep on my stomach, but I _____ lie on my side.

6. I was really weak. When I got out of bed, I _____ stand up.

7. After the operation[11], I _____ lift things weighing less than 2 pounds.

8. I had trouble swallowing[12], so I _____ drink water and broth.

Write about It Rewrite the sentences in Activity 15 with *be able to*.

My head hurt so much that I was barely able to think.

Talk about It Have you ever had any of the health complaints in Activity 15? Tell your classmates.

"Last week, my head hurt so much that I could barely move. I think I hadn't eaten enough."

16 | Error Correction Correct any errors in these sentences. (Some sentences may not have any errors.)

1. Last night I went to bed and could fall asleep right away.

   Last night I went to bed and was able to fall asleep right away.

2. I'm so happy I could go to the picnic next weekend.

3. Sorry I can't come to the dinner last night.

4. She wasn't able to finish the project on time.

5. I studied every day and finally I can pass the test. I got a 90.

6. That runner was really tired. He couldn't barely finish the race.

7. Why can't you come to school yesterday?

8. Someday we can run a whole city on solar power.

9. I worked a lot of hours last week, but I could only make $300.

10. I'm sorry. I can't be able to see you next week.

9.4 Strong Certainty about the Present

We often use modals to show how certain we are that something is true. Charts 9.4 – 9.6 show how different modals express different degrees of certainty.

A

POSITIVE STATEMENTS

1 He answered all the questions correctly. He **must be** pretty smart.

2 She worked all night. She **has to be** exhausted.

3 You **have got to be** kidding. I don't believe you.

NEGATIVE STATEMENTS

4 That **can't be** true.

5 You **couldn't possibly understand** this.

6 You don't know about that place? You **must not live** around here. (NOT: ~~You mustn't live around here.~~)

We use some modals to express strong certainty about things in the present. Usually our belief is based on other information (or evidence) we have.

- We can use *must*, *have / has to*, and *have / has got to* when we are almost sure that something is true, as in **1 – 3**.

- We often use *can't*, *couldn't*, and *must not* to express disbelief or surprise, as in **4 – 6**. We do not usually contract *must not* in this case.

WARNING! We do not use these modals in this way to talk about the future. (NOT: ~~He couldn't come to work tomorrow.~~)

---

[11] **operation:** the act of cutting into the body to fix or remove something   [12] **swallowing:** making food or drink move down your throat

17 | Expressing Strong Certainty with *Must* Match each statement with the correct picture. `9.4 A`

PEOPLE WATCHING

a. He looks nervous. He must have a test.

b. He's in good shape. He must run a lot.

c. She must be a mom.

d. She must be pretty hungry.

e. He must have a headache or something.

f. They sure must like that toy.

1. ____

2. ____

3. ____

4. ____

5. ____

6. ____

Write about It What else do you believe about the people above? Write another statement for each person. Use *must*. Then read your sentences to a partner. Are all of them logical?

1. She must have a small child.

18 | Using Modals for a Strong Degree of Certainty Complete these conversations with *have to*, *have got to*, *must (not)*, *can't*, or *couldn't*. (More than one answer may be possible.) Then practice with a partner. `9.4 A`

SERVICE PROBLEMS

1. A: I'm really sorry. Your order isn't ready yet.

   B: Are you sure? It _____*has got to*_____ be ready. I brought it in two days ago.

   A: Unfortunately, we couldn't finish it because the computer crashed.

   B: But you _____ have more than one computer, right?

   A: We do. But the whole system crashed.

2. A: I'm sorry, but no one can see you today. Can you come back tomorrow?

   B: Are you sure? You _____ be that busy. I mean, there's nobody here.

   A: Oh, it'll get crowded in just a few minutes. Our schedule is full this afternoon.

   B: Maybe I can wait. People _____ cancel sometimes, right?

3. A: Where's the server? I'm starving.

   B: Oh, they're always slow here. You _____ come here very often.

   A: No, I don't. But the food _____ be fantastic.

   B: Why do you say that?

   A: Because the service is so slow, but it's still really popular.

RESEARCH SAYS...

We don't often use *must* in informal speaking. However, when we do, we usually use it to express strong certainty.

 CORPUS

4. A: This _____ be someone else's order.

   B: I'm pretty sure it's yours, actually.

   A: No. It _____ be mine. This lists four cups of coffee and I only ordered one.

5. A: This place is always empty.

   B: I know. Everyone buys books online nowadays. The owners _____ be worried.

   A: Maybe. They _____ pay very much rent, though. This neighborhood is pretty cheap, and they've had the store for years.

Talk about It Where are the people in each conversation in Activity 18? Share your ideas with classmates.

19 | Strong Certainty vs. Obligation Underline the uses of *must* (*not*), *have to*, and *have got to*. Do they express strong certainty or an obligation? Check (✓) your answers. Then practice with a partner. `9.4 A`

A MEETING	STRONG CERTAINTY	OBLIGATION
1. A: You've got to wear a suit and tie to the meeting. B: I know.	☐	✓
2. A: You must be very important! They've seated you at the main table. B: That's because I'm speaking today.	☐	☐
3. A: You must remember Dr. Alton. You met her last year. B: Of course. Nice to see you again.	☐	☐
4. A: We have to present our report at 3. B: That's fine. We'll be ready.	☐	☐
5. A: Mr. Rand is still running the company. But he's got to be 80 years old. B: Hmm. I wonder if he's going to retire.	☐	☐
6. A: We have to wait until 11 before we can take a break. B: OK.	☐	☐
7. A: That must be the new manager. B: It is. I met him yesterday.	☐	☐
8. A: Can you read that sign? B: Yeah. It says, "Every attendee must wear identification."	☐	☐
9. A: The CEO[13] and the CFO[14] must not like each other very much. They haven't spoken all day. B: Yeah, I noticed that.	☐	☐
10. A: I'm so tired. This has to be the last presentation, right? B: Nope. There's one more after this.	☐	☐

FYI

We can use the modals **must**, **have to**, and **have got to** to talk about **certainty** or to talk about **obligation**.

You **must be** pretty smart. (I'm certain.)

You **must be** on time. (This is required.)

Think about It Compare your answers above with your classmates. For each conversation, what helped you decide between the two meanings?

[13] **CEO:** chief executive officer

[14] **CFO:** chief financial officer

20 | Strong Certainty vs. Ability Underline the uses of *can't* and *couldn't* in these conversations. Do they mean "impossible" or "not able"? Write *I* (impossible) or *NA* (not able) above each use. If necessary, look back at Chart 9.1 for information on *can* for ability. [9.4 A]

1. A: Is that Tom in the water?

   B: No way! That can't be Tom!

   A: Why not?

   B: Because he can't swim.

2. A: It can't be 8 already!

   B: I'm afraid it is. Why?

   A: I didn't realize how late it was. Now I can't go shopping.

3. A: This answer can't be right. But I'm not sure what I did wrong.

   B: Sorry, I can't help you with that. I'm terrible at math.

4. A: I think Amin is awake.

   B: No, he couldn't be awake already.

   A: Why not?

   B: He was up until 3 last night. He couldn't fall asleep.

5. A: Where's Bill? He's usually here by now.

   B: He couldn't come to class. He had to pick up his dad from the airport.

   A: Well, he's with someone in the cafeteria right now, but it couldn't be his dad. He looks so young!

Talk about It Practice the conversations above with a partner.

9.5 Weaker Certainty about the Present and Future

We can use the modals *might* (not), *may* (not), and *could* to express weaker certainty about a situation. It means we believe something is possible, but we aren't sure.

We can use *might* (not), *may* (not), and *could* to talk about present situations, as in **1 – 5**.

WARNING! We do not contract *might not* or *may not*. (NOT: ~~mightn't / mayn't~~)

A

POSITIVE STATEMENTS ABOUT THE PRESENT	NEGATIVE STATEMENTS ABOUT THE PRESENT
1 She's not in her office. She **might be** at lunch.	4 These documents **might not** be important, but I'm keeping them just in case.
2 All the lights are off. They **may be closed** today.	5 I always serve a vegetarian dish because some guests **may not eat** meat.
3 You have a fever. You **could have** the flu.	Remember: *Couldn't* expresses stronger certainty (see Chart 9.4).

We can also use *might* (not), *may* (not), and *could* to talk about future situations, as in **6 – 10**.

B

POSITIVE STATEMENTS ABOUT THE FUTURE	NEGATIVE STATEMENTS ABOUT THE FUTURE
6 If they go up too high, gas prices **might affect** the local economy.	9 He's sick. He **might not come** to work tomorrow.
7 The team has been training hard. They **may win** the game tomorrow.	10 There's a lot to do. They **may not finish** by tomorrow.
8 We're hoping for a donation. Additional money **could help** our cause.	

21 | Expressing Weaker Certainty about the Present
Complete each answer below with *might* (*not*), *may* (*not*), or *could* and a verb from the box. (More than one answer may be possible.) **9.5 A**

be	feel	have	know	like

1. Why is Donna smiling?

   It _____ *may be* _____ her birthday.

   She _____ in a good mood.

   She _____ about the bad news.

2. Why is that man wearing a blue uniform?

   He _____ a mail carrier.

   It _____ comfortable to wear.

   He _____ a job at an airport.

3. Why isn't Marco in class today?

   He _____ sick.

   He _____ a doctor's appointment.

   He _____ we have class today.

4. Why is the clerk so unfriendly?

   She _____ good.

   She _____ sick.

   She _____ her job.

5. Why is Sam's face so red?

   He _____ embarrassed.

   He _____ out of breath[15].

   He _____ sick.

Talk about It Talk to a partner. Make statements about these pictures like the statements above using *might* (*not*), *may* (*not*), or *could*.

22 | Making Guesses
Read these facts. Write guesses about why they are true. Use *might* (*not*), *may* (*not*), or *could*. Then compare with a partner. Which are the best guesses? **9.5 A**

Fascinating Facts

1. You burn more calories[16] sleeping than watching TV.

   We might move around a lot when we are sleeping.
   We may not move very much when we watch TV.

2. Women live longer than men.
3. People eat more when they are in groups than they do when they're alone.
4. If one person sees someone in trouble, he or she will usually help. But if a crowd of people sees someone in trouble, sometimes nobody helps.
5. People are about one centimeter taller in the morning than in the evening.
6. It is easier to remember facts if you read them in an unusual, difficult-to-read font[17].
7. Smiling can make you feel happier.
8. People usually do not notice small mistakes in books or movies.

[15] **out of breath:** having trouble breathing, for example, after exercise

[16] **calories:** units for measuring the energy value of food

[17] **font:** a style of printed letters

23 | Weaker Certainty vs. Permission Underline the uses of modals in these conversations. Do they express weaker certainty or permission? (Remember: The modal *may* can express weaker certainty or permission.) Check (✓) your answers. 9.5 A

EMPLOYEES AND EMPLOYERS	WEAKER CERTAINTY	PERMISSION
1. Employees <u>may not make</u> personal phone calls at work.	☐	✓
2. If employees have flexible work hours, they might be less likely to quit.	☐	☐
3. Family problems could distract[18] employees from their work.	☐	☐
4. Employees can retire at the age of 65 and collect full benefits[19].	☐	☐
5. An older employee may have more experience than a younger one.	☐	☐
6. An older employee might not work for a small salary.	☐	☐
7. New employees may not take vacation in their first three months of employment.	☐	☐
8. New employees may not feel comfortable asking for help.	☐	☐
9. A young employee may not be interested in staying at the same company for a long time.	☐	☐
10. A younger employee could have more energy than an older one.	☐	☐
11. Employees cannot leave before 5:00.	☐	☐
12. Employers may hire anyone, as long as they don't practice discrimination[20].	☐	☐

Talk about It Talk with a partner about the sentences above. Do you agree with them? Why or why not?

A: Employees may not make personal phone calls at work.
B: I don't think that's right. People should be able to make a short phone call.

24 | Expressing Weaker Certainty about the Future Tell a partner which things you *may, might,* or *could* do on this list. Explain your answer. (You can use a form like *be going to* to talk about things you are definitely going to do.) 9.5 B

1. take a trip on an airplane	6. buy someone a present
2. buy a car or a bike	7. get a new phone
3. read more than two books	8. get a new computer
4. go to the beach	9. go to a museum
5. visit a different country	10. change your hairstyle

I might take a trip on an airplane next summer. I'm thinking about going to China.
I'm definitely going to buy a bike. I want to start riding to work.

Write about It Write three sentences about three other things you are thinking of doing. Share them with your classmates.

[18]**distract:** to stop you from thinking about what you are doing
[19]**benefits:** money that is paid by a company when someone stops working

[20]**discrimination:** treating someone in an unfair way

25 | Making Guesses Look at the headlines. Do you think these might be real news stories someday? Write a sentence about each headline with *might (not)*, *may (not)*, or *could*. You can use *by* + a year to say when. `9.5 B`

1. Humans Put Building on Moon

   Humans may put a building on the moon by 2020.

2. Scientists Find Cure for Common Cold
3. World Uses More Solar Power than Oil
4. 90% of Homes Have 3-D Televisions
5. Most Cars Run on Autopilot[21]
6. Technology Ends World Hunger
7. Private Spaceship Flies to Mars
8. Governments Stop Printing Paper Money

> **FYI**
>
> We sometimes use the frequency adverbs *never* and *(not) ever* with *may* and *might* to make a negative statement.
>
> Humans **might never put** a building on the moon.
>
> Humans **may not ever put** a building on the moon.

Talk about It Read the sentences you wrote above to a partner. Explain your predictions.

"Humans may put a building on the moon by 2020. Many countries are already able to go to the moon."

9.6 Expectations about the Present and Future with *Should*

A

POSITIVE STATEMENTS

1 The store **should be** open now. It usually opens at 7 a.m.

2 Don't worry. He **should be** here soon. He's almost never late.

NEGATIVE STATEMENTS

3 She lost her keys. I **shouldn't be** surprised—she loses things all the time.

4 The test **shouldn't be** difficult for you. You're very well prepared.

We can use **should** (**not**) to express our expectations about present or future situations, as in **1 – 4**. *Should* expresses moderate certainty—not as strong as *have to* or *must*.

We often contract *should not* as **shouldn't** in negative statements, as in **3 – 4**.

 ONLINE

26 | Expectations with *Should* and *Shouldn't* Match the questions with the answers. Then practice with a partner. `9.6 A`

EXPECTATIONS

1. Will your teacher be late to your next class? ____
2. What will the weather be like tomorrow? ____
3. Where is your best friend right now? ____
4. Who will you see next weekend? ____
5. Will you have a good day tomorrow? ____
6. When will the store open? ____
7. When are you getting home? ____
8. Will you be at work Friday? ____

a. It should be warmer than today.
b. He should be at work.
c. I should. It's my day off.
d. It should open at 7.
e. I shouldn't be. But my boss may call me in.
f. She shouldn't be. She's usually on time.
g. I should be there around 5.
h. I should see my brother. He usually comes over on Sunday.

---

[21] **autopilot:** a device that controls a plane, car, etc., for the pilot or driver

Write about It Write your own responses to these questions. Use *should* or *shouldn't*.

1. How will the weather be tomorrow?
2. What will the teacher cover in your next class?
3. When will you finish your studies?
4. Where will you be three hours from now?

27 | Advice vs. Expectations Do these sentences express advice or an expectation? Check (✓) your answers. `9.6 A`

	Advice	Expectation
1. You really should eat more vegetables. Your diet isn't very healthy.	☐	☐
2. She should have some money left. I gave her quite a bit yesterday.	☐	☐
3. They should be pretty happy. They got everything they wanted.	☐	☐
4. He should be careful. That road is dangerous this time of year.	☐	☐
5. You shouldn't worry about her. She'll be fine.	☐	☐
6. You shouldn't be so tired. You just woke up!	☐	☐
7. They say the storm is over. It should be beautiful tomorrow.	☐	☐
8. You shouldn't have any trouble finding my house. It's right on the corner.	☐	☐

28 | Using Modals for Certainty and Expectation Use the modals in this box to complete the conversations below. Some modals can work in more than one place. Look back at Charts 9.4–9.6 for all the uses. `9.6 A`

STRONG CERTAINTY		EXPECTATIONS	WEAKER CERTAINTY	
must (not)	can't	should(n't)	might (not)	could
have (got) to	couldn't		may (not)	

1. A: Look! I see a whale!

   B: I don't know what that is, but it _____ be a whale. We never see whales around here.

2. A: What is that awful noise?

   B: I don't know. The neighbors are out of town, so it _____ be them.

3. A: Why are all the lights off?

   B: It _____ be closed. There's no one here.

   A: Hmm. I wanted to buy some batteries.

   B: We _____ need any. I bought some just a few days ago.

4. A: Did you finish Chapter 5?

   B: I did. I stayed up all night.

   A: You _____ be exhausted!

   B: Yeah, I am. But that chapter _____ be on the test, so I wanted to finish it.

5. A: Peter ate all the cherries and left all the chocolates.

   B: He _____ like chocolate very much.

whale

STRONG CERTAINTY		EXPECTATIONS	WEAKER CERTAINTY	
must (not)	can't	should(n't)	might (not)	could
have (got) to	couldn't		may (not)	

6. A: I _____ be here tomorrow. I have to pick up my uncle from the airport,

   but I'm not sure what time.

   B: That's OK. We _____ be fine without you for one day.

7. A: So what do you think? Are they going to win?

   B: I'm afraid they _____. They're not playing very well.

Think about It Compare your answers in Activity 28 with a partner. Explain your modal choices.
Then practice the conversations with your partner.

9.7 Expressing Certainty with Linking Verbs

A

SEEM, LOOK, AND SOUND

1a He **must be** tired. He keeps making mistakes.
1b He **seems** tired. He keeps making mistakes.

2 A: Did you like the cake? It **looked** delicious.
  B: It was!

3 A: I'm afraid to take that class. It **sounds** really difficult.
  B: Really? I think it **sounds** interesting.

Sometimes we use the linking verbs **seem**, **look**, and **sound** to express fairly strong certainty, as in **1a – 1b**. This is similar to a **modal** meaning.

We usually use:

• *look* for things we can see, as in **2**

• *sound* for things we have heard or read about, as in **3**

Notice: We usually use adjectives after linking verbs.

B

LOOK LIKE AND SOUND LIKE

4 This **looks like** a good idea. I think we should try it.

5 The new plan **sounds like** an answer to our problems.

6 They're ahead by two goals. It **looks like** they are going to win.

7 It **sounds like** you'll really enjoy it.

We can also use **look like** and **sound like** to express certainty. These expressions are often followed by:

• a **noun phrase**, as in **4 – 5**

• a **clause**, as in **6 – 7**

GO ONLINE

29 | Using *Seem*, *Look*, and *Sound* Complete these conversations. Use the correct form of *seem*, *look*, or *sound* and an adjective from the box. (More than one answer may be possible.) Then practice with a partner. **9.7 A**

IMPRESSIONS

1. A: I cut my finger last night.

   B: Ooh. That _____*looks painful*_____.

   A: It is. I had to get four stitches[22].

2. A: That guy never does any of his work. He _____ really _____.

   B: Actually, he has two jobs. I think he's just too tired to do his schoolwork.

3. A: Why is Ben eating lunch by himself?

   B: I don't know, but he _____. Let's invite him to eat with us.

angry
annoying
disappointed
lazy
lonely
lost
painful
scary

[22] **stitches:** short pieces of thread that doctors use to sew the edges of a cut together

4. A: There's no way I'm going on that roller coaster. It _____!

   B: Oh, come on.

5. A: Did you hear Lee this morning? He _____ really _____.

   B: I know! I wonder who he was yelling at.

6. A: I felt bad for Tony when he lost the race. He _____ so _____.

   B: Yeah. Poor guy.

7. A: My neighbor is practicing the piano again. She practices every night at 11.

   B: That _____.

   A: It is. Especially since she's not very good at it.

8. A: You _____. Can I help you?

   B: Yes, thanks. I can't find Market Street.

Think about It Work with a partner. Look at each sentence you completed in Activity 29. How could you rewrite it using a modal?

Write about It Write six sentences with *seem*, *look*, and *sound* about people and things you know. Use adjectives from this box or your own ideas. Then share your sentences with your classmates.

delicious	exciting	fun	happy	intelligent	nice
easy	friendly	great	helpful	interesting	wonderful

Myung Ja looks happy today.   *The new James Bond movie sounds exciting.*

30 | Using *Look Like* and *Sound Like* Use the correct form of *look like* and *sound like* to complete the responses. Then practice with a partner. [9.7 B]

1. A: Did you hear those guys cheering?

   B: Yep. It _____*sounds like*_____ the Tigers are winning.

2. A: Where is Christine?

   B: I don't know. It _____ she's absent today.

3. A: I read four chapters last night! I'm really tired.

   B: It _____ you were up late.

4. A: Carla was packing her suitcase this morning.

   B: Hmm. It _____ she's going away.

5. A: Who is that?

   B: I don't know. She _____ she might be a professor.

6. A: Do you know when the meeting is going to be over?

   B: Everyone is standing up. It _____ they're finishing now.

7. A: He's always complaining about his job lately.

   B: I know. It _____ he's going to quit.

8. A: Let's go out for dinner tonight.

   B: That _____ a good idea.

9.8 Expressing Certainty with Adverbs

Another way to express certainty is with **adverbs**. Different adverbs express different degrees of certainty.

definitely / clearly = I am certain.

apparently = I'm almost certain. The evidence suggests this is true.

probably = This is very possible.

maybe / perhaps = This is possible.

Notice the placement of adverbs, as in **1 – 8**.

A

SENTENCES WITH A SIMPLE VERB

	subject	adverb	main verb	
1	My sister	**probably**	**knows**	the answer.
2	She	**apparently**	**works**	for that company.

SENTENCES WITH *BE* AS A MAIN OR HELPING VERB

	subject	*be*	adverb	
3	We	are	**definitely**	going to change our plans.
4	This	is	**clearly**	very important.

NEGATIVE SENTENCES

	subject	adverb	negative verb	
5	Sam	**probably**	**won't be**	home tonight.
6	The discussion	**clearly**	**isn't going**	well.

SENTENCES WITH *MAYBE / PERHAPS*

	adverb	subject	verb	
7	**Maybe**	they	**took**	the bus.
8	**Perhaps**	Lela	**isn't**	interested.

 GO ONLINE

31 | Adding Adverbs Read the first sentence of each pair. Add *clearly, apparently, probably, definitely,* or *maybe* to the second sentence. (More than one answer may be possible.) **9.8 A**

                                  probably

1. The student is failing his classes. He doesn't understand the material.

2. They took a popular dish off the menu. There are going to be a lot of complaints.

3. Pablo has a lot of soccer trophies[23]. He's a good player.

4. The students finished the test in ten minutes. It was too easy.

5. The children left most of their food on the plates. They didn't like it.

6. I'm not sure where she is. She went to the store.

7. The audience is laughing and cheering. They love the show.

8. That coffee shop has opened five new stores in this area. It is doing very well.

9. Everyone is reading that book lately. It is a big seller.

Think about It Take turns reading your sentences above aloud with a partner. If your adverb choices are different, discuss whether they both make sense.

---

[23]**trophies:** silver cups, etc., that you get for winning a sports event

32 | Using Adverbs to Write Formal Statements Rewrite these sentences using *clearly, apparently, probably, definitely,* or *perhaps* instead of *must* or *may*. (More than one answer may be possible.) ┃9.8 A┃

IN COURT

1. The defendant must be worried.

   The defendant is definitely worried.

2. The jury must not believe him.
3. The defendant's lawyer must be nervous.
4. The judge must be tired.
5. The defendant's lawyer may ask for a break soon.
6. This trial[24] may last for many days.
7. The witness must know the defendant.
8. The police officer may speak tomorrow.

33 | Using Modals, Verbs, and Adverbs Use the words in this box to complete the text below. You will use one word twice. If necessary, look back at Charts 9.4, 9.5, and 9.7. ┃9.8 A┃

might	seems	clearly	maybe
must	looks	definitely	probably

The Grand Canyon

The Grand Canyon _____*must*_____ be one of the most
                        1
beautiful places in the world. Millions of people visit every year.

It _____ like most visitors stay up near the rim of
        2
the canyon rather than hiking down the trails. The steep trails

are _____ too difficult for many people. But if
        3
you're an experienced hiker, you _____ want to try
                                      4
hiking down. If you don't like to hike, _____ you'd
                                            5
enjoy a helicopter tour. It is _____ expensive,
                                  6
but thrilling!

Most people visit the South Rim of the canyon. It is easy to get there, and there are many places to stay

nearby. However, if you don't like crowds, the North Rim is _____ a better choice for you.
                                                                7
It takes a long time to drive to the North Rim, so there are fewer visitors. If it _____ like you
                                                                                        8
will have enough time, the North Rim is _____ worth the trip.
                                            9

Think about It Which words in the box above could fit in more than one place in the text?

Write about It Write four sentences about a beautiful place. Use words from the box above. Then read your sentences to a partner.

[24]**trial:** the process in a court of law

9.9 Used To for Past Habits and States

A

POSITIVE STATEMENTS

1 My mother **used to make** our lunches every morning.

2 My friends and I **used to take** the bus to school on Mondays and Wednesdays.

3 I **used to live** in Paris. I moved to New York three years ago.

4 He **used to have** a moustache. He shaved it off last week.

5 In high school, I **worked** hard to get good grades.
(NOT: ~~I used to work hard to get good grades.~~)

NEGATIVE STATEMENTS AND QUESTIONS

6 That **didn't use to bother** us.

7 A: **Did** you **use to have** long hair?
B: Yeah, it was pretty long.

We use **used to** + the **base form of a main verb** to talk about past habits, as in **1** and **2**. It means that something happened regularly in the past, but it doesn't happen now—something has changed.

Used to can also describe states or situations that are different now from the past, as in **3** and **4**.

WARNING! We can't use *used to* with every past verb. We don't use it to simply talk about events that began and ended in the past, or if the state or action only happened once, as in **5**.

Notice that we use the base form **use** in negative statements, as in **6**, and questions, as in **7**.

B

USING *NOW*, *THEN*, AND *ANYMORE*

8 He **used to be** rich, but **then** he lost all his money. **Now** he has to work two jobs. He's **not** very happy **anymore**.

We can use *used to* with expressions like *now*, *then*, and *not . . . anymore* to emphasize the change between past and present, as in **8**.
- *Now* and *then* usually come before the subject.
- We use *anymore* at the end of a clause.

C

ADVERBS OF FREQUENCY WITH *USED TO*

9 We **always used to visit** my grandparents during summer vacation. We **sometimes used to stay** until September.

10 I **never used to** exercise.

We can use **adverbs of frequency** before *used to*, as in **9**.

Never makes a sentence negative, as in **10**. It is more common than *didn't use to*.

🔊 **34 | Pronunciation Note: *Used To/Use To*** Listen to the note. Then do Activity 35.

In everyday speech, we reduce *used to* to "usta." As a result, *use to* and *used to* sound the same.

COMPARE

1a She **used to live** on another street.

1b She **didn't use to live** near here.

1c **Did** she **use to live** near you?

🔊 **35 | Identifying *Used To* and *Use To*** Listen to the sentences and circle the correct form. Notice that the forms sound the same. 9.9 A

COMPLAINTS ABOUT HOW THINGS HAVE CHANGED

1. used to	use to	3. used to	use to	5. used to	use to	7. used to	use to
2. used to	use to	4. used to	use to	6. used to	use to	8. used to	use to

🔊 **Talk about It** Listen again. Take notes about the complaints you hear. Do you agree with any of the complaints? Tell your classmates.

"One complaint was, 'People used to be more polite.' I agree with that."

36 | Using *Used To* for Past Habits and States Work with a partner. Ask questions with *did . . . use to* for each of these things. `9.9 A`

CHILDHOOD

1. walk to school
2. play outside all day
3. eat breakfast with your parents
4. have to go to bed early

5. hide when you were in trouble
6. suck your thumb
7. like dinosaurs
8. have a lot of toys

A: *Did you use to walk to school?*
B: *Sometimes. But I usually took the bus.*

Write about It Write five sentences with *used to* about your habits, routines, likes, and dislikes from the past.

I didn't use to enjoy reading.

37 | *Used To* vs. the Simple Past Read these sentences about great soccer stars. Rewrite the **bold** verb with *used to* if possible. `9.9 A`

SOCCER GREATS

Pelé

1. Pelé **grew up** in poverty in Brazil.
2. He **earned** extra money by working in tea shops.
3. He **practiced** soccer using a sock stuffed with newspapers.
4. He **tried out** for Santos Football Club when he was 15 years old.

Zinedine Zidane

5. Zidane's parents **immigrated** to France from Algeria.
6. He **practiced** his soccer skills in the streets of Marseille.
7. When he was 14 years old, he **joined** the Association Sportive de Cannes Football youth division.

Diego Maradona

8. Maradona **received** his first soccer ball as a gift when he was 3 years old.
9. He **became** a ball boy for a professional team when he was 12.
10. During halftime, he **amazed** audiences with his tricks with the ball.

Think about It Which sentences above could you NOT rewrite using *used to*? Why?

38 | Using Expressions to Compare Time Complete the comparisons with *then, now,* or *anymore*. `9.9 B`

CHANGING PLACES

1. This area used to be farmland. ___Now___ it is covered with homes and shopping malls. You don't see farms around here _____.

2. This store used to be very busy. _____ they built the big shopping mall, and _____ people don't come here _____.

3. This school used to be much smaller. _____ there are a lot more students. It's not easy to get into classes _____.

4. That house used to be in good shape. Nobody lives there _____, and the paint is peeling and the grass is brown.

5. This restaurant didn't use to be very popular. _____ they changed the menu. _____ it's crowded every night.

6. It used to be easy to get into this university. _____ thousands of students apply every year. It's hard to get admitted _____.

Write about It Write two or three sentences about changes in these places: your hometown, your neighborhood, your favorite restaurant, and your school. Use *used to*, *now*, *then*, and *anymore*.

39 | Adverbs of Frequency with *Used To* Think of a teacher you had. Use these ideas to write about things that teacher *sometimes*, *always*, and *never* used to do. Add two ideas of your own. `9.9 C`

A TEACHER FROM THE PAST

1. assign a lot of homework
2. sing in class
3. show videos
4. give us free time in class
5. allow students to eat in class
6. allow students to sleep in class

He always used to assign a lot of homework.

9.10 Using Modals in Speaking

A

COMMON EXPRESSIONS WITH *CAN* AND *CAN'T*

The expressions in **1 – 13** are very common in spoken English.

The negative expressions with *can't* are more common than the positive ones.

1 I can't help it. (= I can't control myself.)

2 I can't wait. (= I'm excited about it.)

3 I can wait. (= I don't mind waiting.)

4 I can't stand it. (= I hate it.)

5 I can stand it. (= It doesn't bother me.)

6 I can't imagine. (= I have no idea.)

7 I can imagine. (= I can picture the situation.)

8 I can't afford it. (= I don't have enough money to buy it.)

9 I can afford it. (= I have enough money to buy it.)

10 I can't believe it. (= I don't think it's true. OR "Wow!")

11 I can believe it. (= It's easy for me to think it's true.)

12 I can't deal with it. (= I can't manage the situation.)

13 I can deal with it. (= I can manage the situation.)

B

USING MODALS IN SHORT ANSWERS

14 A: Will he **come** to the meeting?
B: He **can't**. He doesn't have time.

15 A: Is the plumber going to **come** today?
B: She **may**. But she hasn't called.

16 A: Does Mark **have** the keys?
B: He **must**. He had them this morning.

17 A: **Is** he at work?
B: He **might be**. He left about 20 minutes ago.

18 A: **Is** she **talking** on the phone?
B: She **must be**. There's no one else in the room.

We can use most **modals** as short answers to questions, as in **14 – 16**.

Notice: When we use a modal as a short answer, we understand that the modal refers back to the main **verb** in the question.

When the main verb is *be* or when we use a present progressive form, we use modal + *be* in the short answer, as in **17 – 18**.

40 | Using Expressions with *Can* and *Can't* Complete each response with *can* or *can't*. `9.10 A`

1. A: Do you like working nights?

   B: No! I ___can't___ stand it.

2. A: Is he going to buy that car?

   B: Maybe. He _____ afford it, but he's not sure he wants it.

3. A: Should you be eating all that chocolate?

   B: I shouldn't. But I _____ help it!

4. A: Would you rather come back tomorrow?

   B: No, it's OK. I _____ wait.

5. A: Where is Mark?

   B: I _____ imagine. I'm surprised he's not here.

6. A: The Rangers lost the game.

   B: I _____ believe it! They always win.

7. A: There's so much work to do around here.

   B: Don't worry. I _____ deal with it.

8. A: Are you going to Hawaii?

   B: Yes, next week. I _____ wait!

41 | Using Expressions with *Can* and *Can't* Complete these conversations with expressions from Chart 9.10. Two answers are positive and the rest are negative. `9.10 A`

1. A: Shh. Don't talk so loud.

   B: Sorry. I _____can't help_____ it. My voice gets loud when I'm excited.

   A: Why are you so excited?

   B: My husband just bought a new car. I _____ to see it!

2. A: What's the matter?

   B: I have so much housework and yard work to do. I just _____ it.

   A: Why don't you pay someone to help you?

   B: I'd love to, but I _____ it.

3. A: Please turn off that noise. I _____ it!

   B: It's great music. It's not noise.

   A: Yes, it is. I _____ why you listen to that stuff.

4. A: I _____ that the rent is so high now! It used to be much cheaper to live here.

   B: I know. But don't worry. We _____ it. I just got a raise.

5. A: Just think, Sara is traveling around the world right now.

   B: I _____ that. She always was adventurous.

Write about It Choose four of the expressions from Chart 9.10 A. Work with a partner to write a conversation that includes the four expressions. Then read your conversation to another pair.

42 | Using Modals for Short Answers Write a short answer for each question. Use *can't*, *couldn't*, *may*, *might*, and *must* (+ *be*). (More than one answer may be possible.) `9.10 B`

1. A: Will you lend me a thousand dollars?

   B: I _____. I don't have that much money!

2. A: Is your friend working today?

   B: He _____. He usually works on Tuesday, and that's today.

3. A: Are you going out for dinner on Friday?

   B: I _____. It depends on whether I get paid.

4. A: Are you going to vote next month?

   B: I _____. I'm not a citizen yet.

5. A: Does your teacher have a computer at home?

   B: She _____. She works a lot at home.

6. A: Are you going to bed early tonight?

   B: I _____. I need the sleep.

7. A: Is your friend coming to the movie with us?

   B: She _____. I'm not sure yet.

8. A: Did you read this chapter last night?

   B: I _____. I had other homework.

Talk about It Ask and answer these questions with a partner. Use a short answer with a modal, and give more information about your answer.

1. Are you going out for dinner this weekend?

   "I might. I'm going to see how I feel Saturday night."

2. Are you doing something fun next summer?

3. Are you going to study tonight?

43 | Using Modals for Short Answers Write a question for each answer so that the answer is true for you. Don't use the modal in the question. Then add more information to the answer. **9.10 B**

1. _____

   I might. _____

2. _____

   I couldn't. _____

3. _____

   I used to. _____

4. _____

   I can't. _____

5. _____

   I should. _____

6. _____

   I have to. _____

Talk about It Take turns asking and answering the questions you wrote above with a partner.

9.11 Using Modals in Writing

A	***CAN* AND *MAY* FOR POSSIBILITY** **1** February **can be** very cold in this area. Temperatures often **drop** below zero. (= Perhaps not every day in February is cold.) **2** Active worker bees only **live** for a few weeks, but the queen bee **may live** for a year or more. (= Not every queen bee lives more than one year.) **3** Many visitors **come** through the museum's doors, but they **may not see** all of the exhibits.	We usually use the **simple present** to talk about facts and make general statements. However, we sometimes use the modals **may** and **can** to make our writing more exact, as in **1 – 2**. With the modal, the statement describes what happens some of the time (not always). We also use the negative form of *may* this way, as in **3**.
B	***WOULD* FOR PAST HABITS** **4** When I was young, I **would fall** asleep on the sofa and wake up in my bed. **5** In my old neighborhood, the kids **would play** in the street until sunset. **6** My father **used to work** until 7 or 8 in the evening. We **would** always **wait** until he got home to eat dinner. I **used to get** so hungry! But Mom **wouldn't let** us eat dinner until he got there.	We sometimes use **would** in writing to describe past habits and things we often did. However, we usually introduce the past time before using *would*. For example: • In **4 – 5**, **When I was young** and **In my old neighborhood** introduce the past context. • In **6**, the first sentence with **used to** tells us that we are talking about the past. It is very common to use *used to*, *would*, and the simple past together. **WARNING!** We cannot use *would* to describe a past state. *He used to live in Miami.* (NOT: ~~He would live in Miami.~~)

306

44 | Using *Can* and *May* Read this text. Rewrite the underlined part of the sentences using *can* or *may*. (Sometimes the modal is given in parentheses.) `9.11 A`

Barcelona

<u>It's very hot</u> and humid in Barcelona in the summer. If you go in August,
¹
<u>you see</u> a lot of empty streets because so many of the local people are on
²
vacation. And if you try to go shopping in the middle of the day,

<u>you discover</u> that the grocery store is closed. Fortunately, <u>you always find</u>
³   ⁴
lots of fresh fruit and vegetables at the farmers' market downtown. On the

wide street called The Ramblas, <u>you find</u> flowers and birds for sale. Even at
⁵
night, <u>the street is</u> full of people. The beaches south of the city are lovely, but
⁶
<u>you want to bring</u> sunscreen. It's almost always sunny!
⁷

1. (can) _____It can be very hot and humid in Barcelona in the summer._____

2. (may) _____

3. (may) _____

4. (can) _____

5. _____

6. _____

7. _____

Write about It Write a paragraph about where you live. Use *may* and *can* in two or three sentences.

45 | Noticing *Would* and *Used To* Read this text. Circle the examples of *would* and *used to*. Underline the verbs in the simple past. `9.11 B`

LAURA INGALLS WILDER

Laura Ingalls Wilder grew up in the late 1800s. She wrote many books about her childhood that children still read today. When Laura was a little girl, she lived in a cabin in the woods. Her father used to hunt and fish for most of their meat. He would bring the meat home, and then the family would work together to prepare the meat for winter. One day he brought home a bear. Laura's mother used to grow onions, potatoes, and carrots. She would store the vegetables in the cool cellar below the house. The family would live through the winter on the food they had prepared and stored in the spring. One winter was very long and cold, and the family almost didn't survive.

Think about It Why did the writer choose *used to* and *would* for some of the verbs in the text above? Which verbs have to be in the simple past? Were there any other verb forms used? Why?

46 | Using _Would_ Read these sentences. Rewrite six of the sentences with _would_ instead of _used to_. Two of the sentences would not be correct with _would_. 9.11 B

Ancient Rome

1. Much of western and central Europe used to be part of the Roman Empire.
2. The Romans used to build roads to the areas they conquered.
3. They used to bring their advanced plumbing technology with them.
4. They used to fight huge battles with thousands of soldiers.
5. Rich Romans used to eat food imported from Asia and other parts of Europe.
6. They used to lie on couches while they ate.
7. They used to decorate their houses with colorful mosaics[25].
8. Rome used to be the center of power in the Western world.

mosaic

WRAP-UP Demonstrate Your Knowledge

A | DISCUSSION Work with a group. Write as many sentences as you can to make guesses about each picture below. Use words from the box.

must (not)	might (not)	definitely	seems
have (got) to	may (not)	clearly	looks (like)
can't	could	apparently	
couldn't		probably	

1. _It might be New York. It's clearly cold._

B | WRITING Use these sentence starters to write about the past. Use _could, couldn't, (not) be able to, used to,_ and _would_.

1. When I was three years old,
2. Five years ago,
3. Before I came to this school,
4. When I first started learning English,
5. Before my parents met,
6. Before there were televisions,
7. Before there were airplanes,
8. In the 1800s,
9. During ancient times,
10. Before there were computers,

Choose one of the sentence starters above and develop it into a topic sentence. Write a paragraph.

[25] **mosaics:** pictures made from small pieces of glass

ABILITY

Present / Future		
• simple modal	can / can't	She **can play** the piano very well.
• phrasal modal	am / is / are able to	They **are able to attend** all of the meetings.
	will be able to	We**'ll be able to fix** this mistake very soon.
Past		
• simple modal	could / couldn't	When I was young, I **could speak** a little Chinese.
• phrasal modal	was / were able to	They **were able to attract** new customers.

CERTAINTY

STRONGER CERTAINTY

Present		
• simple modals	must (not)	It's 10 degrees. You **must be** cold!
	can't	You **can't be done** yet. The test is 30 pages.
	couldn't	This **couldn't be** mine. I lost mine.
• phrasal modals	has / have to	It's 6:00. They **have to be** home by now.
	has / have got to	He's not here, so he**'s got to be** at the office.
Present / Future		
• verbs	seem	She **seems** very tired lately. She falls asleep in class.
	look (like)	They **look** happy. They're all laughing.
	sound (like)	He **sounded** upset. I don't know what was wrong.
• adverbs	clearly	She's **clearly** the top student in the class.
	definitely	They're **definitely** not going to come.
	probably	They are **probably** out of town.
	apparently	He **apparently** doesn't have any money.
Present / Future		
• simple modals	should / shouldn't	Can you wait? She **should be** here any minute.
• simple modals	could	He **could be** in the library, but I doubt it.
	might (not)	She **might know** the answer. Why don't you ask her?
	may (not)	I **may have** time to help you tomorrow. I'll let you know.
• adverbs	maybe	**Maybe** he's coming later.
	perhaps	**Perhaps** we should stop now.

(EXPECTATION)

WEAKER CERTAINTY

PAST HABITS

PAST STATES

Past		
• phrasal modal	used to	My brother **used to tease** me a lot.
• simple modal	would	When I was a kid, my parents **would take** us to the park every weekend.
• phrasal modal	used to	The neighborhood **used to be** very quiet.

10 Adjectives and Other Forms That Describe Nouns

The beautiful thing about learning is nobody can take it away from you.

—B. B. KING, AMERICAN MUSICIAN (1925–)

Talk about It What does the quotation above mean? Do you agree or disagree?

WARM-UP

A | Match each picture with a dictionary definition below.

Weather Conditions

a. b. c.

d. e. f.

____ 1. A breeze is a **light** wind.

____ 2. A blizzard is a very **bad** storm <u>with snow and strong winds</u>.

____ 3. A tornado is a **violent** storm <u>with a very strong wind</u> *that blows* <u>*in a circle*</u>.

____ 4. Smog is **dirty, poisonous** air *that can cover a whole city*.

____ 5. An avalanche is a **large** amount <u>of snow</u> *that slides quickly* <u>*down a mountain*</u>. It can be **dangerous**.

_a_ 6. A hurricane is a storm <u>with very strong winds and heavy rain,</u> <u>over or near the ocean</u>.

B | The words in **blue** above are adjectives. The <u>underlined</u> words are prepositional phrases. The *italicized* words are adjective clauses. Based on the examples, answer these questions.

1. Can we use two **adjectives** together?
2. Does an **adjective** always come before a noun?
3. Does a <u>prepositional phrase</u> always begin with the word *of*?
4. Does an *adjective clause* come after a noun?
5. Do **adjectives**, <u>prepositional phrases</u>, and *adjective clauses* give information about nouns?

C | Look back at the quotation on page 310. Identify any forms used to describe nouns.

10.1 Overview of Adjectives and Other Forms That Describe Nouns

A

We have many different ways to describe or give more information about nouns (people, places, things, and ideas). This unit looks at how we use adjectives, prepositional phrases, and adjective clauses to describe nouns, as in **2 – 4**.

noun

1 a **car**

adjective + noun

2 an **old car**

noun + prepositional phrase

3 a **car** with a racing stripe

noun + adjective clause

4 a **car** that can carry six surfboards

B

adjective   prepositional phrase
5 Cape Town is a **great place** for a holiday.

adjective   adjective clause
6 I live in a **small town** that doesn't have many stores.

noun phrase
7 Jan has **a good idea for our discussion.**

noun phrase
8 She's **an excellent judge of character.**

In a sentence, we often use more than one way to give information about a noun, as in **5 – 6**.

A noun + its descriptive words = a **noun phrase**, as in **7 – 8**.

Remember: A determiner (*a*, *the*, *my*, *this*, etc.) also gives important information about a noun. A determiner is part of a noun phrase, as in **7 – 8**.

1 | Noticing Descriptive Words Underline the descriptive words in each phrase. Then match each phrase with a picture below. Write the descriptive phrase under the picture. **10.1 A–B**

1. a <u>blue</u> car
2. an old car without a roof
3. a car that was in an accident
4. a red car that goes on water

5. a new car with stripes
6. a car with grass on it
7. a red car with big wheels
8. a red car with four people

a. *a car with grass on it*

b. _____

c. _____

d. _____

e. _____

f. _____

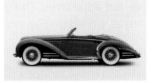
g. _____

h. _____

Talk about It What do you like or dislike about each car in Activity 1? Tell your classmates.

Think about It In the descriptions in Activity 1, find an example of these ways to describe nouns:

- determiner + adjective + noun   *a blue car*
- determiner + noun + prepositional phrase
- determiner + noun + adjective clause

2 | Understanding Descriptive Words in Conversation Check (✓) the correct picture for each conversation. Then practice with a partner. `10.1 A–B`

IN A RESTAURANT

1. A: Can I help you?
   B: Yes, **a small coffee with cream**, please.

□   ☑

2. A: What's the special tonight?
   B: We're serving **a baked fish with tomatoes and onions**.

□   □

3. A: What can I get for you?
   B: **A hamburger with lettuce and tomato**, please.

□   □

4. A: Could we have **a table for two near the window**, please?
   B: Sure. Follow me.

□   □

IN AN OFFICE SUPPLY STORE

5. A: What kind of chair are you looking for?
   B: **A chair with wheels**.

□   □

6. A: Can I help you?
   B: Yes, I need **some white paper for my printer**.

□   □

7. A: Are you looking for something special?
   B: Yeah, I need **a printer that prints on both sides of the page**.

□   □

8. A: What kind of pens do you want?
   B: I need **some pens that don't have caps**.

□   □

Think about It Look again at each **bold** noun phrase in Activity 2. Write the words in the correct column.

NOUN PHRASES				
Determiner	Adjective	Noun	Prepositional phrase	Adjective clause
1. *a*	*small*	*coffee*	*with cream*	
2.				
3.				
4.				
5.				
6.				
7.				
8.				

10.2 Using Adjectives and Noun + Noun Combinations

A

ADJECTIVE + NOUN

1 My **favorite sport** is football.

2 That was a **terrible meal**.

LINKING VERB + ADJECTIVE

3 **My room** is getting **cold**.

4 **You** look **familiar**.

INDEFINITE PRONOUN + ADJECTIVE

5 Did you buy **anything new**?

6 He cooked **something delicious**.

We use **adjectives** to give important information about a noun. We generally use adjectives in three main places:

- before a noun (after a determiner), as in **1 – 2**
- after a linking verb in a statement, as in **3 – 4**. The adjective describes the subject of the sentence. Common linking verbs are:

be	feel	grow	seem
become	get	look	

- after (not before) an indefinite pronoun, as in **5 – 6**

For a list of common adjectives, see the Resources, page R-11.

B

NOUN + NOUN

7 I just had a **phone conversation** with her.

8 I haven't had my **morning coffee** yet.

9 Do you have a **credit card**?

10 My brother is a **university student**.

ADJECTIVE + NOUN + NOUN

11 He's a **professional football player**.

12 It's a **beautiful beach area**.

13 Did you get a **new cell phone**?

We can also use a **noun** to describe another noun. The first noun functions like an adjective: it gives information about the second noun, or main noun, as in **7 – 10**.

Notice that we often use an adjective before a noun + noun combination, as in **11 – 13**.

For a list of common noun + noun combinations, see the Resources, page R-11.

GO ONLINE

3 | Noticing Adjectives Read these comments and underline the adjectives. `10.2 A`

COURSE NAME	STUDENT COMMENTS ON PROFESSORS
Biology 124	1. <u>Excellent</u> professor! Dr. Franklin is very <u>nice</u> and always helpful. His class can be difficult but I definitely recommend it.
Biology 124	2. Dr. Franklin's lectures are very clear and his *PowerPoint* presentations are awesome. His tests aren't easy, but go to class and do the homework, and you'll be fine.
Biology 124	3. Great professor! His lectures are interesting because he tells a lot of personal stories. Tests are very long but that's not really a bad thing.
Management 103	4. Awesome teacher! She's very helpful and enthusiastic about the subject. I can't think of anything negative about her class.
Management 103	5. One of my favorite professors! The class is easy and enjoyable.
Public Speaking 101	6. I just want to say that I'm a very shy person but this class was terrific. There was nothing scary about it at all. Professor Lane really helped me overcome[1] my fear of public speaking.

Think about It Group the adjectives from the sentences above in this chart.

Adjective + noun	Linking verb + adjective	Indefinite pronoun + adjective
excellent professor	is nice	

Write about It Write three sentences about a teacher you liked. Use adjectives in your sentences.

4 | Using Adjectives in Different Places Put the words in the correct order to make statements. Check (✓) *Compliment* or *Criticism*. Then compare answers with your classmates. Do you agree? `10.2 A`

	COMPLIMENT	CRITICISM
1. a/is/nice/person/he *He is a nice person.*	✓	☐
2. food/good/tastes/this _____	☐	☐
3. wasn't/answer/clear/your _____	☐	☐
4. apartment/I/love/new/your _____	☐	☐
5. looks/nice/your/hair _____	☐	☐

[1] **overcome:** to control something

	COMPLIMENT	CRITICISM

6. good/you/coffee/make ☐ ☐

_____

7. she/person/is/a/lazy ☐ ☐

_____

8. did/you/great/a/job ☐ ☐

_____

9. wasn't/good/there/anything/on TV ☐ ☐

_____

10. never/do/anything/for me/nice/you ☐ ☐

_____

11. looks/perfect/it ☐ ☐

_____

Talk about It Work with a partner. Choose one compliment and one criticism in Activity 4, and use each of them to create a short conversation.

5 | Usage Note: Placement of Adjectives Read the note. Then do Activity 6.

Most **adjectives** can go either before a noun or after a linking verb. However:

ADJECTIVE + NOUN	**LINKING VERB + ADJECTIVE**
A few adjectives normally go **before a noun only**. Examples of these adjectives include:	A few adjectives normally go **after a linking verb only**. Examples of these adjectives include:

entire	introductory	maximum
former	main	previous

afraid	alone	glad	ready	sure
alive	asleep	ill	sorry	well

The **entire class** is here. (NOT: ~~The class is entire.~~) | The boy **was afraid.** (NOT: ~~He was an afraid boy.~~)

6 | Using Adjectives in the Correct Place Choose an adjective from the box to complete each conversation below. Then practice with a partner. **10.2 A**

afraid	entire	glad	previous	tired	well
asleep	full	northern	sorry	unusual	

1. A: Why aren't you going outside?
   B: Because it's dark and I'm _____*afraid*_____.

2. A: Where do you live in the city?
   B: In the _____ part.

3. A: Where do you live now?
   B: 223 Ridgewood Road.
   A: And what was your _____ address?
   B: 182 Center Street.

4. A: Jack didn't look right today.
   B: Yeah, I don't think he's _____.

5. A: Is Barbara at home?
   B: Yes, but she's _____.

6. A: Do you want to do something tomorrow?
   B: I'm _____ but I have a meeting all day.

7. A: Thank you for the beautiful sweater.

   B: I'm _____ you like it.

8. A: How was the movie?

   B: I don't know. I didn't get to see it.

   A: What happened?

   B: The theater was already _____ when I got there.

9. A: Do you know this city very well?

   B: I should. I've lived here my _____ life.

10. A: You look _____.

   B: I am. I'm taking seven classes this semester.

   A: Is that _____?

   B: Yeah, four or five is more common.

Think about It Which adjectives in Activity 6 can you use both before a noun and after a linking verb?

7 | Using Noun + Noun Combinations Choose a noun from the box to complete each question. (More than one noun may be possible.) **10.2 B**

1. Do you have a _____road_____ map of this area?
2. Did you take a long _____ trip last year?
3. Does anyone help you with your _____ work?
4. Are you a _____ fan²?
5. Do you have _____ insurance?
6. What is your favorite _____ memory?
7. How long was your _____ vacation from school?
8. Do you usually carry _____ identification?
9. Do you make your own _____ arrangements?
10. Do you hope to be a _____ owner someday?
11. Do you enjoy going to _____ museums?
12. Do you have a _____ degree?

art
baseball
business
childhood
health
photo
road
school
summer
train
travel
university

Talk about It Ask a partner the questions above. (Just say "I'd rather not answer that" if you don't want to answer a question.)

Think about It Answer these questions.
1. Which questions above use an adjective before a noun + noun combination?
2. What other adjectives could you use in each question?

Do you have a(n) [electronic/good/clear/new] road map of this area?

8 | Forming Noun + Noun Combinations Use the words in this box to make as many different noun + noun combinations as you can. Then compare your list with a partner. **10.2 B**

business	environment	hospital	manager	office	record	school	teacher
emergency	guide	library	notebook	paper	room	supplies	worker

Write about It Choose three of the noun + noun combinations you made above and use each in a sentence.

²**fan:** a person who likes, for example, a singer or a sport very much

10.3 Using a Series of Adjectives

A

We use **adjectives** to give many different types of information. For example:

TYPE OF INFORMATION	EXAMPLES
OPINION	beautiful, delicious, familiar, favorite, interesting, safe, terrible, tired
SIZE	big, enormous, huge, large, little, short, small, tall, tiny
SHAPE	flat, oval, round, square
AGE	ancient, elderly, new, old, young
COLOR	black, brown, green, red, white, yellow
NATIONALITY	Canadian, Chinese, Spanish
MATERIAL	cotton*, paper*, plastic*, sandy, wool*
PURPOSE / TYPE	international, national, private, public, social

*Words like *cotton, paper, plastic,* and *wool* function as both nouns and adjectives.

B

ADJECTIVES + NOUN

1 This restaurant serves **fresh, simple** meals.

2 My phone has a lot of **interesting new** features.

We sometimes (but not often) use two or three adjectives before a noun, as in **1 – 2**. When two adjectives come before a noun, people sometimes put a comma between them.

> It's not easy to know when to add a comma between two adjectives that come before a noun. For now, just be aware that you will see this done.

LINKING VERB + ADJECTIVES

3 We were **tired** and **hungry**.

4 Bicycles are **safe, fun,** and **economical**.

After a linking verb, we add *and* between two adjectives, as in **3**. We use commas between three adjectives; we use *and* before the last adjective, as in **4**.

C

ORDER OF ADJECTIVES

5 He gave me a **beautiful ceramic** bowl.

6 She teaches **traditional Chinese** cooking.

7 I just found an **interesting new** website.

8 I want to go somewhere with **white sandy** beaches.

9 This restaurant serves **simple, delicious** food.

10 Everyone should have **good, clean** water.

When we use two or more adjectives together, they often (but not always) follow the order in Section A above. For example:

- We usually use an adjective of opinion before other types of adjectives, as in **5 – 7**.
- We usually use an adjective of color before an adjective of material, as in **8**.

We often use two adjectives of opinion together, as in **9 – 10**. The more general adjective usually comes first. In this case, we usually use a comma between the adjectives.

9 | Categorizing Adjectives Underline the adjectives in these statements and check (✓) *True* or *False*. Then group the adjectives in the chart on page 319. (More than one answer may be possible.) **10.3 A**

	TRUE	FALSE
1. I've been really <u>busy</u> lately.	☐	☐
2. I'm taking an interesting course this semester.	☐	☐
3. I think it's really noisy in here.	☐	☐
4. I just learned something new.	☐	☐
5. I never do anything wrong.	☐	☐
6. My previous school was in a different city.	☐	☐

	TRUE	FALSE
7. I had a big breakfast this morning.	☐	☐
8. I love Japanese food.	☐	☐
9. I don't like using plastic shopping bags.	☐	☐
10. I don't eat enough green vegetables.	☐	☐
11. I've had a lot of hard jobs.	☐	☐
12. I'm tired now.	☐	☐
13. The earth is flat.	☐	☐
14. The United Nations is an international organization.	☐	☐

Opinion	Size	Shape	Age	Color	Nationality	Material	Purpose/ Type
busy							

Think about It Which type of adjective seems to be the most common? Which adjectives were hard to put in a category?

Write about It Rewrite each false statement in Activity 9. Use a different adjective to make the statement true.

10 | Using a Series of Adjectives Choose a series of adjectives from the box to complete the sentences below. Add commas and use *and* where necessary. (More than one answer may be possible.) `10.3 B`

big/beautiful	clean/safe	good/hot	pleasant/residential
busy/industrial	friendly/cozy	helpful/nice/caring	spacious[3]/clean/comfortable
busy/main	friendly/helpful	nice/quiet	

○ ○ ○

Hotel Kashmir

1. Great place to stay in Agra. The staff was _____*friendly and helpful*_____, and my
   room was _____.

2. This was my favorite hotel in India. It's on a _____ street
   yet close to a _____ road.

3. Agra is a _____ city, but the hotel is in a _____
   _____ area. It's a _____ place to stay.

[3] **spacious:** with a lot of space inside

4. The hotel itself is a _____ house with a nice garden,

and there was very _____ water.

5. This hotel has a _____ atmosphere, and its staff is

_____ as well.

Think about It Which series of adjectives in Activity 10 need commas? Why?

Think about It Writers use a series of adjectives when they need to get a lot of descriptive information into a few words. Can you think when this might be necessary?

Talk about It Talk to a partner. Describe the last hotel where you stayed.

11 | Which Adjective Comes First? What type of information do you think each **bold** adjective gives? Choose your answers from the box. (Some adjectives are difficult to categorize.) `10.3 C`

opinion	size	shape	age	color	nationality	material	purpose/type

1. I own a **beautiful Persian** carpet. ___opinion___ ___nationality___

2. Kimchi is a **traditional Korean** dish. _____ _____

3. Can you hand me that **big plastic** spoon? _____ _____

4. I went to a **large private** school. _____ _____

5. You can't live without **good, clean** water. _____ _____

6. **Small, solar-powered** cars will be available in the future. _____ _____

7. There's a **new green** space around my house. _____ _____

8. Fast food is **tasty, convenient,** and **cheap**. _____ _____ _____

9. A banana is a **long, curved, yellow** fruit. _____ _____ _____

10. The National Council of La Raza (NCLR) is a **large national Hispanic** organization. _____ _____ _____

Think about It Which adjectives above were hard to put in a category? What does this suggest about why the order of adjectives isn't always the same?

12 | Error Correction Correct any errors in these sentences. (Some sentences may not have any errors.)

1. Friends are always honest supportive and loyal.

2. The leader of a country needs to be intelligence and truthful.

3. My parents' house is modern, and comfortable.

4. Good neighbors are caring, collaborative[4], and sociable.

5. Chinese food is healthy delicious.

6. I try to write good and interesting paragraphs.

[4] **collaborative:** able to work with others on a project

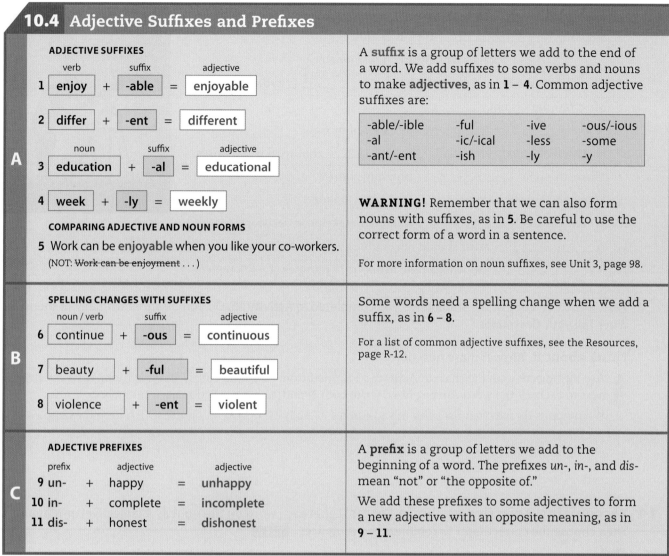

A

ADJECTIVE SUFFIXES

	verb	suffix		adjective
1	enjoy	+ -able	=	enjoyable
2	differ	+ -ent	=	different

	noun	suffix		adjective
3	education	+ -al	=	educational
4	week	+ -ly	=	weekly

COMPARING ADJECTIVE AND NOUN FORMS

5 Work can be **enjoyable** when you like your co-workers.
(NOT: ~~Work can be enjoyment . . .~~)

A **suffix** is a group of letters we add to the end of a word. We add suffixes to some verbs and nouns to make **adjectives**, as in **1 – 4**. Common adjective suffixes are:

-able/-ible	-ful	-ive	-ous/-ious
-al	-ic/-ical	-less	-some
-ant/-ent	-ish	-ly	-y

WARNING! Remember that we can also form nouns with suffixes, as in **5**. Be careful to use the correct form of a word in a sentence.

For more information on noun suffixes, see Unit 3, page 98.

B

SPELLING CHANGES WITH SUFFIXES

	noun / verb	suffix		adjective
6	continue	+ -ous	=	continuous
7	beauty	+ -ful	=	beautiful
8	violence	+ -ent	=	violent

Some words need a spelling change when we add a suffix, as in **6 – 8**.

For a list of common adjective suffixes, see the Resources, page R-12.

C

ADJECTIVE PREFIXES

	prefix	adjective		adjective
9	un-	+ happy	=	unhappy
10	in-	+ complete	=	incomplete
11	dis-	+ honest	=	dishonest

A **prefix** is a group of letters we add to the beginning of a word. The prefixes *un-*, *in-*, and *dis-* mean "not" or "the opposite of."

We add these prefixes to some adjectives to form a new adjective with an opposite meaning, as in **9 – 11**.

GO ONLINE

13 | Noticing Suffixes How is each adjective formed? Complete this chart. Then complete each sentence on page 322 with an adjective from the chart. (More than one answer may be possible.) `10.4 A`

Adjective	= Verb/Noun + suffix
1. attractive	= _____attract_____ + __ive__
2. available	= _____ + _____
3. awesome	= _____ + _____
4. careless	= _____ + _____
5. comfortable	= _____ + _____
6. emotional	= _____ + _____
7. fashionable	= _____ + _____
8. foolish	= _____ + _____
9. harmful	= _____ + _____

Adjective	= Verb/Noun + suffix
10. healthy	= _____ + _____
11. important	= _____ + _____
12. monthly	= _____ + _____
13. national	= _____ + _____
14. poisonous	= _____ + _____
15. powerful	= _____ + _____
16. professional	= _____ + _____
17. reasonable	= _____ + _____
18. successful	= _____ + _____

1. Looking at the stars through a telescope is an _____ sight.
2. Smoking is _____ to your health.
3. _____ clothes usually aren't fashionable.
4. Chocolate will kill some animals. It is _____ to them.
5. Most fast food is not _____.
6. Not all _____ people earn a lot of money.
7. Heat and electricity are usually _____, not weekly, expenses.
8. There are some _____ programs on TV.
9. You should never become _____ at work.
10. When you are _____, you often make poor decisions.
11. A _____ artist should never give away his or her work.
12. It's _____ to walk a mile in about 15 minutes (1.6 kilometers).

Talk about It Look at the statements you completed in Activity 13. Do you disagree with any of them? Why? Tell your classmates.

Think about It Answer these questions.

1. Are the adjectives in the chart in Activity 13 formed from nouns or verbs? Write *N* (noun) or *V* (verb) next to each. (If the word can be either, write both *N* and *V*.) Use a dictionary if necessary.
2. What nouns do we often use with the adjectives in Activity 13? Do an online search to find examples.

attractive: woman, people, images, face, personality

14 | Recognizing Adjective vs. Noun Forms Label each word on the right as *A* (adjective) or *N* (noun). Then choose the correct form to complete the sentences. `10.4 A`

DESCRIBING WEBSITES

1. This website produces _____ podcasts⁵ of stories translated into Spanish.   ____ freedom   ____ free

2. This is a _____, educational website just for children.   ____ safe   ____ safety

3. This poetry website provides examples of _____ styles of poetry.   ____ different   ____ difference

4. This website offers university courses with both _____ and practical value.   ____ academy   ____ academic

5. This website is a _____ resource for teachers.   ____ wonder   ____ wonderful

6. People of all ages will find a _____ of weekend activities on this website.   ____ variety   ____ various

7. This website provides _____ activities on math and geography.   ____ interactive   ____ interaction

8. These free lectures and podcasts are a _____ resource for students.   ____ value   ____ valuable

⁵**podcasts:** recordings that you can take from the Internet and watch or listen to on your computer or MP3 player

9. Learn how to run a _____ business through these free online courses. ___ successful ___ success

10. This website has a science _____ for everyone. ___ active ___ activity

15 | Making Spelling Changes Complete these questions with the adjective form of the word in parentheses. If necessary, use a dictionary to make the spelling changes. 10.4 B

1. Do you feel _____ on an airplane? (nerve)

2. What's the name of a _____ movie? (fun)

3. Have you ever met anyone _____? (fame)

4. How can you learn about _____ differences? (culture)

5. Do you like to read _____ materials? (science)

6. What are three _____ things that everyone needs? (base)

7. Are you in _____ health? (excellence)

8. Can you study in a _____ room? (noise)

9. What is an example of a _____ disaster? (nature)

10. Are you a _____ person? (create)

11. Were you _____ when you were a child? (cooperate)

> **STUDY STRATEGY**
>
> There is no easy way to know which suffix to add to a word. You learn suffixes by seeing the words and using them. Reading a lot helps. You can also look in a dictionary.

Talk about It Ask a partner the questions above.

16 | Spelling Note: The Prefix *In-* Read the note. Then do Activity 17.

When we add the prefix *in-* to some adjectives, we make a spelling change.

- When the adjective begins with *p* or *m*, the prefix *in-* changes to **im-**:
  possible   impossible   mature   immature

- When the adjective begins with *r*, the prefix *in-* changes to **ir-**:
  regular   irregular   relevant   irrelevant

- When the adjective begins with *l*, the prefix *in-* changes to **il-**:
  logical   illogical   legal   illegal

17 | Using Adjective Prefixes Add a prefix to make a new adjective with the opposite meaning. Make any necessary spelling changes. (Use a dictionary to check the meaning of any words you don't know.) 10.4 C

un-					
afraid	_____	comfortable	_____	fashionable	*unfashionable*
attractive	_____	connected	_____	interested	_____
breakable	_____	conscious	_____	kind	_____
certain	_____	equal	_____	professional	_____
clear	_____	fair	_____	safe	_____

in- / im- / ir- / il-					
patient	_____	replaceable	_irreplaceable_	separable	_____
practical	_____	resistible	_____	significant	_____
rational	_____	reversible	_____	sincere	_____
regular	_____	secure	_____	valid	_____
relevant	_____	sensitive	_____		

dis-					
agreeable	_____	interested	_____	orderly	_____
connected	_____	loyal	_____	respectful	_____
graceful	_____	obedient	_____	similar	_____

Think about It Which adjectives in Activity 17 can use more than one negative prefix? Can you explain the differences in the meaning of each pair of adjectives?

Write about It Read these questions. Use five of the adjectives in Activity 17 to write five more questions. Then ask a partner the questions.

1. What do you think is fashionable these days? What's unfashionable?
2. What is irreplaceable to you?
3. Do you own something unbreakable?
4. Have you ever been disloyal to a good friend?
5. What food is irresistible to you?
6. _____
7. _____
8. _____
9. _____
10. _____

18 | Error Correction Correct any errors in these sentences. (Some sentences may not have any errors.)

1. My wife is a kindness woman.
2. Traveling by plane is very convenience.
3. A success person is willing to work long, hard hours.
4. When I am loneliness, I try to do something fun with my friends.
5. My sister is an optimist person.
6. You need many different skills to be succeed in the world.
7. We are not safety here.
8. There are many things you can do to stay health.
9. I think confident makes us cheerful and grateful.
10. Life needs to be colorful and adventure.

10.5 Introduction to -ing and -ed Adjectives

We sometimes use the *-ing* and *-ed* forms of verbs as adjectives. With adjectives for feelings, we can often use both forms, but we use them in different ways, as in **1a – 2b**.

A

X CAUSES A FEELING

1a A bear is a **frightening** animal.
A bear is **frightening**.
(A bear causes fright.)

2a That man is an **amazing** skier.
That man is **amazing**.
(The man causes amazement.)

X FEELS SOMETHING

1b Tom was a **frightened** little boy.
Tom felt **frightened**.
(Something makes Tom feel fright.)

2b She performed to an **amazed** audience.
The audience felt **amazed**.
(Something makes the audience feel amazement.)

With many other *-ing* and *-ed* forms, only one form commonly functions as an adjective, as in **3a – 4b**.

3a We moved the meeting to the **following** week.

3b Not used as an adjective: ~~followed~~

4a This problem is **complicated**.

4b Less common: The problem has a number of **complicating** factors.

GRAMMAR TERMS: We call the *-ing* form of a verb the **present participle**. The *-ed* form of a verb is the **past participle**.

19 | Noticing -ing and -ed Adjectives Underline the *-ing* and *-ed* adjectives and complete the sentences with your own ideas. Then compare with your classmates. `10.5 A`

1. _____ is an interesting book.

2. _____ is a tiring activity.

3. _____ is a confusing topic for an essay.

4. _____ is an exciting sport.

5. I am interested in _____.

6. I feel tired when _____.

7. I feel confused when _____.

8. I feel excited when _____.

20 | Using *-ing* and *-ed* Adjectives Complete the sentences below with adjectives from the box. (More than one answer may be possible.) `10.5 A`

encouraging	exciting	increasing	outstanding	relaxing

1. Climbing a mountain is not a _____*relaxing*_____ way to spend your vacation.
2. Traveling around the world would be an _____ adventure.
3. Do we need to worry about the _____ number of people who try to climb Mount Everest every year?
4. I could use a few _____ words before I take my driver's test.
5. This is an _____ book. You really should read it.

> **RESEARCH SAYS...**
>
> Common *-ing* adjectives include *amazing, boring, encouraging, exciting, following, increasing, interesting, outstanding,* and *working.*
>
> CORPUS

complicated	determined	disappointed	exhausted	organized

6. An _____ person can find things quickly.
7. A _____ person doesn't give up easily.
8. A _____ math problem is difficult to solve.
9. It's not unusual to feel _____ when you don't reach a goal.
10. He was _____ after taking a long hike in the mountains.

> **RESEARCH SAYS...**
>
> Common *-ed* adjectives include *advanced, ashamed, bored, complicated, confused, determined, disappointed, educated, excited, exhausted, frightened, interested, pleased, surprised,* and *tired.*
>
> CORPUS

21 | *-ing* or *-ed* Adjective? Complete each conversation with an adjective from the box. Then practice with a partner. `10.5 A`

1. A: That was really scary.
   B: I don't know. I thought it was sort of _____.

   exciting/excited

2. A: I have a surprise for you but don't get too _____.
   B: What is it?
   A: We're going to San Francisco!

3. A: Let's do something different because this is really _____.
   B: I agree.

   boring/bored

4. A: What did you think of the movie?
   B: I didn't really like it but I wasn't _____ at all.

5. A: How was the show?
   B: It was pretty _____.

   amazing/amazed

6. A: Did you see the car hit the fence?
   B: Yeah, I'm _____ the driver didn't get hurt.

7. A: Are you nervous about the exam?

   B: No, I feel pretty _____.

relaxing/relaxed

8. A: Do you want to do something special?

   B: No, let's just stay here and have a _____ day.

10.6 Multi-Word Adjectives

A

We sometimes put two or more words together to make a **multi-word adjective**, as in **1 – 7**. Some common combinations include:

1	ADJECTIVE + NOUN	a **last-minute** plan, a **full-length** movie, a **high-risk** investment, a **fast-food** restaurant
2	NOUN + ADJECTIVE	a **smoke-free** office, an **ice-cold** drink, a **world-famous** singer
3	ADJECTIVE + ADJECTIVE	a **bluish-gray** car, a **dark-gray** suit, a **light-blue** sweater
4	ADJECTIVE + *-ING* FORM	a **high-ranking** person, a **long-lasting** friendship, an **English-speaking** country
5	NOUN + *-ING* FORM	a **confidence-building** activity, a **hair-raising** experience, a **mouth-watering** smell
6	ADJECTIVE + *-ED* FORM	an **open-ended** question, a **ready-made** meal, an **old-fashioned** kitchen
7	NOUN + *-ED* FORM	a **world-renowned** doctor, a **health-related** issue, **sun-dried** fruit

B

8 I'm looking for a **full-time** job.

9 He's a **good-looking** man.

10 The test had a lot of **open-ended** questions.

11 I have more health problems now that I'm **middle aged**.

12 This phone **isn't** very **user friendly**.

When a multi-word adjective comes before a noun, we usually write it with a hyphen (-), as in **8 – 10**.

We don't usually use a hyphen when a multi-word adjective follows a linking verb, as in **11 – 12**.

22 | Noticing Multi-Word Adjectives

Underline the multi-word adjective in each sentence. Then group the multi-word adjectives in the chart on page 328. [10.6 A]

1. A sloth is a <u>strange-looking</u> animal.
2. Spinach is an iron-rich food.
3. Most people have long-distance service on their phones.
4. This isn't a very user-friendly website.
5. Jogging in waist-high water is good for you.
6. Driving through the mountains can be a nerve-racking experience.
7. It's easy to move a free-standing mirror.
8. Physically inactive people have more health-related problems.
9. Not all trees have dark-green leaves.
10. The average life expectancy of a family-owned business is 24 years.
11. Businesses spend a lot of money on eye-catching advertisements.
12. My advice for the new employees is to stay open minded.

sloth

Adjective + noun	
Noun + adjective	
Adjective + adjective	
Adjective + *-ing* form	*strange-looking*
Noun + *-ing* form	
Adjective + *-ed* form	
Noun + *-ed* form	

Talk about It What other multi-word adjectives can you think of for each group above?

Write about It Choose three of the multi-word adjectives in the chart above. Use them in your own sentences.

23 | Using Multi-Word Adjectives Choose a multi-word adjective from the box to complete each sentence below. Add a hyphen if necessary. 10.6 B

big name	funny looking	side view	time consuming
bright yellow	home cooked	Spanish speaking	year round
family owned	life prolonging	sugar free	world famous

F Y I

We sometimes use another adjective with a multi-word adjective.

I'm looking for a **permanent** full-time job.

The test had a lot of **difficult** open-ended questions.

1. IZZE is a _____ *sugar-free* _____ soda. They make it with fruit juice.

2. People in Brazil speak Portuguese. Brazil is not a _____ country.

3. My grandfather started this company 100 years ago. It is a _____ business.

4. Britain, New Zealand, and Australia have _____ schools. This means there are shorter summer vacations and more frequent breaks.

5. People everywhere have heard of Barack Obama. He's _____.

6. Writing good tests is a difficult, _____ task.

7. The red-shanked douc is a _____ monkey that looks a lot like a clown.

8. Cars have _____ mirrors so you can see passing cars.

9. Most people have heard of Apple. It's a _____ company.

10. I usually eat a lot of meals out, so I always enjoy a _____ meal.

11. In some countries, taxis are _____. That makes them easy to see.

12. Exercising regularly is a _____ activity.

Think about It In which sentences above did you use a multi-word adjective without a hyphen? Why?

10.7 Prepositional Phrases That Describe Nouns

A

	noun	prepositional phrase	
1	They have	a house	with	a pool.

preposition + noun phrase

2 You'll love the white sandy **beaches** of Cape Town.
(Which beaches?)

3 The school has made several **changes** in the schedule. (What kind of changes?)

4 Berries are a great **source** of vitamins.
(What kind of source?)

5 He didn't give a **reason** for the gift.
(What kind of reason?)

6 It's a small **city** with narrow streets.

7 What are the **causes** of climate change?

Like an adjective, we can use a **prepositional phrase** to give more information about a **noun**, as in **1**. The prepositional phrase comes after the noun.

A prepositional phrase often answers the question *what kind* or *which one*, as in **2 – 5**.

Common prepositions include:

as	by	from	like	on	with
at	for	in	of	to	

Notice that we sometimes add an **adjective** or **noun** before the noun in a prepositional phrase, as in **6 – 7**.

B

Remember: Not every prepositional phrase functions like an adjective. Many give information about an action or a whole sentence.

COMPARE

8a | My **brother** in Canada | is a doctor. | (Which brother? In Canada. = acts like an adjective)

8b | I visited my father | **in Canada**. | (Visited where? In Canada. = acts like an adverb)

We sometimes use several prepositional phrases after a noun, as in **9 – 10**. Each prepositional phrase adds information to the noun before it.

9 | What is the salary | of the top football player | in the world?

10 | There has been a noticeable increase | in the number | of cars | on the road.

GO ONLINE

24 | Noticing Prepositional Phrases Underline the prepositional phrases in these sentences. Circle the noun that each prepositional phrase describes. Then check (✓) *True* or *False* for you. **10.7 A**

	TRUE	FALSE
1. I have had more than 15 (years) of education.	☐	☐
2. I have an apartment with big windows.	☐	☐
3. I'm a member of an organized group or club.	☐	☐
4. I've met a few people from Germany.	☐	☐
5. I have great respect for my parents.	☐	☐
6. I have a strong interest in science.	☐	☐
7. I have a large collection of jazz music.	☐	☐
8. I have studied the history of China.	☐	☐
9. I have some experience as a teacher.	☐	☐
10. I enjoy unusual food like squid[6] and okra[7].	☐	☐

[6] **squid:** an animal that lives in the ocean. It has a soft body and ten long legs

[7] **okra:** a vegetable with long green pods that are used in soups and stews

	TRUE	FALSE
11. I have recently made some important changes in my life.	☐	☐
12. I think freedom of expression is important.	☐	☐
13. I have a good sense of humor.	☐	☐
14. I know a lot about life in Saudi Arabia.	☐	☐

Talk about It Which sentences in Activity 24 are true for you? Compare with a partner.

Think about It How many adjectives can you find in the sentences in Activity 24? Make a list and compare with a classmate. Which adjectives come before the noun in the prepositional phrase?

25 | Usage Note: Learning Noun + Preposition Combinations Read the note. Then do Activity 26.

We often use nouns with specific prepositions. It's helpful to learn the two words together.

NOUN + *OF*		NOUN + *IN*	NOUN + *FOR*	NOUN + *ON*
cause of	quality of	change in	explanation for	data on
cost of	result of	confidence in	reason for	effect on
development of	role of	difference in	respect for	emphasis on
effect of	sense of	experience in	responsibility for	focus on
form of	series of	increase in	room for	impact on
history of	source of	interest in	time for	influence on
importance of	understanding of	role in	way for	research on
knowledge of	way of	success in		
process of				

Notice that some nouns combine with more than one preposition.

What is the **role of** the United Nations Security Council?
My aunt played an important **role in** my childhood.
For many people, moving to a new country also gives them a new **way of** life.
The company offers new **ways for** people to connect.

26 | Learning Nouns + Prepositional Phrases Choose a noun from the Usage Note above to complete each question. You may need to use a plural form of the noun. (More than one noun may be possible.) `10.7 A`

of

1. Do you have a good _____*sense*_____ of direction?

2. Do you have a good _____ of English grammar?

3. What is the _____ of a college education?

4. What are the _____ of wind on water?

5. What is one common _____ of war?

6. What is one common _____ of stress?

wind on water

in

7. Have you noticed any _____ in your memory recently?

8. Has there been an _____ in the price of food over the past ten years?

9. Do you have any _____ in computer programming?

for

10. Is there _____ for a cell phone in your pocket?

11. What is a good _____ for celebration?

12. Why is it important to have _____ for differences?

on

13. Would you enjoy doing _____ on animal behavior?

14. Did your parents put an _____ on grades when you were young?

15. Where can you get _____ on the changing population?

animal behavior

Talk about It Ask a partner the questions in Activity 26.

A: Do you have a good sense of direction?
B: I guess so. I don't usually get lost.

27 | Noticing Prepositional Phrases in a Row Read the building descriptions and follow these steps.

`10.7 B`

• Underline the prepositional phrases that describe nouns. (Remember: Not every prepositional phrase describes a noun.)

• Circle the noun that each prepositional phrase describes.

• Look at the pictures on page 332. Match each picture with the correct building name.

Famous Buildings

Citigroup Center

1. The Citigroup Center in New York is a tall, modern building with a triangle at the top.

Flatiron Building

2. New York's Flatiron Building is a tall, triangular building at the intersection of two streets.

Casa Milà

3. The Casa Milà in Barcelona is a fascinating example of the work of the architect Antoni Gaudí. There is usually a long line to get in, but there is a great view of the city from the rooftop.

Bank of Asia

4. This famous building is in Bangkok. Some people say that its robotic appearance is a symbol of the modernization of banking.

Sydney Opera House

5. The design of the Sydney Opera House in Sydney, Australia, copies the appearance of the sailboats in Sydney Harbor. The view of the harbor from the inside of the building is breathtaking.

Oriente Station

6. The design of this beautiful train station in Lisbon, Portugal, is light and airy. The designer, Santiago Calatrava, wanted people to feel close to nature while they were in his building.

Hundertwasserhaus

7. Artist/architect Friedensreich Hundertwasser designed this multi-colored apartment building in Vienna, Austria. It has windows of various shapes in many sizes. There are a total of 19 terraces for residents in the building.

National Aquatics Center (Water Cube)

8. The National Aquatics Center's cube shape is a representation of the Chinese symbol for Earth. The outer wall is designed like a pattern of bubbles from soap.

a. _Hundertwasserhaus_

b. _____

c. _____

d. _____

e. _____

f. _____

g. _____

h. _____

Talk about It Work with a partner. Describe other famous buildings you know of. Try to use prepositional phrases.

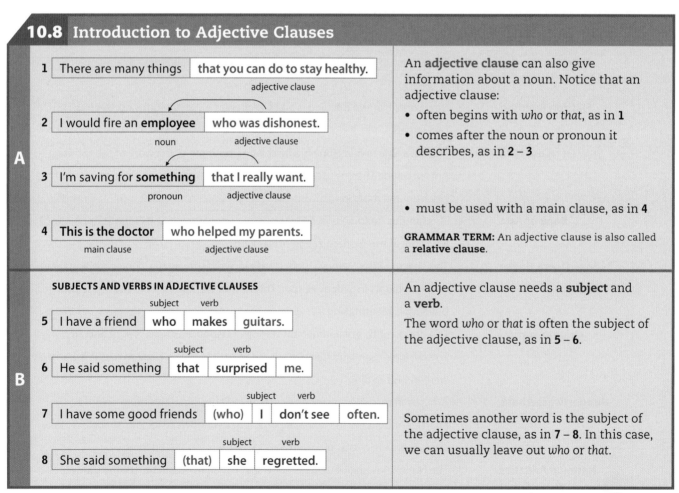

10.8 Introduction to Adjective Clauses

A

1 There are many things | that you can do to stay healthy.
  adjective clause

2 I would fire an **employee** | who was dishonest.
  noun adjective clause

3 I'm saving for **something** | that I really want.
  pronoun adjective clause

4 **This is the doctor** | who helped my parents.
  main clause adjective clause

An **adjective clause** can also give information about a noun. Notice that an adjective clause:

- often begins with _who_ or _that_, as in **1**
- comes after the noun or pronoun it describes, as in **2 – 3**

- must be used with a main clause, as in **4**

GRAMMAR TERM: An adjective clause is also called a **relative clause**.

B

SUBJECTS AND VERBS IN ADJECTIVE CLAUSES

5 I have a friend | subject: who | verb: makes | guitars.

6 He said something | subject: that | verb: surprised | me.

7 I have some good friends | subject: (who) I | verb: don't see | often.

8 She said something | subject: (that) she | verb: regretted.

An adjective clause needs a **subject** and a **verb**.

The word _who_ or _that_ is often the subject of the adjective clause, as in **5 – 6**.

Sometimes another word is the subject of the adjective clause, as in **7 – 8**. In this case, we can usually leave out _who_ or _that_.

332

28 | Noticing Adjective Clauses Circle the adjective clauses and underline the main clauses. Then match each definition with a picture. `10.8 A`

DEFINITIONS OF ANIMALS

1. <u>A frog is a small green animal</u> (that lives in and near water.) _c_

2. A grasshopper is an insect that can jump high in the air. ____

3. A hippopotamus is a large African animal that has thick skin and lives near the water. ____

4. A jellyfish is an animal with a soft, pale body that lives in the ocean. ____

5. A lizard is a small animal that has four legs and a long tail. ____

6. A moth is an insect with big wings that flies at night. ____

a.

b.

c.

d.

e.

f.

DEFINITIONS OF TOOLS/EQUIPMENT

7. A printer is a machine that prints words and pictures from a computer. ____

8. A helmet is a hard hat that keeps your head safe. ____

9. A javelin is a long, pointed stick that people throw as a sport. ____

10. A padlock is a lock that you use on things like gates and bicycles. ____

11. A compass is an instrument for finding direction, with a needle that always points north. ____

12. A hammer is a tool that you use to hit nails into things. ____

g.

h.

i.

j.

k.

l.

All dictionary entries are from the *Oxford Basic American Dictionary for learners of English*
© Oxford University Press 2011.

Think about It In the sentences above, draw an arrow from each adjective clause to the noun it describes.

A frog is a small green animal (that lives in and near water).

Think about It What adjectives and prepositional phrases does the writer use to describe each thing in the sentences above?

frog = small/green

29 | Usage Note: Choosing *Who* or *That* Read the note. Then do Activities 30 and 31.

> To give more information about a person, we can begin an adjective clause with *who* or *that*.
>
> He's the person **who helped me.**   There are some people here **that you should meet.**
> She's not the one **that got the job.**   I have some friends **who you know.**
>
> To give more information about a thing, we often begin an adjective clause with *that*.
>
> That's the dog **that bit me.**   I heard something **that you should know.**
> Could you hand me the book **that's on the table?**   I found the key **that you lost.**

30 | Adding Information Complete each sentence with an adjective clause on the right. `10.8 A–B`

1. Friendship is a relationship __*h*__

2. Anger is a feeling ____

3. A good friend is someone ____

4. A freshman is a student ____

5. Freshman composition is a course ____

6. A hero is a person ____

7. A dolphin is an intelligent animal ____

8. The Coast Guard is an organization ____

9. An explorer is someone ____

10. A school counselor is a person ____

a. who is in the first year of college.

b. who has done something brave or good.

c. that everyone experiences in life.

d. that lives in the ocean.

e. who students can go to for help.

f. that helps people who are in danger at sea.

g. who travels around a new place to learn about it.

h. that takes time to build.

i. who is loyal.

j. that students take in their first year of college.

Talk about It Do you disagree with any of the statements above? Why? Tell your classmates.

Think about It In which sentences above can you leave out *who* or *that*? Why?

31 | Using *Who* or *That* Circle the correct pronoun(s). Then practice with a partner. `10.8 A–B`

1. A: Do you know Mr. Lucas?
   B: Yeah, he's the teacher ((who) / (that)) gave me
      an F in Biology.

2. A: *Ci vediamo domani.*
   B: Uh, I don't understand a word (who / that)
      you are saying.
   A: Oh, sorry. You don't speak Italian, do you?
   B: No, unfortunately.

3. A: Who's Anna?
   B: She's someone (who / that) I met at school.

4. A: Do we have to go out tonight?
   B: But you're the one (who / that) didn't want
      to stay at home.

5. A: What's all this stuff?
   B: It's everything (who / that) I want to sell.

6. A: Is there something special (who / that) you
      are looking for?
   B: No, I'm just looking.

7. A: Do you know anyone (who / that) wants an
      old TV?
   B: Sure. I'll take it.

8. A: Don't leave yet. There's something
      (who / that) I think you should see.
   B: But I'm in a hurry.
   A: OK then. I'll show you later.

Think about It In which sentences above can you only have one answer? Why? In which sentences can
you leave out *who* or *that*? Why?

10.9 Using Adjectives and Other Forms That Describe Nouns in Speaking

A	**1** A: Which book do you want?
	  B: **The one about the economy.**
	2 A: Here are your books.
	  B: Oh. Those aren't **the ones** I wanted.
	3 A: Which keys are yours?
	  B: **The ones on the table.**
	4 A: This is a really silly movie.
	  B: Yeah, sorry. I'm **the one** who wanted to see it.
		We use **the one(s)** + a **prepositional phrase** or an **adjective clause** to identify a particular noun from a group of similar nouns, as in **1 – 4**. We can use it to answer the question *which*.
		
		For more information on *one(s)*, see Unit 4, page 123.

B	**5** A: Hey, you're standing on my foot!
	  B: Whoops! **Sorry!** (Sorry! = I'm sorry.)
	6 A: My cell is 555-0199.
	  B: **Sorry?** (Sorry? = Excuse me, I didn't understand.)
	  A: You wanted my cell number. It's 555-0199.
	7 A: **Nice shirt!**
	  B: Thanks.
	8 A: **Great meal!**
	  B: I'm glad you liked it.
		We often respond to another person or introduce a topic with a single **adjective** or an adjective + noun, as in **5 – 8**.

C	**9** A: Did you get the **stuff** that I sent?
	  B: Yeah, it just arrived.
	10 A: Is there **anything** I can get you?
	  B: I'd love a glass of water.
	11 A: Here. I brought you **something** special.
	  B: Oh, this is **something** I've always wanted.
		We sometimes use an **adjective clause** to add more information to:
		• a noun with a general meaning, such as *thing* or *stuff*, as in **9**
		• an indefinite pronoun, such as *anything* or *something*, as in **10 – 11**

GO ONLINE

32 | Identifying *Which One(s)* Listen and write the missing words. Circle the person or thing in the picture that Speaker B identifies. Then practice with a partner. `10.9 A`

1. A: Are those your shoes?

   B: No, mine are the ones _____.

2. A: Which key opens the garage door?

   B: The one _____.

3. A: Is your brother the one _____?

   B: No, he's on the left.

4. A: Who's that man?

   B: You mean the one _____?

   A: Yeah.

   B: I don't know.

5. A: Which questions do I need to answer?

   B: Just the ones _____.

6. A: Which sandwich is the one _____?

   B: The one _____.

33 | Using Adjectives in Conversation Use the adjectives in the box to complete the conversations below. (More than one answer may be possible.) `10.9 B`

Big	Delicious	Nice.	Sorry?	Super!	Terrible.
Boring	Fine.	Poor	Sorry.	Sure.	

1. A: Could you open the door for me?

   B: _Sorry?_

   A: The door. Could you open it, please?

   B: _____

2. A: _____ James.

   B: Why? What happened?

   A: He wrecked his car yesterday.

3. A: Ouch! That hurt.

   B: _____

4. A: _____ day today.

   B: I know. I hope I get the job.

5. A: I don't want to go out today.

   B: _____ Stay here.

6. A: _____ meal.

   B: I'm glad you enjoyed it.

7. A: What's for dinner?

   B: Pizza.

   A: _____

8. A: Did you draw this?

   B: Yeah.

   A: _____

   B: You really think so?

   A: Yeah. I like it a lot.

9. A: How was your day?

   B: _____

   A: What happened?

   B: I lost my wallet.

10. A: _____ movie.

    B: Yeah, it almost put me to sleep.

Talk about It Listen and check your answers. Were your choices the same? Then practice the conversations with a partner.

Think about It Which adjectives above are used alone and which are used with a noun?

34 | Adding Information to General Nouns and Indefinite Pronouns Listen and write the missing adjective clauses. Then practice with a partner. `10.9 C`

1. A: Is there anything special _____?

   B: No, let's just stay home.

2. A: Do we have any plans for today?

   B: Nope. You can do anything _____.

3. A: There's something _____.

   B: Sorry. I'm in a hurry. Can you tell me later?

   A: I guess so.

4. A: Are you going to finish painting the door today?

   B: I don't have time.

   A: Come on. You never finish anything

   _____.

5. A: Do you know anyone _____?

   B: No. Why do you ask?

   A: Because I'm going there next month.

6. A: Is there any stuff here _____?

   B: Yeah, you can take the magazines.

7. A: Are you going to the meeting tonight?

   B: I can't. There's some stuff

   _____ at home.

8. A: There are two things _____

   about Anita.

   B: What?

   A: She's quiet but she can be demanding.

9. A: We're having a guest for dinner.

   B: Is it someone _____?

   A: I can't tell you. It's a surprise.

10. A: What's that big black thing you

   _____?

   B: It's just an old radio. I don't want

   it anymore.

   A: I can see why.

Think about It How many adjective clauses above use *who* or *that*? Can those words be left out? Why or why not?

10.10 Using Adjectives and Other Forms That Describe Nouns in Writing

A

PREPOSITIONAL PHRASES

1 The Internet is a useful **tool** for education.

2 Decisiveness is an important **quality** of a good boss.

3	A child's **education**	during the first years	of life
	is very important.		

4	She has a master's **degree**	in business
	from the University	of North Carolina.

Prepositional phrases are common in written English, especially after a noun with a general meaning, such as *way*, *idea*, *method*, *tool*, *quality*, etc., as in **1 – 2**.

Writers often use two or three prepositional phrases together, as in **3 – 4**.

B

COMPARING SPOKEN AND WRITTEN LANGUAGE

5 A: Are you a writer?
B: No, I'm an actor.
A: Oh, yeah? What kind of stuff?
B: A lot of TV.
A: Anything I'd know?
B: Maybe. (from the movie *Sideways*)

6 I have a well-known **actor friend** who has been in a number of TV shows that you probably have seen.

In conversation, we often describe a noun with just one adjective or other form, as in **5**.

In writing, we tend to combine a lot of information into longer, complete sentences, as in **6**. **Adjectives**, **noun + noun combinations**, **prepositional phrases**, and adjective clauses are four ways we can put more information into a sentence.

ADJECTIVES AND OTHER FORMS THAT DESCRIBE NOUNS **337**

35 | Using Prepositional Phrases Choose a prepositional phrase to complete each sentence. `10.10 A`

1. One of the most dangerous ways _____ is by car.

2. Foreign travel makes you question your way _____.

3. People have many different ways _____.

4. Many people _____ change careers.

5. Relaxing before you go to bed will help to improve the quality _____.

6. The cell phone is a convenient tool _____.

7. The goal _____ is to make money.

8. Wearing white coats became a tradition _____.

9. The students _____ stayed awake for 24 hours.

10. This study shows the differences _____ among residents of Paris, Madrid, and London.

11. Doctors say you should eat a variety of types _____.

12. The Internet gives people instant access to large amounts _____.

13. A number of studies have shown that walking _____ gives you energy.

14. It sometimes takes a disaster for people to see the need _____.

for change
for doctors
for work
in cell phone behavior
in the research study
in the woods
in their fifties
of any business
of dealing with stress
of doing things
of food
of information
of traveling
of your sleep

Think about It In which sentences above are two or more prepositional phrases used together? What noun or pronoun does each prepositional phrase describe?

Write about It Choose a sentence above. Write two to three more sentences to support or explain it.

36 | Using Prepositional Phrases in a Text Complete the article below with the prepositional phrases from the box. `10.10 A`

about kindness and taking care of the planet	of animated films	of the world's greatest directors
at drawing	of art	of young people
at the Japanese Academy Awards	of audiences and critics[8]	with magical abilities
of airplanes	of his own	

HAYAO MIYAZAKI: DIRECTOR OF ANIMATED FILMS

Many people regard Hayao Miyazaki as one _of the world's greatest directors_
                                                            1
_____. Viewers love his imaginative animation,
            2
adventurous characters, and thrilling plots[9]. He is famous not just in Japan but
throughout the world.

   Miyazaki began his career as an animator in 1963. His skill _____ earned him the
                                                                            3
admiration[10] _____. He directed his first feature anime[11] film 16 years later. Then he
            4

[8] **critics:** people who say that someone or something is good or bad
[9] **plots:** the things that happen in stories, plays, or movies
[10] **admiration:** the feeling that someone or something is very good
[11] **anime:** Japanese style of cartoons or animation

338

started a movie company _____ in 1985. In 2001, his movie *Spirited Away* won

Best Film _____. It was also the first anime film to win an American

Academy Award.

   Miyazaki's movies are often about the adventures _____

_____. As a boy, Miyazaki loved to draw pictures _____.

In his movies, people can sometimes fly. One character even turns into a bird. His movies also teach

lessons _____. Miyazaki's movies aren't cartoons;

they are works _____.

Think about It Circle the adjectives the writer used in Activity 36. Put a box around any nouns used to describe other nouns. In which sentences did the writer use two prepositional phrases together? Underline the noun that each prepositional phrase describes.

37 | Noticing Different Forms of Adjectives Read these job descriptions. Then group the **bold** descriptive words in the chart below. `10.10 B`

CAFÉ HELP

We are hiring **full-time counter staff** for our **busy café**. We ask for a **high level** of **friendly customer service** from our staff. Patience, punctuality[12], and an **outgoing personality**—all these **positive qualities** will help. Both **morning shifts**[13] and **evening shifts** are available. All applicants must be at least 18 years old. Please send your resume, including **phone number**, and also tell us something about your idea of **excellent customer service**!

CONSTRUCTION COMPANY SEEKS CARPENTERS

Previous experience is essential. The **successful applicant must be good** with **hand tools** and **reliable**. Must be able to lift **heavy objects**. We are a **well-run**, **progressive company** with opportunities for growth and advancement.

Multi-word adjective + noun + noun	Adjective + noun + noun	Multi-word adjective + adjective + noun	Adjective + noun	Linking verb + adjective	Noun + noun
full-time counter staff					

Talk about It Which job above sounds more interesting to you? Why? Tell your classmates.

---

[12] **punctuality:** the quality of arriving or doing something at the right time, not late

[13] **shifts:** periods of time in the working day

The Importance of Early Learning

VERSION 1

An American study shows the importance of early education. The study involved 111 young children.

Researchers put the children in two groups. One group of children attended an all-day program at a childcare center. It offered some programs. The other group did not attend the childcare center. However, both groups went to public school.

The two groups were similar when they were babies, but different after the age of about 18 months. As babies, both groups had similar results in tests. However, the children in the childcare program scored much higher in tests after the age of 18 months.

The children took tests again at the ages of 12 and 15 years. Again, the children had better test scores.

The study suggests that education is important for all later development. Children may be more successful if they have early education. They may do better in school, go to college, and get better jobs. The researchers believe their study shows a need to spend money on public education. They believe these kinds of programs could create better success in schools.

VERSION 2

A major American study from the University of North Carolina shows the importance of early education for poor children. The long-term study involved 111 young children from poor families.

Researchers put the children in two groups. One group of children attended an all-day program at a high-quality childcare center. It offered some social, health, and educational programs. The other group did not attend the childcare center. However, both groups went to public school after the age of 5.

The two groups were similar when they were babies, but different after the age of about 18 months. As babies, both groups had similar results in tests for mental and physical skills. However, the children in the educational childcare program scored much higher in tests after the age of 18 months.

The children took tests again at the ages of 12 and 15 years. Again, the children who had been in the childcare center had better test scores.

The study suggests that education during the first months and years of life is important for all later development. Poor children may be more successful if they have early education. They may do better in school, go to college, and get better jobs. The researchers believe their study shows a need for the government to spend money on public education at an early age. They believe these kinds of programs could create better success in American schools.

Think about It What kinds of words, phrases, and clauses did the writer add to Version 2 above?

ADJECTIVES	PREPOSITIONAL PHRASES	ADJECTIVE CLAUSES
major	from the University of North Carolina	
	for poor children	

WRAP-UP Demonstrate Your Knowledge

A | DISCUSSION What are the characteristics of a good teacher? In a group, consider the qualities in this box or other qualities. Decide on the top three qualities. Then say why and give examples from your own experience. Share the results of your discussion with the class.

expects a lot from students	has a sense of humor	is very strict
explains things clearly	has knowledge of his or her subjects	makes the class interesting
gives a lot of homework	is considerate of students' feelings	spends time to help students

B | WRITING Describe your best friend. What is special about this person, and why is he or she your best friend?

My best friend is Thomas, and he is someone who can always make me laugh. We met when we were working together a few years ago. He's a little quiet, so we didn't become friends right away. But after a while, I realized he had a really clever sense of humor. That's when we started spending more time together. . . .

Exchange descriptions with a partner and answer these questions.

1. Does your partner's description give a clear mental picture of the subject? What other information do you want to know?

2. How did your partner use adjectives and other forms to describe nouns? Identify the uses.

C | RESEARCH Look at the back cover of several books to find excerpts of praise for the book from different sources. Find examples of the types of adjectives, noun + noun combinations, prepositional phrases, and adjective clauses from this unit, and share them with your classmates.

"A funny, profound, emotionally generous, and wonderfully human story." —Joe Lansdale
"A truly interesting, engaging, and fascinating memoir." —Lou Schuler

D | WEB SEARCH Look online for an interesting apartment for rent. Print out the advertisement, and underline the words, phrases, and clauses that describe nouns. Then write an advertisement for your ideal apartment.

Apartment for Rent

This <u>amazing</u> unit is in a <u>prime</u> <u>14th Street</u> location <u>with elevator and laundry</u> <u>in the building</u>. This <u>bright</u> unit has <u>big</u> windows and a <u>private</u> patio!!!! The windows are a <u>unique</u> feature <u>that you will not find anywhere else</u>. There is a lot of <u>closet</u> space and an <u>additional</u> <u>storage</u> loft. The kitchen has <u>new</u> <u>full-sized</u> appliances. Don't miss out on this <u>great</u> deal! Call or txt today for more information on your <u>new</u> home!! Contact Franklin at 555-1212.

10.11 Summary of Adjectives and Other Forms That Describe Nouns

We use adjectives, prepositional phrases, nouns, and adjective clauses to give more information about a **noun** (a person, place, thing, or idea).

		noun			
I went to	a	restaurant.			

		noun	noun		
I went to	a	family	restaurant.		

		adjective	noun		
I went to	an	American	restaurant.		

		adjective	multi-word adjective	noun	
I went to	an	American	fast-food	restaurant.	

		adjective	multi-word adjective	noun	adjective clause
I went to	an	American	fast-food	restaurant	that has a playground.

		adjective	multi-word adjective	noun	adjective clause	prepositional phrase
I went to	an	American	fast-food	restaurant	that has a playground	for children.

11

Adverbs and Prepositional Phrases

Live simply, that others may simply live.

—MAHATMA GANDHI,

INDIAN LEADER

(1869–1948)

Talk about It What does the quotation above mean? Do you agree or disagree?

WARM-UP

A | Check (✓) the sentences that describe your study habits. Then compare answers with your classmates and share other study habits.

Study Habits

☐ 1. I usually take notes in class.
☐ 2. I often look up new words in a dictionary.
☐ 3. I review my textbook before class.
☐ 4. Unfortunately, I don't always do my homework.
☐ 5. I study regularly outside of class.
☐ 6. I pay attention during class.
☐ 7. I like to study with a group of friends.
☐ 8. Surprisingly, I prefer to study in noisy places.

B | The words in blue above are adverbs. The words in green are prepositional phrases. Based on these examples, what can you say about adverbs and prepositional phrases? Check (✓) *True* or *False*.

	TRUE	FALSE
1. Adverbs always end in *-ly*.	☐	☐
2. We can use adverbs in different places in a sentence.	☐	☐
3. We use some adverbs and prepositional phrases to give information such as *when*, *where*, *how*, and *how often*.	☐	☐
4. We use some adverbs to give an opinion about the information in a statement.	☐	☐

C | Look back at the quotation on page 342. Identify any adverbs or prepositional phrases.

11.1 What Is an Adverb?

A

1 The movie started **late**. (when)

2 The train is **always** late. (how often)

3 No one is going to be **there**. (where)

4 Some people learn languages **easily**. (how)

5 We were **very** tired. (to what degree)

We often need to explain *when*, *how often*, *where*, *how*, or *to what degree* something happens. We can use **adverbs** to do this, as in **1 – 5**.

B

       adverb   adjective

6 I feel | **pretty** | good.

       adverb   adverb

7 They left | **very** | quickly.

       verb   adverb

8 Did you | look | **outside?**

       verb phrase   adverb

9 You | need to do your homework | **now.**

       adverb   whole sentence

10 **Unfortunately,** | I'm busy tomorrow.

An adverb can add information to:

- an adjective, as in **6**
- another adverb, as in **7**
- a verb or verb phrase, as in **8 – 9**
- a whole sentence or clause, as in **10**. Notice that these adverbs sometimes give the speaker's opinion about the information in the sentence.

Notice: We use adverbs in several different places in a sentence.

C

WHEN

11 She arrived **in the evening**.

12 He'll probably get here **before lunch**.

WHERE

13 He lives **at home**.

14 There's a good restaurant **near here**.

HOW

15 She didn't want to go **with me**.

16 I'm going to go **by myself**.

WHY

17 They canceled the meeting **because of the weather**.

18 **Thanks to the Internet**, I can do all my research from home.

We often use a **prepositional phrase** to explain *when*, *where*, *how*, or *why*, as in **11 – 18**. In these sentences, the prepositional phrase functions like an adverb.

GO ONLINE

1 | Noticing Adverbs Decide if the **bold** adverb in each conversation explains *when*, *how often*, *where*, *how*, or *to what degree*. Check (✓) your answers. Then practice with a partner. `11.1 A`

	WHEN?	HOW OFTEN?	WHERE?	HOW?	TO WHAT DEGREE?
1. A: David, I need you here **immediately**. B: I'll be right there.	✓	☐	☐	☐	☐
2. A: Have you been checking your messages? B: Yes, **obsessively**[1].	☐	☐	☐	☐	☐

[1] **obsessively:** without being able to stop

	WHEN?	HOW OFTEN?	WHERE?	HOW?	TO WHAT DEGREE?
3. A: I'll see you **later**. B: OK. Sounds good.	☐	☐	☐	☐	☐
4. A: That's a nice sweater. B: Thanks. I made it years **ago**.	☐	☐	☐	☐	☐
5. A: You look **really** familiar. Have we met before? B: I don't think so.	☐	☐	☐	☐	☐
6. A: Could you please give this package to Mr. Jones? B: Certainly. I'll deliver it **personally**.	☐	☐	☐	☐	☐
7. A: Is anyone here yet? B: Yeah, a few people. They're waiting for you **upstairs**.	☐	☐	☐	☐	☐
8. A: Could you wait **outside**, please? B: Of course. Is there a problem? A: I'm not really sure.	☐	☐	☐	☐	☐
9. A: What are you doing now? B: Setting up my new computer. A: Well, be sure you follow the instructions **carefully**.	☐	☐	☐	☐	☐
10. A: Have you ever been to Canada? B: **Once**, but it was a long time ago.	☐	☐	☐	☐	☐
11. A: Do you talk to Amanda very often? B: No, but she sends text messages **hourly**.	☐	☐	☐	☐	☐
12. A: How do you find anything here? B: It's a mess, isn't it? I just can't throw anything **away**.	☐	☐	☐	☐	☐

Think about It Circle any other adverbs in the sentences in Activity 1. What kind of information do they give?

2 | What Does the Adverb Describe? What part of the sentence does each **bold** adverb describe? Draw an arrow to it. Then check (✓) *Agree* or *Disagree* for each statement. `11.1 B`

Sentences from Student Essays

	AGREE	DISAGREE
1. A good teacher must be able to explain things **clearly**.	☐	☐
2. You can play tennis **indoors**.	☐	☐
3. All public buildings should be **easily** accessible².	☐	☐
4. Employers should treat all of their employees **equally**.	☐	☐

² **accessible:** possible to enter

		AGREE	DISAGREE

5. **Hopefully**, scientists will find life on other planets. ☐ ☐

6. Card games are a good form of entertainment because you can play them **anywhere**. ☐ ☐

7. Feeling a lot of stress is a **very** good thing. ☐ ☐

8. The average life expectancy[3] has increased **greatly** since 1900. ☐ ☐

9. Learning languages is not an **especially** difficult thing to do. ☐ ☐

10. Today people can communicate **instantly** by using email. ☐ ☐

11. In stressful situations, you should try to breathe **slowly**. ☐ ☐

12. Running your own business can be **extremely** rewarding. ☐ ☐

Think about It Replace each **bold** adverb in Activity 2 with a different one. Do your classmates agree or disagree with your new statement?

"A good teacher must be able to explain things simply."

3 | Noticing Prepositional Phrases What does each **bold** prepositional phrase explain? Write *when*, *where*, *how*, or *why* above the phrase. `11.1 C`

Ray Charles

where
1. The musician Ray Charles was born **in the United States** in 1930.

2. **At the age of 5**, he began to lose his sight[4], and **by age 7**, he was completely blind[5].

3. **At the Florida School for the Deaf[6] and the Blind**, he learned to play the piano, organ, saxophone, clarinet, and trumpet.

4. **After the death of his mother**, he quit school. He tried to make a living **as a musician**, but it wasn't easy.

5. Charles never worked **in just one style of music**. He played country music, rhythm and blues, and gospel music.

6. **After years of copying other musical styles**, Charles began to create his own style. He called it *soul music*.

7. **In 1980**, he performed **in the movie *The Blues Brothers***.

8. **Over the years**, Charles won 12 Grammy Awards **for original music**.

9. He died **from liver[7] disease at his home in Beverly Hills**.

RESEARCH SAYS...

Prepositional phrases are the most common way we explain *when*, *where*, etc.

Common prepositions are *at*, *by*, *for*, *in*, *of*, *on*, *to*, and *with*.

CORPUS

---

[3] **life expectancy:** how long we believe someone or something will live
[4] **sight:** the ability to see

[5] **blind:** not able to see
[6] **deaf:** not able to hear
[7] **liver:** the part of the body that cleans the blood

Think about It How many prepositional phrases do you see in each sentence in Activity 3? Is it possible to put two or more prepositional phrases together in a row?

Talk about It Was any of the information in the article in Activity 3 surprising to you? Discuss with a partner.

4 | Usage Note: Adjective or Adverb? Read the note. Then do Activity 5.

An adverb adds information to a verb, an adjective, an adverb, or an entire sentence or clause. An adjective adds information to a noun. Sometimes a word or prepositional phrase can function like an adverb in one context and like an adjective in another context.

FUNCTIONS LIKE AN ADVERB	FUNCTIONS LIKE AN ADJECTIVE
1a I don't have any classes **on Tuesday**.	**1b** My class **on Tuesday** is bigger than my class **on Friday**.
2a My brother works **hard**.	**2b** My brother is a **hard** worker.
	2c The test was **hard**.

5 | Adjective or Adverb? Does each **bold** word or prepositional phrase function like an adjective or an adverb? Check (✓) your answers. `11.1 A–C`

	ADJECTIVE	ADVERB
1. The window **in my bedroom** is broken.	✓	☐
2. I'm going to study **in my bedroom**.	☐	☐
3. Why do you drive so **fast**?	☐	☐
4. You're a **fast** learner.	☐	☐
5. You shouldn't work so **hard**.	☐	☐
6. That test was **hard**.	☐	☐
7. Try to get here **early**, please.	☐	☐
8. Let's have an **early** lunch today.	☐	☐
9. Most of my friends **at school** are from this area.	☐	☐
10. I've made a lot of good friends **at school**.	☐	☐
11. I think there's someone **at the door**.	☐	☐
12. Who's the man **at the door**?	☐	☐
13. Who put the picture **on the wall**?	☐	☐
14. The picture **on the wall** is of my grandparents.	☐	☐

Write about It Choose a prepositional phrase, and write your own pair of sentences like the ones above. Ask your classmates to identify how the prepositional phrase functions in each sentence (like an adverb or like an adjective).

A

EXPLAINING *WHEN*

1 They're having dinner **now**.

2 No one has arrived **yet**.

3 That happened **in the past**.

4 I'll see you **in a while**.

COMPARE

5a They **arrived** after lunch. (simple past)

5b I'll **be** there after lunch. (future with *will*)

5c He usually **takes** a nap after lunch. (simple present)

6a She **met** him a long time ago. (simple past)

6b **Have** you **met** him lately? (present perfect)

We can use certain **adverbs** and **prepositional phrases** in time expressions to explain *when* something happens, as in **1 – 4**.

We use many time expressions with more than one verb form, as in **5a – 5c**.

However, we use some time expressions together with particular verb forms (simple past, present perfect, etc.), as in **6a – 6b**.

B

EXPLAINING *HOW OFTEN*

7 **Sometimes** we stayed late but not **always**.

8 He's **always** leaving his clothes on the floor.

9 They're **usually** a few minutes late.

10 It's important to exercise **regularly**.

11 **Year after year**, she won the competition.

We can use adverbs of frequency and certain prepositional phrases to explain *how often* something happens, as in **7 – 11**. Examples include:

• always, constantly, continuously, over and over
• usually, regularly, normally
• often, frequently, again and again
• sometimes, occasionally, from time to time
• rarely, seldom, infrequently
• never, no longer
• hourly, daily, monthly, year after year

C

PLACEMENT OF TIME AND FREQUENCY EXPRESSIONS

12 A: Do you have any meetings this week?
B: **On Tuesday** I'm meeting with the design team, and **on Wednesday** I have a budget meeting.

13 She **never goes** there.

14 They **are constantly** bothering me.

15 Some people **are always** happy.

16 I don't cook **in the evening** when I'm tired.

We use different time and frequency expressions in different places in a sentence. For example, we use some of them:

• at the beginning of a clause or sentence, as in **12**
• before a single main verb, as in **13**
• after the first helping verb, as in **14**
• after the verb *be*, as in **15**
• at the end of a clause or sentence, as in **16**

6 | Noticing Time Expressions Underline the time expressions in these conversations. Then practice with a partner. `11.2 A`

1. A: Do you want some coffee?
   B: No, thanks. Not <u>now</u>.

2. A: Hey, James. Where are you?
   B: Relax. I'll be there in a second.

3. A: Bye. I'll call you later.
   B: OK. Bye.

4. A: Have you eaten yet?
   B: No, I just got home five minutes ago.

5. A: What do you want to do?
   B: I don't know, but we need to decide soon.

6. A: Is Anna there?
   B: No, but she'll be back in a few minutes.

7. A: What's the matter?

   B: I'm in trouble again.

   A: So what else is new?

8. A: John is coming over in a while.
      Do you want to join us?

   B: Sure. I haven't seen him in years.

9. A: Ready for your job interview on Friday?

   B: I think so.

10. A: Can I talk to you?

    B: Yes, but just for a second. I'm late for class.

11. A: Is Emma here?

    B: No, but she should get here before long.

12. A: Have you looked outside lately?

    B: No. Why?

    A: It's snowing.

Think about It What verb form did the speaker use with each time expression in Activity 6?

1. I don't want any coffee now. (simple present)

7 | Explaining *How Often* Circle the correct frequency expression to complete each sentence. 11.2 B

MAKING TRUE STATEMENTS

1. The average person laughs **constantly** / **occasionally**.

2. Too many people talk on the phone while they are driving.
   This is **frequently** / **infrequently** the cause of accidents.

3. It's important to brush your teeth **from time to time** / **regularly**.

4. You can learn the words to a song by repeating them
   monthly / **over and over**.

5. It's not unusual for a husband and wife to argue
   from time to time / **hourly**.

6. Many people pay their bills **hourly** / **monthly**.

7. Children **usually** / **continuously** start walking around age 1.

8. If you store honey in a tight jar, it will **never** / **usually** go bad.

9. An annual flower blooms[8] and then dies, but a perennial blooms **again and again** / **once**.

10. Languages are **constantly** / **never** in contact with each other and affect each other in many ways.

11. Many languages have 50,000 words or more, but people **infrequently** / **normally** use the same few
    hundred words in everyday conversation.

12. The earth moves around the sun **continuously** / **infrequently**.

Talk about It What other frequency expressions could you use in each sentence above? Share ideas with
your classmates.

8 | Usage Note: Using Noun Phrases like Adverbs Read the note. Then do Activity 9.

We sometimes use just a **noun phrase** to explain *when*, *how long*, or *how often*. We almost always use
these noun phrases at the very beginning or very end of a sentence or clause.

1 You should eat breakfast **every morning**.

2 **Next week** I can't travel.

3 Are you going anywhere **today**?

4 I've been here **all day**.

5 We shop there **all the time**.

6 Maybe I should come back **another time**.

[8] **bloom:** to produce a flower

9 | Using Noun Phrases and Prepositional Phrases like Adverbs Look at the answers to these questions. Label each one as *NP* (noun phrase), *A* (adverb), or *PP* (prepositional phrase). Then circle the answers that are true for you. Add your own answer if necessary. **11.2 B**

Personal Survey

1. When did you last eat something?

   a. a few minutes ago *NP*   c. yesterday

   b. an hour ago   d. other: _____

2. How often do you work out?

   a. six times a week   c. once a week

   b. twice a week   d. other: _____

3. When are you going to take your next vacation?

   a. this time next year   c. in a couple of years

   b. this spring   d. other: _____

4. How often do you change your passwords?

   a. never   c. every day

   b. every few months   d. other: _____

5. How often do you use your phone to make actual phone calls?

   a. rarely   c. 30 minutes a month

   b. quite a bit   d. other: _____

6. When did you last go to a movie theater?

   a. last month   c. years ago

   b. last year   d. other: _____

7. How long have you lived here?

   a. my whole life   c. since 2011

   b. for a couple of years   d. other: _____

8. How long have you been in this room?

   a. all morning   c. for about an hour

   b. all afternoon   d. other: _____

Talk about It Compare your answers above with your classmates. Who has the most unusual answer?

Think about It What other time expressions could you use to answer each question above?

Write about It Work with a partner. Write a short quiz like the one above using the question words *when* and *how often*. Then give your quiz to your classmates.

   1. How often do you miss class?

     a. never   c. from time to time

     b. almost never   d. frequently

10 | Noticing the Position of Expressions Underline the time and frequency expressions in these paragraphs. Then answer the questions below. 11.2 C

When Do You Function⁹ Best?

I am a morning person. I get up <u>at 5:00</u> <u>every morning</u>. My mind is fresh and clear then. I feel energetic. I like to exercise early in the morning and do things around my apartment. Then I feel ready to go to work. I can get a lot of things done at this time of day.

    After lunch, things slow down for me. I don't work very well between 2:00 and 3:00. By the end of the workday, I am very tired. I don't usually go out in the evening because I just don't have any energy. Instead, I relax at home. By 9:30, I can't keep my eyes open anymore. I know that some people feel wide awake at night, but I'm not like that at all.

> **WARNING!**
> A few time adverbs have the same form as adjectives: *early*, *late*, *daily*, *weekly*, *monthly*, and *yearly*.
>
> We left **early**. (adverb)
> I had an **early** breakfast. (adjective)

QUESTIONS

1. Which sentences have two time or frequency expressions in a row? Which expression comes first—the more specific one or the more general one?

2. How many sentences begin with a time expression?

3. Which time or frequency expression does the writer use after a helping verb?

4. Which time or frequency expressions does the writer use at the end of a clause or sentence?

Write about It When do you function best? Write several sentences to read to your classmates.

11.3 Explaining *Where*

A

1 Your friends are **upstairs**.

2 Go **away**.

3 What's happening **outside**?

4 A: A large coffee, please.
   B: For **here**?
   A: No, make it to go.

We often use **adverbs** of place to explain *where* someone or something is, as in **1 – 4**. This information usually comes at the end of a sentence. Common adverbs of place include:

ahead	backward	down	here	outside
away	behind	far	inside	somewhere
back	close	forward	nearby	there

B

5 I left my things **at home**.

6 The World Court is **in the Netherlands**.

7 He yelled at me **in front of the whole office**.

We can also use certain **prepositional phrases** to explain *where*, as in **5 – 8**. Some common prepositions used this way are:

at	home, school, work, war, sea, college
in +	the kitchen, the city, China, the world, my backyard
on	Fifth Avenue, the floor, the ground, the table
to	school, work, the hospital, the store

8 She worked **in Singapore** **in 2012**.
(in Singapore = where; in 2012 = when)

Notice that we often use several prepositional phrases together, as in **8**. These expressions may give different kinds of information.

9 Please **put the milk** **in the refrigerator**.
(NOT: ~~Please put in the refrigerator the milk.~~)

WARNING! We don't normally use an expression of place between a verb and its object, as in **9**.

⁹**function:** to work or do other tasks

11 | Noticing Place Expressions Underline the expressions that explain *where* in these conversations. Then practice with a partner. `11.3 A–B`

1. A: Do you work <u>here</u>?
   B: Yeah. Let me show you around.

2. A: Are you in the attic? What are you doing up there?
   B: I'm looking for something.

3. A: Where are you going now?
   B: Relax. I'm not going far. I'll be back in a second.

4. A: What's the matter?
   B: I can't find my glasses. I know I put them somewhere.
   A: Did you look in the kitchen?
   B: I've looked everywhere.

5. A: The door is open. Do you think it's OK to go inside?
   B: I don't know. It's kind of dark in there. You go ahead. I'll follow right behind in a few seconds.

6. A: What's that on the ground?
   B: I don't know. Don't get close to it. It might be dangerous.

7. A: Where have you been?
   B: Nowhere.
   A: You mean you've been at home all day?
   B: That's right.

8. A: Could everyone please step forward?
   B: Why? What's going on?
   A: Nothing. But you're blocking the sidewalk.

9. A: What are you cooking?
   B: Don't look! Go away! It's a surprise.

10. A: Is there anything interesting in the news?
    B: Not really.

11. A: Is this your laptop?
    B: Oh, thanks. I've been looking all over for it.

12. A: Can I borrow your phone?
    B: Sure, but don't forget to bring it back.

13. A: How's the fish? Is it OK?
    B: Actually, it's a little raw inside.

14. A: How many people were at your old school?
    B: About a hundred.
    A: Really! That's small.
    B: How many go here?
    A: About two thousand.

> **FYI**
>
> Many words function in more than one way. For example, the word *inside* can function as an adverb, a preposition, an adjective, or a noun.
>
> He went **inside**. (adverb)
> We saw smoke **inside the house**. (preposition)
> He put the letter in his **inside** pocket. (adjective)
> He locked the door from the **inside**. (noun)

Think about It How many time expressions can you find in the conversations above? Circle them.

12 | Explaining *Where* Complete the article below with the correct expressions of place from the box.

`11.3 A–B`

above the ground	on the wheel
away	to a mechanic
in its place	to the side of the road
in the hubcap	under the car
in your car	

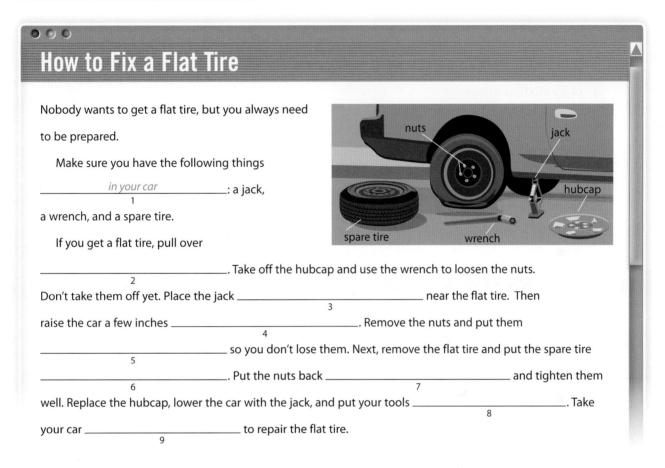

How to Fix a Flat Tire

Nobody wants to get a flat tire, but you always need to be prepared.

Make sure you have the following things _____*in your car*_____ : a jack,
                                          1
a wrench, and a spare tire.

If you get a flat tire, pull over

_____. Take off the hubcap and use the wrench to loosen the nuts.
           2
Don't take them off yet. Place the jack _____ near the flat tire. Then
                                              3
raise the car a few inches _____. Remove the nuts and put them
                                    4
_____ so you don't lose them. Next, remove the flat tire and put the spare tire
           5
_____. Put the nuts back _____ and tighten them
           6   7
well. Replace the hubcap, lower the car with the jack, and put your tools _____. Take
                                                                                        8
your car _____ to repair the flat tire.
                     9

13 | Usage Note: Using Place, Time, and Frequency Together Read the note. Then do Activities 14 and 15.

We often use **place expressions** with **time expressions** or **frequency expressions**. The expression of place usually comes first.

		where	when	
1	We left	**for school**	at 8:00.	

		where	when	
2	Have you looked	**outside**	lately?	

		where	how often	
3	I read the newspaper	**online**	every morning.	

14 | Explaining *Where* and *When* Complete these sentences with information about yourself, and share them with your classmates. `11.3 A–B`

PERSONAL BACKGROUND

1. I was born _____
   (where / when)
   _____.

2. I went to high school _____
   (where / when)
   _____.

3. I worked _____
   (where / when)
   _____.

4. I met my best friend _____
   (where / when)
   _____.

5. My parents met _____
   (where / when)
   _____.

6. Yesterday I went _____
   (where / when)
   _____.

> **F Y I**
>
> For most places, we use *to* + determiner + noun: *to the store, to my friend's house.*
>
> For a small group of places, we use *to* + noun: *to work, to school.* This means *to my regular place of work, to my school.*
>
> For a few others, we can use the noun alone: *home, downtown, uptown.*

15 | *Where* or *When*? Do these underlined words and phrases answer the question *where* or *when*? Write your answers above the words and phrases. `11.3 A–B`

Starting a New Job

It's important to make a good impression <u>on your first day</u> *(when)* <u>at a new job</u>.

<u>Here</u> are some tips to help you:

- Be sure to arrive <u>at work</u> <u>on time</u>.
- <u>Before your first day</u> <u>at work</u>, find out about the company's dress code[10].
- What are the lunch-hour rules <u>at your new job</u>? Find out. For example, do people eat <u>at their desks</u>, or does everyone take a full hour <u>outside the workplace</u>?
- You should never make personal phone calls <u>from your office</u> <u>during work hours</u>.
- Don't send personal emails <u>from your office computer</u>.
- <u>At the end of your first day</u> <u>at work</u>, make sure your desk is neat.

> **F Y I**
>
> A prepositional phrase can function like an adverb in one context and like an adjective in another context.
>
> I was **at work** by 7:00.
> (= adverb; I was *where* at 7:00?)
>
> I met a lot of people on my first day **at work**.
> (= adjective; *which* first day?)

Think about It In which sentences above does the time information come before the place information? Why is that?

[10] **dress code:** a set of rules about what you are allowed to wear

11.4 Explaining *How*

A

1 She **has done** well so far.
2 Please **come** quickly.

PLACEMENT OF ADVERBS OF MANNER

3 **Don't forget to speak** slowly.
4 My parents **dropped by** unexpectedly.
5 We **need to finish** this work quickly.
6 Can we **do this** together?

7 They **ate** dinner quickly.
(NOT: ~~They ate quickly dinner.~~)

We can use **adverbs** of manner to describe how something is done, as in **1 – 2**.

We often use these adverbs of manner:
- after the **complete verb**, as in **3 – 4**
- after the **complete verb** and its **object**, as in **5 – 6**

WARNING! We don't usually use an adverb between a verb and its object, as in **7**.

B

FORMING ADVERBS OF MANNER

adjective		-ly		adverb
8	sad	+	-ly	=	sadly
9	strange	+	-ly	=	strangely
10	careful	+	-ly	=	carefully

We form many adverbs of manner by adding -ly to an adjective, as in **8 – 10**.

WARNING! Not all words ending in -ly are adverbs. Some are adjectives, such as *friendly*, *costly*, and *lovely*.

For a list of spelling rules, see Activity 17.

C

11 I don't want to go **by myself**.
12 **With difficulty**, he climbed out of the tiny car.
13 A: Can I take your order?
B: Just a cup of coffee, please. **With extra cream**.
14 She left the house **without a word** to anyone.
15 They left **in a hurry**.
16 He works **as a waiter**.

We can also use certain **prepositional phrases** to explain *how*, as in **11 – 16**. Some common prepositions used this way are:

as		a waiter, a child, a team, a student
by		car, bus, mistake, myself
in	+	a hurry, a low voice, a new way
with		people, friends, water, difficulty, a smile
without		a doubt, a word, question, hesitation

 GO ONLINE

16 | Using Adverbs of Manner   Circle the adverbs that best describe you. Then compare with a partner.

`11.4 A`

YOUR BEHAVIOR

1. I usually eat **quickly** / **slowly**.
2. I do my homework **carefully** / **carelessly**.
3. I tend to walk **fast** / **slowly**.
4. My friends and I usually study **alone** / **together**.
5. I usually treat other people **nicely** / **rudely**.
6. I drive **cautiously** / **recklessly**[11].
7. Normally I speak **loudly** / **softly** in class.
8. When I was a child, I played sports **awkwardly** / **gracefully**.
9. I usually dress **elegantly** / **simply**.
10. I speak my first language **poorly** / **well**.

> **WARNING!**
>
> The word *good* is an **adjective**. The related adverb is *well*.
>
> He's a **good** singer. (adjective)
> He sings **well**. (adverb)
>
> Some adverbs of manner and adjectives have the same form:
>
> **fast**–fast
> **hard**–hard
> **wrong**–wrong

[11] **recklessly:** dangerously and without thinking

Think about It Can you change the placement of the adverb of manner in any of the sentences in Activity 16? Why or why not?

Write about It Write three more sentences about your behavior. Use an adverb of manner from Activity 16 in each sentence.

I tend to read slowly.

17 | Spelling Note: Spelling -*ly* Adverbs Read the note. Then do Activities 18–20.

We can form **adverbs** from many adjectives.

	ADJECTIVE	ADVERB
1 For many adverbs, simply add *-ly* to the adjective.	natural	natural**ly**
2 When the adjective ends in *-le*, change the *-e* to *-y*.	sim**ple**	sim**ply**
3 When the adjective has two syllables and ends in *-y*, change the *-y* to *-i* and then add *-ly*.	craz**y**	craz**ily**
4 When the adjective ends in *-ic*, add *-ally*.	bas**ic**	bas**ically**

WARNING! Some adjectives end in *-ly*. We can't change these adjectives into adverbs. We use a **prepositional phrase** instead; for example, *friendly* becomes *in a friendly way*.

18 | Spelling -*ly* Adverbs Write the adverb form of each adjective. Then use ten of the adverbs to complete the sentences below. (More than one answer may be possible.) `11.4 B`

ADJECTIVE	ADVERB	ADJECTIVE	ADVERB
1. greedy	*greedily*	10. enthusiastic	_____
2. angry	_____	11. irritable	_____
3. brave	_____	12. accidental	_____
4. thoughtful	_____	13. hungry	_____
5. weary	_____	14. happy	_____
6. rude	_____	15. loud	_____
7. anxious	_____	16. frantic	_____
8. easy	_____	17. repeated	_____
9. hasty	_____	18. comfortable	_____

HOW DID THEY SAY IT?

1. "Can I have three more cookies?" Kate asked _____*greedily*_____.

2. "No, no, no," the man said _____.

3. "I'm really nervous about the exam," Matt said _____.

4. "I can't walk any farther," the child said _____.

5. "Why did you throw my computer out the window?" the woman asked _____.

6. "My vacation starts tomorrow," Rob said _____.

7. "Stop, thief!" the woman yelled _____.

8. "Come on, everyone. This is going to be fun!" Sam said _____.

9. "Is there anything to eat?" the child asked _____.

10. "Someone has been hurt! We need a doctor now!" Mary yelled _____.

19 | Using -*ly* Adverbs Choose an adverb from Activity 18 to complete these sentences. (More than one answer may be possible.) `11.4 B`

Good Advice

1. Don't answer test questions _____*hastily*_____. Slow down and you'll make fewer mistakes.

2. Don't let children play with matches[12]. They might _____ start a fire.

3. Use new words _____. That will help you learn them.

4. Don't speak _____ to anyone. You may regret what you say.

5. In a dangerous situation, act _____ but don't do anything foolish.

6. In a store, don't speak _____ on your cell phone. No one else wants to hear your conversation.

7. It's important to dress _____ when you take a long plane trip.

8. Don't speak _____ to your elders. Speak politely.

> **F Y I**
>
> Sometimes we can use an adverb before a main verb to give emphasis to other words in the sentence. Compare:
>
> Don't answer the test questions **hastily**.
>
> Don't **hastily answer** the test questions.

Think about It Can you change the placement of the adverb of manner in each sentence above? Why or why not?

Write about It Write three sentences with good advice. Use an adverb of manner in each sentence.

20 | Using -*ly* Adverbs Rewrite the questions. Use the adverb form of the **bold** adjective. `11.4 B`

1. Are you a **careful** writer?   Do you write _____*carefully*_____?
2. Are you a **positive** thinker?   Do you think _____?
3. Do you want to be a **good** writer?   Do you want to write _____?
4. Are you an **attentive**[13] listener?   Do you listen _____?
5. Are you a **confident** speaker?   Do you speak _____?
6. Have you ever done something **courageous**[14]?   Have you ever acted _____?
7. Are you an **independent** person?   Do you like to make decisions _____?
8. Are you a **careless** driver?   Do you drive _____?
9. Are you an **enthusiastic** sports fan?   Do you cheer _____?
10. Are you **irritable** in the morning?   Do you behave _____ in the morning?
11. Is learning a new language **easy** for you?   Do you learn new languages _____?
12. Are you a **selfish** person?   Do you ever act _____?

Talk about It Ask a partner the questions in the second column above.

[12] **matches:** short pieces of wood that you use to light a fire
[13] **attentive:** watching, listening to, or thinking about someone or something carefully
[14] **courageous:** brave; not afraid

21 | Usage Note: *By/Without* + Gerund Read the note. Then do Activity 22.

We sometimes use a prepositional phrase formed with **by** + a **gerund** or *without* + a **gerund** to express *how*.

1 I learn new words **by repeating them.**   4 She left **without saying goodbye.**

2 You can log in **by using your password.**   5 Don't cross the street **without looking both ways.**

3 You can help **by making lunch.**   6 You can't play the game **without knowing the rules.**

22 | Using Prepositional Phrases to Explain *How* Match each question with an answer. `11.4 C`

HOW SHOULD YOU DO IT?

1. How should you answer the phone in English? _b_   a. With great care.

2. How should you talk on the phone in public? ____   b. By saying hello.

3. How should you choose a husband or wife? ____   c. Without making any noise.

4. How should you come into class late? ____   d. In a soft voice.

5. How should you climb a mountain? ____   e. By shaking hands and saying hello.

6. How do people often greet each other in business   f. Without looking down.
   situations? ____   g. Without eating the whole bag.

7. How can you see the surface of the moon? ____   h. Without yelling.

8. How can you get good grades? ____   i. With a telescope.

9. How should you eat potato chips? ____   j. By studying hard.

10. How should you speak to an angry child? ____

Write about It Write three of your own questions that begin with *how should you*. Ask your classmates your questions.

23 | Explaining *How* Complete each definition below with a word or phrase from the box. `11.4 A-C`

by radio or television	in an angry way	loudly	quietly	with great force
by using your hands	lightly	quickly	strongly	with your arms and head first

DICTIONARY DEFINITIONS

1. **demand** to say _____ *strongly* _____ that you must have something: *The workers are demanding more money.*

2. **dive** to jump into water _____: *Sam dove into the pool.*

3. **argue** to talk with someone _____ because you do not agree: *My co-workers argue a lot about schedules.*

4. **whisper** to speak _____ to someone so that others cannot hear you: *He whispered so that he wouldn't wake up the baby.*

5. **broadcast** to send out sound or pictures _____: *The Olympics are broadcast live around the world.*

6. **exclaim**   to say something suddenly and _____ because you are

    surprised or angry: *"I don't believe it!" she exclaimed.*

7. **dab**   to touch something _____ and quickly: *She dabbed the cut with*

    a cotton ball.

8. **dart**   to move _____ and suddenly: *He darted across the road.*

9. **fling**   to throw something carelessly or _____: *She flung her coat on the chair.*

10. **grope**   to try to find something _____ when you cannot see: *He groped*

    for the light switch.

24 | Explaining *When*, *Where*, and *How* Underline the words and phrases that explain *when, how long, where,* and *how*. Write *when, how long, where,* or *how* over the words. (Look back at Charts 11.2, 11.3, and 11.4 for more information if necessary.)

How to Calculate Your Life Expectancy

Note: This quiz is just for fun!

1. Start with the number 79.   *79*

2. Are you male? *Subtract 3.* Are you female? *Add 4.*   ____

                   where

3. Do you live <u>in a large city</u>? *Subtract 2.* Do you live in a small town? *Add 2.*   ____

4. Do you live with a relative or friend? *Add 5.* Do you live alone? *Subtract 1.*   ____

5. Do you eat fresh fruit and vegetables every day? *Add 3.*   ____

6. Do you sleep more than ten hours a night or fewer than five? *Subtract 2.*   ____

7. Do you exercise hard for at least 30 minutes three or four times a week? *Add 2.*   ____

8. Do you plan to work behind a desk for most of your life? *Subtract 3.* Are you physically active at work? *Add 2.*   ____

9. Do you expect to work after age 65? *Add 3.*   ____

10. Do you get angry easily? *Subtract 3.* Are you easygoing and relaxed most of the time? *Add 3.*   ____

11. Are you usually happy? *Add 1.*   **TOTAL** ____

Talk about It Answer the questions above to find your life expectancy. Share your results with your classmates.

11.5	**Explaining *Why***	
A	1 We didn't leave the house **because of the weather**. 2 There were 50,000 deaths last year **due to car crashes**. 3 **Thanks to the Internet**, we can now get information quickly.	We can use certain **prepositional phrases** to explain *why* (or give a reason), as in **1 – 3**. These are more common in writing. For more information on giving reasons, see Unit 12, Chart 12.3, page 383.

25 | Explaining *Why* Complete each sentence with a reason from the box. `11.5 A`

GIVING REASONS

1. People live longer today in part __*because of advances in medicine*__.
2. _____, many people spend one or two hours a day just driving to their jobs.
3. Many areas aren't getting enough rain _____.
4. She's a great singer, and _____, she's had many opportunities to travel.
5. They couldn't fit the box into the car _____.

because of advances in medicine
because of climate[15] change
because of crowded roads
because of its size
because of that

6. The city is becoming crowded _____.
7. _____, Europe has become largely multilingual.
8. Men are more likely to miss a day of work _____.

due to a cold or flu
due to the arrival of foreigners
due to the growing population

9. The beaches are crowded _____.
10. _____, I'm in good shape now.
11. _____, I can wake up to music.

thanks to the arrival of tourists
thanks to my clock radio
thanks to yoga

Write about It Think of another way to complete each sentence above.

People live longer today in part because of better food.

11.6 Explaining *To What Degree*

A

ADVERBS OF DEGREE

1	I'm	extremely very somewhat a bit	**upset** with you.

high ↑ ↓ low

WITH ADJECTIVES OR ADVERBS

2 He's **perfectly capable** of doing it.

3 I think I did **pretty well** on the test.

4 I'm **fairly certain** about this.

5 Where can I hang my jacket? It's **slightly wet**.

WITH VERBS

6 We **completely forgot**.

7 I don't **quite understand** this.

8 The car **nearly hit** the wall.

We can use **adverbs** of degree to explain *to what degree*. We use different adverbs to express different degrees of strength, as in **1**.

We can use adverbs of degree with adjectives and other adverbs, as in **2 – 5**. Some common examples include:

high ◄─────────────────► low

completely exactly extremely perfectly	awfully pretty quite really so very	fairly rather somewhat	a (little) bit kind of slightly

We can use some adverbs of degree with verbs, as in **6 – 8**. Some common examples include:

high ◄─────────────────► low

absolutely completely definitely totally	quite really	almost nearly

GRAMMAR TERM: Adverbs of degree are also called **intensifiers**.

GO ONLINE

---

[15] **climate:** the normal weather conditions of a place

26 | Noticing Adverbs of Degree Underline the adverbs of degree in these conversations. Then practice with a partner. `11.6 A`

1. A: How do you feel today?
   B: <u>Pretty</u> good. And you?
   A: I don't know. I'm kind of tired.
2. A: Is something wrong?
   B: No, I'm just a bit hungry.
3. A: This is so pretty!
   B: I'm glad you like it.
4. A: It's sort of hot in here.
   B: Yeah, it is a bit.
5. A: This is a serious problem.
   B: You're absolutely right.
6. A: What are you doing?
   B: Packing my suitcase.
   A: So you're definitely going?
   B: Yep. I've already called a taxi.
7. A: What's the value of the euro now?
   B: I'm not exactly sure.

8. A: How was the weather in London?
   B: Terrible. It almost ruined my trip.
9. A: When are you leaving?
   B: Right now. Are you coming with me?
   A: Hold on. I'm almost ready.
10. A: Can I use your computer tonight?
    B: It works somewhat differently from yours, but help yourself.
11. A: When will you have the answer?
    B: I should be able to find out pretty quickly.
12. A: How was your trip?
    B: It was OK, but I couldn't completely enjoy myself because of work.
13. A: I don't understand the homework assignment.
    B: I don't quite understand it myself.
14. A: How did you do on the test?
    B: Really well. I don't think I made any mistakes.
    A: Good for you.

Think about It Does each adverb of degree above describe an adjective, another adverb, or a verb?

27 | Usage Note: Placement of Adverbs of Degree Read the note. Then do Activity 28.

> When an **adverb** of degree describes an adjective or another adverb, it usually comes before the adjective or adverb.
>
>   I'm not quite **certain**.   They left rather **quickly**.   She told the story somewhat **differently**.
>
> When *almost*, *nearly*, *quite*, and *really* describe a single verb, they usually come before the main verb. When there is one (or more) helping verb, they usually come after the first helping verb.
>
>   He almost **fell down**.   They had nearly **forgotten**.   I don't quite **believe** her.
>
> A few adverbs of degree can come before the main verb, after the main verb, or after an object.
>
>   I completely **agree**.   I **agree** completely.   I **don't understand you** completely.

28 | Placing Adverbs of Degree Write the adverb of degree in parentheses in the correct place in the sentence. (More than one answer may be possible.) Then check (✓) *True* or *False* for you. `11.6 A`

Personal Statements

	TRUE	FALSE
pretty 1. I'm a good student. (pretty)	☐	☐
2. I'm hard-working. (incredibly)	☐	☐

	TRUE	FALSE
3. I like ice cream. (really)	☐	☐
4. I usually do my homework carefully. (fairly)	☐	☐
5. I missed the bus today. (nearly)	☐	☐
6. I don't understand the news in English. (quite)	☐	☐
7. I have lived here for a long time. (very)	☐	☐
8. I have changed over the past year. (completely)	☐	☐
9. I am certain about my future. (absolutely)	☐	☐
10. I prefer food that is spicy. (slightly)	☐	☐

Think about It Which adverb of degree in Activity 28 can you use in more than one place in the sentence?

Write about It Rewrite the false statements in Activity 28 to make them true for you.

29 | Usage Note: *Too* and *Enough* Read the note. Then do Activity 30.

We often use **too** <u>before</u> an adjective or adverb to mean "more than is good or possible."

These shoes are **too small**.   He speaks **too quickly**.   The test was not **too hard**.

We can use the adverb *enough* <u>after</u> an adjective, adverb, or verb. *Enough* means "to the necessary amount or degree."

These shoes aren't **big enough**.   She doesn't speak **clearly enough**.   She doesn't **read enough**.

We can use an **infinitive** in a sentence with *too* and *enough*. The infinitive shows a result.

I'm too **tired to study**.   She speaks too **softly to hear**.
The kids are **old enough to stay home alone**.   I didn't get up **early enough to go to the gym**.

30 | Using *Too* and *Enough* Complete these conversations with the word in parentheses and *too* or *enough*. Then practice with a partner. 11.6 A

1. A: Who did you vote for?

   B: I didn't vote. I'm not _____. (old)

2. A: What do you think of my cake?

   B: It's _____ to eat. (pretty)

   A: Oh, come on. Have a piece.

3. A: What's that music?

   B: I can't tell. It's not _____. (loud)

4. A: How was your vacation?

   B: Absolutely wonderful, but it ended

   _____. We didn't have time

   to see everything. (soon)

5. A: Can you translate this Spanish song for me?

   B: Oh, sorry. My Spanish isn't

   _____. (good)

6. A: What's for dinner?

   B: I don't know. I'm _____ to cook.

   (tired)

7. A: OK. I'm finally ready to go.

   B: It's _____ to go to the store.

   (late) It's closed.

8. A: Who's that over there? Can you see?

   B: No. He's not _____. (close)

9. A: Are you _____ to help
    me move this sofa? (strong)

    B: I think so. Let's try.

10. A: Wait for me. You're getting
    _____ ahead. (far)

    B: Sorry. I'll slow down.

31 | Using *Too/Enough* with Infinitives Write ten logical questions using ideas from this chart. Use each infinitive in the right column only once. (Different questions are possible.) `11.6 A`

Are you	fit[16] enough humble[17] enough old enough strong enough tall enough too busy too nervous too old too shy too smart too tired	to apologize when you make a mistake? to ask for help? to be fooled? to give answers in class? to lift a friend? to reach the top shelf? to remember when no one had a cell phone? to run a marathon? to see your friends? to start a new career? to stay up late?

> **F Y I**
>
> Remember: We can also use *too* and *enough* before nouns to compare amounts.
>
> This doesn't cost **too much money**.

Talk about It Ask a partner the questions you wrote above.

A: Are you fit enough to run a marathon?
B: Well, I'm in good shape, but I don't think so.

11.7 Other Uses of Adverbs

A

1 There is **certainly** no secret formula for being a good boss.

2 I'll be at the meeting, **of course**.

3 **Without a doubt**, Yosemite is one of the most beautiful spots in the U.S.

4 We'll **probably** take the train.

5 Yosemite is **maybe** one of the most beautiful spots in the U.S.

6 I planned to leave by 7:00, but I **actually** didn't leave until 9:00.

7 I know Sarah's coming. **In fact**, she's bringing all the food.

8 **Luckily**, no one got hurt in the accident.

9 **Unfortunately**, it rained all day.

10a This story is true, **really**.

10b This story is **really** long.

11a **Clearly** we're going to be late.

11b You need to explain your ideas **clearly**.

We sometimes use an **adverb** or **prepositional phrase** to show our attitude or feelings about the information in a clause or sentence. For example, we may:

- show certainty, as in **1 – 3**
- show doubt, as in **4 – 5**

- emphasize that something is true or factual, as in **6 – 7**

- make an evaluation or judgment, as in **8 – 9**

Notice that many of these adverbs can also function as **adverbs of degree** or **manner**, as in **10a – 11b**.

GO ONLINE

---

[16] **fit:** healthy and strong

[17] **humble:** not thinking that you are better than other people

32 | Noticing Adverbs In these sentences, which adverbs show the writer's attitude or feelings about the information in the sentence? Circle them. Then write them under the correct group in the chart below. `11.7 A`

Sentences from Student Essays

1. Many people fear or dislike anger, but anger is (actually) a very important emotion.
2. Sadly, we had to leave the area when I was only three.
3. It was really the best advice that I had ever received.
4. We need to address the causes of climate change. Fortunately, advances in technology will help us do this.
5. I have read a lot of books about Mahatma Gandhi. He has definitely inspired me in my life.
6. I try to put some money in the bank every month. Perhaps I will use this money to start a business or go back to school.
7. Recreation[18] can make families and friends closer. Taking a trip or playing a sport gives them something to remember for the rest of their lives. Of course, not all these memories will be good.
8. There are certainly many important problems in the world today.
9. Obviously, you have more space in the suburbs than in the city.
10. The Internet will bring people around the world closer together. In fact, it already does every day.
11. Without a doubt, Yosemite is one of the most beautiful spots in the U.S.
12. Coal[19] is a major source of air pollution. Unfortunately, we can't live without it.
13. When I think about my future, I plan big things. Maybe I will be a fashion designer or perhaps an art buyer.
14. At the age of 25, he had no money and no job. Clearly he needed to change his situation.

Certainty	Doubt	Actuality/Truth	Evaluation
		actually	

Think about It Are there any words or phrases in the sentences above that say *when, where, how, why,* or *to what degree*? Underline them and say what kind of information they give.

very—to what degree

---

[18] **recreation:** relaxing and enjoying yourself, when you are not working

[19] **coal:** a black mineral used as fuel

33 | Using Adverbs in Conversation Circle the best adverb to complete each conversation. Then practice with a partner. 11.7 A

1. A: Do you still have five dollars?

   B: **Actually / Of course**, I have eight dollars, not five.

2. A: Do you really enjoy swimming?

   B: I love it. I would do it every day, but I can't, **luckily / sadly**.

3. A: I had a good time tonight, **really / unfortunately**.

   B: Good. So did I.

4. A: Do you want to come over on Tuesday?

   B: Um, **actually / maybe**, I have football practice on Tuesday.

   A: Well, **certainly / maybe** Wednesday then.

   B: I'm kind of busy Wednesday.

5. A: You did the dishes!

   B: **Maybe / Of course** I did the dishes. I always do the dishes.

6. A: Why am I always the last person to get here?

   B: **Actually / Luckily**, Carlos and David aren't here yet.

7. A: Is there anything left to eat?

   B: **Fortunately / Probably**, I saved something for you.

8. A: Are you really going to sell your car?

   B: Sure. **In fact / Really**, two people have already looked at it.

9. A: Do you need to sit down?

   B: No, I'm OK, **obviously / really**.

10. A: What are you going to do next year?

    B: I don't know. I might take some time off.

    A: What for?

    B: **Clearly / Maybe** to do some traveling.

Do you still have five dollars?

Are you really going to sell your car?

34 | Using Adverbs Rewrite each sentence or pair of sentences using one of the adverbs in the box. 11.7 A

1. I don't think he will come back.

   He probably won't come back.

2. I am sure she will be here soon.
3. You aren't happy here. That's obvious.
4. I'm telling you the truth. I didn't do it.

5. The traffic was terrible this morning, but I still got to my job interview on time. That was lucky.
6. I really mean it. You should stay in bed today.
7. I don't know the answer to your question. That's the truth.
8. We might go to Spain next summer.

certainly
clearly
honestly
probably

actually
luckily
maybe
seriously

Talk about It Work with a partner. Choose one of the sentences you rewrote in Activity 34, and use it to create a short conversation. Present your conversation to the class.

A: *When is Jake coming back?*
B: *You know, he probably won't come back. He wasn't feeling well.*
A: *Oh, too bad!*

11.8 Using Adverbs in Speaking

A		
1 A: When are you leaving? B: **In a minute**.		In conversation, speakers sometimes use **adverbs** or **prepositional phrases** alone, as in **1 – 3**.
2 A: Let's stay home tomorrow. B: **Seriously?** A: Yeah, I'm kind of tired.		
3 A: I think it's going to rain again. B: Yeah, **probably**.		

B		
SOFTENING A SUGGESTION		Speakers sometimes use an adverb to soften a suggestion, as in **4 – 5**. These are usually adverbs showing doubt, but we also use *just* in this way, as in **6**.
4 A: I think I'll leave now. B: It's raining pretty hard. **Maybe** you should wait until later.		
5 A: What time is it? B: It's late. You should **probably** get going.		
6 A: Could I **just** interrupt you for a minute? B: Sure. What do you need?		

35 | Using Adverbs Alone Listen and complete these conversations with the missing words. Then practice with a partner. `11.8 A`

1. A: I like your new haircut.

   B: _____

   A: Yeah, it looks very good on you.

2. A: Do you really think I can do it?

   B: _____

3. A: Are you sure you want to go?

   B: _____

4. A: Will you be ready to leave in ten minutes?

   B: Yeah, _____.

5. A: Do you still want to look at my pictures?

   B: Oh, yeah. _____. Of course.

6. A: I'm proud of you.

   B: _____

   A: Yes. You did a great job.

7. A: Do you want dinner now?

   B: No, _____.

8. A: Did you like the movie?

   B: _____

9. A: How did the meeting go?

   B: _____

10. A: Are you hungry?

    B: Yes, _____.

Talk about It Practice the conversations above again. This time, respond with a different adverb or prepositional phrase.

A: *I like your new haircut.*
B: *Really?*

36 | Softening a Suggestion Add *probably, perhaps, maybe,* and *just* to soften the suggestions in the box, and use each suggestion in a conversation below. Then practice with a partner. `11.8 B`

> Well, you should tell him about it.   You should apologize.   You should lie down for a while.
> You need to leave home earlier.   You should call him.

1. A: Toshi hasn't called in days. I hope he's OK.

   B: *Perhaps you should call him.*

2. A: Why is Isabel so angry?

   B: I forgot to go to her picnic and now she won't talk to me.

   A: _____

3. A: My head's killing me.

   B: _____

4. A: I just can't get to class on time.

   B: _____

5. A: Does your father know about your accident?

   B: No, I don't think so.

   A: _____

11.9 Using Adverbs and Prepositional Phrases in Writing

Writers use certain **adverbs** and **prepositional phrases** to connect sentences in a piece of writing, as in **1**. We call them **linking expressions**.

1 | I spend a lot of time planning for the future. | However, | this is usually more stressful than helpful. |

sentence 1   sentence 2

A

2 It's fun to look for cultural differences when you travel. For example, people in a different place may eat very different food.

3 I would need a good reason to fire an employee. For instance, I would fire someone who stole from the company.

4 As a child, I wanted to become a great athlete or movie star. However, now my goals are more realistic.

5 At first I couldn't communicate in Spanish very well. However, after several months, my Spanish got better.

Like traffic lights and road signs, linking expressions signal (or tell the reader) the kind of information that is coming. The most common linking expressions in academic writing are *for example* and *however*.

• We use *for example* or *for instance* to signal an example of something mentioned earlier, as in **2 – 3**.

• We use *however* to signal that contrasting information is coming next, as in **4 – 5**.

B

6 Most children take their first steps between 10 and 16 months. At this age, the child is still somewhat unstable.

7 A fad is something that is very popular for a short time. One summer everyone wears the same kind of shirt. The next summer, people wear something totally different.

Writers sometimes use time, place, and manner expressions at the beginning of a sentence to connect the sentence back to a previous sentence and to add details, as in **6 – 7**.

GO ONLINE

37 | Adding Examples in Writing Match the sentences on the left with examples on the right. `11.9 A`

THE ENGLISH LANGUAGE

1. Many words in English come from other languages. ____

2. We are constantly adding new words to the language or new meanings to old words. ____

3. The main part of a word is called the root. Many words in English come from the same root. ____

4. Some prefixes, such as *in-* and *un-*, can reverse the meaning of a word. ____

5. Many words in English have more than one meaning. ____

6. Synonyms are words that are similar in meaning. ____

7. We form an acronym by using the first letters of a group of words. ____

a. For example, the word *incomplete* is the opposite of *complete*.

b. For example, the words *biography*, *biology*, and *biochemistry* come from the root *bio*, which means "life."

c. The word *so*, for example, can mean "consequently," "thus," "to a great extent," "also," "apparently," or "true."

d. The word *scuba*, for example, means "self-contained underwater breathing apparatus."

e. For instance, computers introduced a new meaning for the word *mouse*.

f. The word *chocolate*, for example, comes from the Aztec word *xocolatl*, which means "bitter water."

g. For instance, you can use the word *large* in place of *big* with little change in meaning.

38 | Using Linking Expressions Complete each sentence with *however* or *for example*. `11.9 A`

1. It's not always possible to exercise every day. _____, most people should be able to go for a walk or play a sport several times a week.

2. Sometimes a little stress is good for me. _____, feeling a little stress before an exam makes me study harder.

3. A few years ago, experts thought that computers would replace books. Now, _____, they are saying that books won't disappear.

4. I'm usually quite tired in the afternoon. By evening, _____, I usually feel pretty alert and energetic.

5. In my culture in the past, a girl's parents chose a husband for her. Today, _____, this happens less often.

6. I moved here with my family ten years ago. At first I was very unhappy because I didn't know anyone. _____, after I started school, I made lots of new friends and I didn't feel lonely anymore.

7. In many parts of the world, the average life expectancy has increased greatly. _____, in the U.S., life expectancy was 47 years in 1900. Today it is 77 years.

8. A few bilingual people speak two languages equally well. Normally, _____, bilingual people speak one language more fluently.

9. I would need a good reason to fire an employee. _____, I would fire someone who kept missing work without a good excuse.

10. When you sleep, you dream about 20 percent of the time. _____, a person who sleeps for eight hours dreams for about 96 minutes.

11. I am very hard-working and I get along well with other people. _____, I am not very organized.

39 | Connecting Ideas in Writing Complete each sentence with your own ideas. Then compare with your classmates. (Many different answers are possible.) `11.9 A`

1. There are many different ways to greet someone. For example, _____.
2. There is always something interesting to do here. For example, _____.
3. There are many things that can make a person angry. For instance, _____.
4. Some great cities are not very well known. For instance, _____.
5. The way people live has changed tremendously[20] in the past 50 years. For example, _____

   _____.

6. Traveling alone can be fun. However, _____.
7. Air travel is relatively safe. However, _____.
8. It's not easy to learn a foreign language. However, _____.
9. Many people would like to work fewer hours. However, _____.

40 | Using Time and Place Expressions to Connect Ideas Read two versions of each essay. Underline the new information in Version 2. Then answer the questions below. `11.9 B`

Version 1	Version 2
THE AIRCAR	**THE AIRCAR**
Would you like to drive and fly? You may be able to. Ken Wernicke is building a car that you can both drive and fly. He calls it an Aircar. Wernicke's Aircar is wide enough to fly but narrow enough to fit on the road. This unusual car will have a maximum speed of 310 miles per hour (499 kilometers per hour). It will go 65 miles per hour (105 kilometers per hour). This two-person vehicle will be able to travel 1,300 miles (2,092 kilometers) or 2,000 miles (3,219 kilometers).	Would you like to drive <u>to the airport</u> and then fly to another city—without ever leaving your car? Someday you may be able to. Ken Wernicke is building a car that you can both drive and fly. He calls it an Aircar. Wernicke's Aircar is wide enough to fly but narrow enough to fit on the road. In the air, this unusual car will have a maximum speed of 310 miles per hour (499 kilometers per hour). On the highway, it will go 65 miles per hour (105 kilometers per hour). With two 50-gallon (189-liter) fuel tanks, this two-person vehicle will be able to travel 1,300 miles (2,092 kilometers) in the air or 2,000 miles (3,219 kilometers) on the road.
THE FIRST AIRPLANE	**THE FIRST AIRPLANE**
Orville Wright flew the first successful airplane. He and his brother Wilbur took turns as pilot and flew. They went a little bit farther. Wilbur was able to travel 852 feet. The two brothers from Ohio had invented powered flight.	On December 17, 1903, Orville Wright flew the first successful airplane for 120 feet on a beach in Kitty Hawk, North Carolina. He and his brother Wilbur took turns as pilot and flew three more times that day. On each flight, they went a little bit farther. On their final flight, Wilbur was able to travel 852 feet in 59 seconds. The two brothers from Ohio had invented powered flight.

1. How is Version 1 of each story different from Version 2?
2. In Version 2 of each story, which time, place, and manner expressions does the writer use at the beginning of a sentence? What purpose do they serve? Write *when*, *where*, or *how* next to each expression.

[20] **tremendously:** a lot

WRAP-UP Demonstrate Your Knowledge

A | GIVING ADVICE Choose an adverb of manner. List five things you should do using the adverb of manner. Then read your list to the class, and ask your classmates to add more ideas.

carefully
- *You should drive carefully.*
- *You should answer questions on a test carefully.*
- *You should choose a spouse carefully.*

B | WRITING Study the pictures and complete the accident reports with your own ideas. (Many different answers are possible.) Try to use all of the adverbs and prepositional phrases in the box.

Accident Report #1

Employee's name: Sandra Woods

Describe accident: ___On Saturday,___

___Sandra Woods had almost finished with___

___the lunch service.___

_____

_____

_____

_____

_____

_____

_____

_____

_____

actually
almost
however
luckily
maybe
on the floor
pretty
suddenly
usually

Accident Report #2

Employee's name: Jeff Sawyer

Describe accident: _____

_____

_____

_____

_____

_____

_____

_____

_____

_____

_____

backward
carelessly
however
probably
really
unexpectedly
unfortunately
without looking

C | RESEARCH Choose a well-known person—someone you admire—and research biographical information about him or her. Then write a short biography about this person for your classmates to read. Be sure to include details about *when*, *why*, and *how*.

D | PRESENTATION Explain to your classmates how to do something simple. Try to use adverbs and prepositional phrases in your presentation.

How to Wash Your Hands
1. *Put water on your hands.*
2. *Add soap to your hands.*
3. *Rub your hands together vigorously for about 20 seconds.*
4. *Rinse your hands well.*
5. *Dry your hands with a paper towel.*

E | WEB SEARCH Look online for the script of a movie you enjoyed seeing. Search in the script for three examples of degree adverbs from Chart 11.6. Copy the sentences with the examples from the script, and ask your classmates to use the sentences to make a new conversation.

from the movie <u>*Moonstruck*</u>*:*
What exactly does your husband do?   *That's very sad.*   *It's really cold.*

11.10   Summary of Adverbs and Prepositional Phrases

TYPE	PURPOSE	EXAMPLES IN BOOK TITLES
TIME	to explain *when*	***Now***, *Discover Your Strengths* by Marcus Buckingham and Donald O. Clifton
FREQUENCY	to explain *how often*	***Seldom*** *Right But Never in Doubt: Essays, Journalism, and Social Commentary* by Joseph Dobrian and Dorothy Parker
PLACE	to explain *where*	*Difficult People: Dealing With Difficult People* ***at Work*** by Colin G. Smith
MANNER	to explain *how* or *in what way*	*How to Take Great Notes* ***Quickly*** *And* ***Easily***: *A Very Easy Guide* by John Connelly
REASON	to explain *why*	***Because of You*** by B. G. Hennessy and Hiroe Nakata
DEGREE	to explain *to what degree* to strengthen or weaken a verb, adjective, or adverb	*The* ***Perfectly*** *Roasted Chicken: 20 New Ways to Roast* by Mindy Fox
ATTITUDE / FEELINGS	to show certainty	*The Underground Baseball Encyclopedia: Baseball Stuff You Never Needed to Know and Can* ***Certainly*** *Live Without* by Robert Schnakenberg
	to show doubt	*Baking Soda: Over 500 Fabulous, Fun, and Frugal Uses You've* ***Probably*** *Never Thought Of* by Vicki Lansky
	to emphasize the truth	*Your First $1000—How to Start an Online Business that* ***Actually*** *Makes Money* by Steve Scott
	to make an evaluation or judgment	***Unfortunately***, *It Was Paradise: Selected Poems* by Mahmoud Darwish, Munir Akash, Carolyn Forché, and Sinan Antoon
LINKING	to connect clauses in a piece of writing	*You're Not Old Until You're Ninety: Best to Be Prepared,* ***However*** by Rebecca Lattimer

12

Adverb Clauses

If you wait for perfect conditions, you'll never get anything done.

—ANONYMOUS

Talk about It What does the quotation above mean? Do you agree or disagree? Why?

WARM-UP

A | Complete this questionnaire. Check (✓) *True* or *False*. Then compare answers with your classmates. Would you be better at starting a new business if you checked more *Trues* or *Falses*?

SHOULD YOU START YOUR OWN BUSINESS?

	TRUE	FALSE
1. I like to try new things **because I enjoy taking risks.**	☐	☐
2. I'll do something by myself **if no one can help me.**	☐	☐
3. **When I make a mistake,** I try to learn from it.	☐	☐
4. I don't get stressed **when I don't have a lot of money.**	☐	☐
5. In the past, **when something went wrong,** I stayed calm and focused.	☐	☐
6. I am willing to listen **when someone disagrees with me.**	☐	☐
7. I'll keep working **until a job is finished.**	☐	☐
8. I have been able to do unpleasant tasks **if they were necessary.**	☐	☐

B | The words in blue in each sentence above form an adverb clause. Based on these examples, what can you say about adverb clauses? Check (✓) *True* or *False*.

	TRUE	FALSE
1. An adverb clause has a subject and a verb.	☐	☐
2. An adverb clause always comes at the end of a sentence.	☐	☐
3. An adverb clause always begins with the word *when*.	☐	☐
4. An adverb clause always uses a present verb form.	☐	☐
5. We always use a comma in a sentence with an adverb clause.	☐	☐

C | Look back at the quotation on page 372. Identify any adverb clauses.

12.1 What Is an Adverb Clause?

A

	main clause	adverb clause
1	You should leave	while you still have time.

2 He was fine **when I last saw him.** (when)

3 She didn't do anything **because it was so hot.** (why)

4 **If you want to call,** our number is 555-0199.
(under what conditions)

			subject	verb	
5	He called	because	he	needed	something.

		subordinator	
6	Call me on my cell phone	if	you go out.

COMPARE

7a We had dinner together **before she left.**

7b **Before she left,** we had dinner together.

We use an **adverb clause** to add information to a **main clause**, as in **1**. This unit looks at how we use adverb clauses to explain *when, why,* or *under what conditions,* as in **2 – 4**.

Notice that an adverb clause:
- has a subject and a verb, as in **5**
- begins with a connecting word called a **subordinator**, as in **6**
- can come before or after the main clause, as in **7a – 7b**

Notice: When the adverb clause comes first, we use a comma (,) to separate it from the main clause, as in **7b**.

B

PRESENT TIME FRAME

8 I **like** football **because** it's fast-paced.
(simple present / simple present)

9 **Come** back **when** you **can stay** longer.
(imperative / *can* + base form)

10 I'm good at tennis **because** I've played it for a long time. (simple present / present perfect)

PAST TIME FRAME

11 He **got** excited **when** he **heard** the news.
(simple past / simple past)

12 I **couldn't believe** it **when** he **told** me the news.
(*couldn't* + base form / simple past)

13 She **was** upset **because** I **had forgotten** to call.
(simple past / past perfect)

MIXED TIME FRAME

14 Here is a picture of me **when** I **was** 12 years old.

15 He **isn't going to go because** he's still sick.

It's important to pay attention to the form of the verbs in the **main clause** and the **adverb clause**.

When both verbs refer to a present time frame, we use present verb forms, as in **8 – 10**.

When both verbs refer to a past time frame, we use past verb forms, as in **11 – 13**.

When both verbs refer to future time, we use verb forms in a special way. See Chart 12.2.

When the verbs in the two clauses refer to different time frames, we use different verb forms, as in **14 – 15**.

 ONLINE

1 | Understanding Adverb Clauses Underline the subject and verb in each **bold** adverb clause. `12.1 A`

Learning to Play the Piano

1. I started playing the piano **when <u>I was</u> 10 years old**.
2. At first I didn't like playing the piano **because I wasn't very good at it**.
3. I didn't like my teacher either **because she made me practice every day**.
4. **Even when I was on vacation**, I had to practice.
5. My first piano teacher was also very impatient. **If I made a mistake**, she always yelled at me.
6. Of course, **when she yelled at me**, I got nervous and made more mistakes.

7. Luckily, **when I was 13 years old**, my family moved to another city and I got a new piano teacher.
8. My new piano teacher was very different from my first teacher. **Whenever I made a mistake**, she raised her eyebrows but she never yelled at me.
9. She also made me practice a lot, but not **while I was on vacation**.
10. **Because I practiced a lot**, I'm now a pretty good piano player.
11. **Whenever I have some free time**, I sit down at the piano.
12. I play a lot of jazz **because it's my favorite type of music**.

Think about It How many different subordinators can you find in the sentences in Activity 1? What are they? Which adverb clauses are followed by a comma? Why?

Talk about It What did you learn about the writer? Without looking back, tell a partner three things.

2 | Identifying the Time Frame
Look again at the sentences in Activity 1. Complete this chart. Write the verb in the main clause, the verb in the adverb clause, and the time frame. `12.1 B`

	Verb in main clause	Verb in adverb clause	=	Time frame: present, past, mixed?
1.	started	was	=	past
2.			=	
3.			=	
4.			=	
5.			=	
6.			=	
7.			=	
8.			=	
9.			=	
10.			=	
11.			=	
12.			=	

3 | Using the Correct Verb Form
Complete each sentence with the correct form of the verb in parentheses. (Hint: In these sentences, the verbs in the main clause and the adverb clause refer to the same time frame.) Then check (✓) *True* or *False* for you. `12.1 B`

		TRUE	FALSE
1.	I _____ like _____ to read in bed before I go to sleep. (like)	☐	☐
2.	I studied English when I _____ a child. (be)	☐	☐
3.	Because I _____ English fairly well, I feel comfortable speaking in public. (speak)	☐	☐
4.	I couldn't go to school last year because I _____ a job. (have)	☐	☐

	TRUE	FALSE

5. When this course _____, I didn't know anyone in my class. (start) ☐ ☐

6. I know a lot about Canada because I _____ there several times. (be) ☐ ☐

7. I like to listen to music while I _____. (study) ☐ ☐

8. I don't like to exercise when it _____ very hot. (be) ☐ ☐

9. I can't study while other people _____. (talk) ☐ ☐

10. I'm not usually hungry in the morning because I _____ dinner late. (eat) ☐ ☐

11. I was tired this morning because I _____ really late last night. (stay up) ☐ ☐

12. I _____ satisfied after I've had a good meal. (feel) ☐ ☐

Write about It Rewrite the false statements in Activity 3 to make them true for you.

I usually watch TV before I go to sleep.

12.2 Adverb Clauses of Time

A

EVENTS THAT HAPPEN AT THE SAME TIME

1 You shouldn't use your phone **while you're driving**.

2 We were eating **when the phone rang**.

3 The phone went dead **as she was dialing his number**.

4 **Whenever I call**, he's busy.

We can use an **adverb clause of time** to explain when something happened or happens.

We use some subordinators to show that two events happen at the same time, as in **1 – 4**.

• *while* = during the time that, as in **1**
• *when* = at the time that, as in **2**
• *as* = while; when; during the time that, as in **3**
• *whenever* = every time that, as in **4**

EVENTS THAT HAPPEN IN A SEQUENCE

5 You can't stop the process **after it begins**.

6 I had just fallen asleep **when the phone rang**.

7 I usually get up **as soon as I hear the alarm**.

8 **Once it started to rain**, they stopped the game.

9 I didn't know her **before I moved here**.

10 **By the time I called**, everyone was asleep.

We use some subordinators to show that one event happens before or after another event.

• *after* = at a later time, as in **5**
• *when* = and then, as in **6**
• *as soon as* = immediately after, as in **7**
• *once* = as soon as; anytime after, as in **8**
• *before* = at an earlier time, as in **9**
• *by the time* = before that time or event, as in **10**

OTHER TIME RELATIONSHIPS

11 I decided to stay **until my parents arrived**.

12 It has been a month **since we talked**.

13 I'm going to stay **as long as I can**.

Other time subordinators include:

• *until* = up to that time, as in **11**
• *since** = from that time until now, as in **12**
• *as long as* = for the length of time that, as in **13**

* When we use *since* in a time clause, the verb must refer to an earlier time (simple past, present perfect, past perfect, etc.).

B

FUTURE TIME CLAUSES

14 I'll wait **until you get here**.

(NOT: ~~I'll wait until you will get here.~~)

15 I'm going to call **as soon as I get there**.

(NOT: ~~I'm going to call as soon as I will get there.~~)

We can also use an adverb clause to tell when something will happen in the future. We use the simple present form in a time clause to express future time, as in **14 – 15**.

GO ONLINE

4 | Noticing Adverb Clauses of Time Check (✓) the sentences that describe you. Then underline the adverb clauses of time. `12.2 A`

Unusual Habits

- [ ] 1. I always count the stairs <u>as I go up</u>.
- [ ] 2. I like to drink several glasses of water while I eat.
- [ ] 3. When I'm alone, I talk to myself.
- [ ] 4. Whenever I'm scared, I laugh.
- [ ] 5. I like to sing when I'm driving alone.
- [ ] 6. When I get out of the shower, I put on a pair of plastic slippers.
- [ ] 7. I have to open the windows as soon as I get in a car, or I'll get carsick.
- [ ] 8. I always turn on a fan before I go to bed, even when it's cold.
- [ ] 9. I bite my tongue whenever I'm concentrating.
- [ ] 10. When I'm out in public, I almost always wear sunglasses.
- [ ] 11. I never answer the phone until it rings three times.
- [ ] 12. As soon as I wake up in the morning, I drink a full glass of warm water.
- [ ] 13. I have to wear socks when I sleep—even if it's hot.
- [ ] 14. Before I go to bed, I eat a couple of crackers so I don't feel hungry.
- [ ] 15. Ever since I was a child, I've been able to fall asleep almost anywhere.

RESEARCH SAYS...

Time clauses are more commonly used after the main clause than before it.

CORPUS

Think about It Which sentences describe two events that happen at the same time? That happen in a sequence?

Talk about It What are some other unusual habits that people have? Share ideas with your classmates.

Write about It Use these adverb clauses to write sentences about your habits.

- Whenever I'm nervous, . . .
- Before I go to sleep, . . .
- Whenever I'm scared, . . .
- . . . while I eat.

5 | Punctuating Time Clauses Underline each time clause and add a comma (,) where necessary. `12.2 A`

Eating Customs

1. **Brazil**
   - <u>When you go into a restaurant</u>, you should greet the people who work there.
   - It's rude to make noise while you are eating.
   - Before they start to eat Brazilians usually say "bom apetite" to their friends.

2. **Turkey**
   - You shouldn't talk when you have food in your mouth.
   - You should keep your mouth closed while you are eating.
   - In a restaurant, you should order your food before you order your drinks. While the kitchen is preparing your food the server can bring your drinks.

FYI

Remember: When the adverb clause comes before the main clause, we use a comma after the adverb clause.

When you get good service in a restaurant, you should leave a tip.

3. Japan
- You shouldn't start eating until everyone is at the table.
- When you eat a bowl of rice or soup you may lift the bowl to your mouth.
- People often say "gochiso-sama deshita" when they finish eating.

4. Korea
- When you are eating with an older person you should wait until he or she starts eating.
- Try not to make any noise while you are chewing[1] your food.
- You shouldn't leave the table before the oldest person finishes eating.

Write about It Write two true sentences and one false sentence about eating customs in your culture. Read your sentences to the class, and ask your classmates to identify the false sentence.

6 | Understanding Subordinators Decide if each pair of sentences is similar in meaning or different. Write *S* (similar) or *D* (different). `12.2 A`

_S_ 1. Make a wish while you blow out the candles.
Make a wish when you blow out the candles.

____ 2. You shouldn't use your phone while you are driving.
You shouldn't use your phone when you are driving.

____ 3. I had just fallen asleep when the phone rang.
I fell asleep just before the phone rang.

____ 4. I decided to stay until my parents left.
I decided to stay before my parents left.

____ 5. He had just arrived when the fire broke out.
He arrived when the fire broke out.

____ 6. You can't stop the process once it begins.
You can't stop the process after it begins.

____ 7. Whenever I talk to her, she always makes me laugh.
She always makes me laugh when I talk to her.

____ 8. I'll tell you all about it when I get back.
I'll tell you all about it after I get back.

____ 9. I've played the piano since I was a child.
I played the piano when I was a child.

____ 10. I don't want to do anything until he gets here.
I don't want to do anything before he gets here.

[1] **chew:** to use your teeth to break up food in your mouth while you are eating

7 | Using Time Subordinators Choose the subordinator in parentheses that best completes each sentence. Then check (✓) the good study habits. **12.2 A**

Good Study Habit or Bad Study Habit?

☐ 1. _____ I have homework, I do it right away.
      (while / until / whenever)

☐ 2. I often study at night _____ I go to bed.
      (since / as soon as / before)

☐ 3. I like to listen to loud music _____ I am studying.
      (since / before / while)

☐ 4. I am ready to start learning _____ I get to class.
      (as soon as / until / since)

☐ 5. I often skip² class _____ I'm tired.
      (by the time / after / when)

☐ 6. I often daydream³ _____ the teacher talks.
      (as / before / after)

☐ 7. I take notes in class _____ my teacher talks.
      (before / whenever / until)

☐ 8. _____ I've read a chapter in my textbook, I never look at it again.
      (before / as / once)

☐ 9. _____ I read a new word, I write it in my notebook.
      (whenever / since / before)

☐ 10. I haven't opened a book _____ the semester started.
      (before / since / when)

Talk about It What are some other good and bad study habits? Share ideas with your classmates.

8 | Usage Note: Reduced Clauses with *When* and *While* Read the note. Then do Activities 9 and 10.

We can sometimes shorten or reduce an adverb clause of time. We can do this when:
- the adverb clause begins with *when* or *while*, and
- the subject of the main clause and the subject of the adverb clause are the same, and
- the adverb clause has a form of the verb *be* (as a helping verb or main verb).

We reduce the clause by removing the subject and the verb *be*.

FULL ADVERB CLAUSES	REDUCED ADVERB CLAUSES
1a She had a job **when she was studying there**.	1b She had a job **when studying there**.
2a We didn't meet anyone **while we were in Rome**.	2b We didn't meet anyone **while in Rome**.

When the main clause and the adverb clause have different subjects, we can't reduce the adverb clause.

  3 She had a job **while her husband** was studying there. (NOT: ~~She had a job while studying there.~~)

---

²**skip:** to not do something that you should do

³**daydream:** to think happy thoughts that make you forget what you should be doing

9 | Using Reduced Clauses Read these sentences and check (✓) *True* or *False*. Where possible, rewrite the sentence with a reduced clause. `12.2 A`

TRUE OR FALSE?

	TRUE	FALSE

1. Scientists often wear a special coat or jacket when they are doing experiments.   ☐ ☐
    Scientists often wear a special coat or jacket when doing experiments.

2. When you quit smoking, your heart rate[4] goes up right away.   ☐ ☐
    The adverb clause can't be reduced.

3. While you're resting, you burn a lot of body fat.   ☐ ☐
    _____

4. Most professional tennis players started playing while they were very young.   ☐ ☐
    _____

5. Many people like to read while they're traveling on public transportation.   ☐ ☐
    _____

6. When you are feeling relaxed, you can usually think more clearly.   ☐ ☐
    _____

7. When you are breathing deeply, your chest expands, or gets bigger.   ☐ ☐
    _____

8. Many university students have jobs while they are in school.   ☐ ☐
    _____

9. Most athletes don't do extra training before they have competitions.   ☐ ☐
    _____

10. Your body will let you know when you are working too hard.   ☐ ☐
    _____

11. Very few people listen to music while they are driving.   ☐ ☐
    _____

12. Most people do things outdoors when the weather is nice.   ☐ ☐
    _____

13. Only very intelligent people dream while they are sleeping.   ☐ ☐
    _____

14. When a parent sings to a baby, the baby's breathing speeds up.   ☐ ☐
    _____

15. Most athletes don't drink enough water when they are exercising.   ☐ ☐
    _____

Think about It Tell a partner which sentences above can't be reduced. Explain why not.

Talk about It Tell your partner why you said true or false for each sentence above.

[4] **heart rate:** the speed at which the heart pumps blood through the body

10 | Using Reduced Clauses Complete these sentences with information about yourself. Then rewrite each sentence with a reduced adverb clause. **12.2 A**

YOUR HABITS

1. I usually _____ listen to music _____ when I am _____ resting _____.

   I usually listen to music when resting. _____

2. I never _____ while I am _____.

   _____

3. I like to _____ while I am _____.

   _____

4. I didn't _____ while I was _____.

   _____

5. I always _____ while I am _____.

   _____

6. I never _____ when I am _____.

   _____

7. I dislike _____ when I am _____.

   _____

8. I enjoy _____ while I am _____.

   _____

Talk about It Ask a partner questions based on the sentences you wrote above. Does your partner have similar habits?

A: *Do you usually listen to music when resting?*
B: *No, I usually like it to be quiet.*

11 | Talking about the Future Complete these conversations with the simple present or a future form of the verb in parentheses. Then practice with a partner. **12.2 B**

1. A: Why hasn't Annie called?

   B: Relax. I'm sure she'll call as soon as she _____ back. (get)

2. A: Could you give this to Andy?

   B: Sure. I'll give it to him when I _____ him tomorrow. (see)

3. A: Aren't you going to be late?

   B: Yes, but I'm not going to leave until Bob _____. (call)

4. A: How was the meeting?

   B: I _____ you about it as soon as I'm back home. (tell)

5. A: Can I borrow a little money from you?

   B: Sure. Is this enough?

   A: Yeah, thanks. I _____ you back as soon as I can. (pay)

6. A: Where are you now?

   B: I'm still pretty far away. I'm probably not going to see you before you

   _____. (leave)

7. A: What time do you get out of work today?

   B: I'm not sure.

   A: Well, I'll come get you when you _____ ready to leave. Just call me. (be)

8. A: What are you going to do while your friends _____ here? (be)

   B: I'll just show them around, take them a few places, you know.

9. A: What did they say? Did you get the job?

   B: I won't know until they _____ me. (call)

10. A: What do you want to do now?

    B: I'm going to take a shower before I _____ anything else. (do)

Think about It Underline the future forms in the conversations in Activity 11. Then look at the uses of future forms in this box. Why is the future form used in each conversation?

USES OF FUTURE FORMS

to talk about a future plan	to make a prediction	to make a promise	to offer some help

12 | Using Future Time Clauses Read these clauses and think about the sequence of events. Combine the clauses using the adverb in parentheses. Use a simple present and a future verb form. (More than one answer may be possible.) `12.2 B`

PLANNING A WEDDING

1. have an engagement party / start planning the wedding (before)

   We're going to have an engagement party before we start planning the wedding.
   We're going to start planning the wedding before we have an engagement party.

2. announce the engagement / tell our families (after)
3. decide on a date / make a budget⁵ for the wedding (once)
4. look for a wedding location / make a guest list (while)
5. choose a location / send the invitations (when)
6. hire a band / decide on the kind of music we want (once)
7. taste the food / not choose the menu (until)
8. ask some friends for advice / hire a photographer (after)
9. not think about wedding clothes / do everything else (until)
10. go shopping for clothes / take my best friend (when)

Think about It Which sentences above are logical when written in either sequence?

13 | Error Correction Correct any errors in these sentences. (Some sentences may not have any errors.)

1. Until I came to this country, then I went to school.
2. I will take care of my parents when they will be older.
3. When the movie finish, I went home.
4. I want to go back home as long as I can.
5. Before leave, you have to sign out.
6. After they got married. They moved to Spain.

⁵ **budget:** a plan for how much money you will have and how you will spend it

7. When I woke up I realized the house was freezing.

8. When I feel sad my sister told me a funny story.

9. I met him six months ago when he start this class.

10. My mother left Hungary in 1998. When she arrived here, she doesn't like it.

11. My sister went to school in Los Angeles. While she studying there, she made a lot of friends.

12. Our needs change as we get older. When we are children, we spend a lot of time with our parents. Since we are teenagers, we do more things with our friends.

13. At home we always did the same thing in the evening. Around 7:00, we had something for dinner, and then as soon as we finish, we played chess.

12.3 Adverb Clauses of Reason

A	main clause reason clause **1** I like Thai food | **because it's spicy.** **2 Since my phone wasn't working, I couldn't call.** **3 Don't bother to call me because I won't answer.** **4 I can't invite you in because I have to leave now.**	We use an **adverb clause of reason** to explain why something in the main clause happens or happened, as in **1**. Adverb clauses of reason usually begin with the subordinators **because** or **since**, as in **1 – 4**.
B	**5 A:** Why didn't you call me back? **B: Because I fell asleep.** **6** The traditional role of fathers is changing. **Since many mothers now work outside the home,** fathers must help out more at home.	In conversation, speakers sometimes leave out the main clause when they answer a question, as in **5**. In writing, however, we need to use a main clause with the adverb clause, as in **6**. Otherwise, the sentence is incomplete.
C	**OTHER WAYS TO EXPLAIN** *WHY* main clause + *so* + main clause **7a They were doing construction on the street outside, so I couldn't sleep.** main clause with *because of* + noun phrase **7b I couldn't sleep because of the construction.**	Notice the other ways we explain why something happens in **7a – 7b**. • *so* = a conjunction • *because of* = a phrasal preposition *Because of* is followed by a noun phrase, not a clause, as in **7b**. The information that follows *because of* is usually shorter or more concise.
D	**CORRECT THE COMMON ERRORS** (See page R-13.) **8 ✗** I was happy because learned something important. **9 ✗** I'm proud of myself because now I could communicate with people in English.	**10 ✗** I was sad because I have to leave soon. **11 ✗** We stayed at home. Because it was so hot.

14 | Noticing Adverb Clauses of Reason
Underline each adverb clause of reason. Then circle the verbs in each main clause and adverb clause. 12.3 A

Sentences from Student Essays

1. I try to eat well and exercise every day. I think I feel better because I do these things.

2. My grandfather didn't spend much time with his children because he worked very long hours.

3. Because we live in a multilingual world, I think everyone should study a foreign language.

4. My favorite game is sudoku because I can play it by myself.

5. In a big city, you can stay out late because there is always something open.

6. I have always wanted to be a teacher. I think this is because I have always had great teachers.

7. People like to use the Internet because it gives them instant access to a lot of information.

8. I avoid coffee and tea late in the day because they will interfere⁶ with my sleep.

9. My watch is special to me because it was a gift from my parents.

10. Since my family is Polish, I want to learn about the history of Poland.

11. Since many people have moved here from other countries, you hear many different languages on the street.

12. Since many mothers are now working outside the home, fathers are helping more with the children.

Think about It Look again at the sentences in Activity 14. Complete the chart. Then answer the questions below.

Verb in main clause	Verb in adverb clause	Verb in main clause	Verb in adverb clause
1. *think, feel*	*do*	7.	
2.		8.	
3.		9.	
4.		10.	
5.		11.	
6.		12.	

QUESTIONS

1. For each sentence, how are the verb forms similar or different in the two clauses?
2. In which sentences do both clauses refer to the same time frame?

15 | Usage Note: Using *Since* in Time Clauses and Reason Clauses Read the note. Then do Activity 16.

We can use *since* to introduce a **time clause** or a **reason clause**, but the meaning of the word is different.

Time clause: I haven't done anything **since I got home.** (*since* = from the time that)
Reason clause: Since no one is here, you should probably lock the door. (*since* = because)

In conversation, we use *since* more often to introduce a time clause. In writing, we use *since* more often to introduce a reason clause.

⁶**interfere:** to stop something from being done well

16 | Adverb Clause of Time or Reason? Underline the adverb clauses in these sentences. Then check (✓) *Time Clause* or *Reason Clause*. `12.3 A`

	TIME CLAUSE	REASON CLAUSE
1. I have wanted to be a doctor <u>since I was a small child</u>.	✓	☐
2. Since the front door wasn't locked, I let myself in.	☐	☐
3. Since it began in the 1980s, the organization has attracted many new members.	☐	☐
4. Since we had to leave right away, we didn't have time to pack a suitcase.	☐	☐
5. We've known her since we were four or five.	☐	☐
6. Since I had already studied English for several years, I got into an advanced class.	☐	☐
7. I haven't been to that museum since it reopened in 2012.	☐	☐
8. Since you need more money, maybe you should get a better-paying job.	☐	☐
9. I've been a fan of Alan Rickman since I saw him in a play several years ago.	☐	☐
10. The new technology led to smaller devices[7] since designers could use smaller batteries.	☐	☐
11. It has been a long time since we went to that restaurant.	☐	☐
12. Since we didn't speak the same language, we spent a lot of time smiling at each other.	☐	☐

17 | Pronunciation Note: *Because* Listen to the note. Then do Activity 18.

In conversation, we often pronounce *because* as /cɔs/ or /cəz/.

1 A: Why aren't you coming with us?
B: **Because** /cəz/ I'm tired.

2 A: How come you're still here?
B: **Because** /cɔs/ I still have work to do.

WARNING! We do not use /cəz/ or /cɔs/ in writing.

---

18 | Listening for Reasons Listen and complete these conversations. Then listen again and check (✓) the pronunciation: *because* or /cɔs/ /cəz/. `12.3 B`

	BECAUSE	/cɔs/ /cəz/
1. Friend A: Why didn't you call?	☐	✓
Friend B: Because *I left my phone at school* .		
2. Friend A: Why are you watching this movie again?	☐	☐
Friend B: Because _____.		
3. Wife: I think we should take flowers or something.	☐	☐
Husband: What for?		
Wife: Because _____.		

---

[7] **devices:** specialized tools or pieces of equipment

	BECAUSE	/cɔs/ /cəz/

4. Wife: Why are you telling me about this?

   Husband: Because _____.

5. Sister: I'm so sorry. Really.

   Brother: Sorry? Why are you sorry?

   Sister: Because _____.

6. Teacher: Why didn't you finish the test?

   Student: Because _____.

7. Teacher: You have very good ideas. Why don't you say more in class?

   Student: Because _____.

8. Teacher: Why are you late?

   Student: Because _____.

9. Teacher: Do you have your homework?

   Student: I'm sorry, I don't.

   Teacher: Well, why not?

   Student: Because _____.

10. Teacher: Why weren't you here yesterday?

    Student: Because _____.

Talk about It Practice the conversations in Activity 18 with a partner. Try using /cɔs/ or /cəz/ instead of *because*.

Talk about It What other reasons could each person give for the questions in Activity 18? Share ideas with your classmates.

Write about It Rewrite each person's answer in Activity 18 as a complete sentence.

I didn't call because I left my phone at school.

19 | Explaining *Why* Rewrite each sentence using a different way to explain *why*. In some cases, you may need to add more information so that the meaning is complete. **12.3 C**

1. The airport shut down because of bad weather.

   The weather was bad, so the airport shut down.   OR
   The airport shut down because the weather was bad.

2. I couldn't go because of an illness.
3. My sister didn't want to go, so I didn't go.
4. I lost my job because of an injury.
5. I joined the chess club because he did.
6. The roads were really bad, so we stayed at home.
7. He had to stop working because he got sick.
8. My sister quit her job because she didn't like her boss.

Think about It How does the information we give change if we use *because of* versus *so*? Which expression lets us give more information?

20 | Error Correction Correct any errors in these sentences. (Some sentences may not have any errors.)

1. My brother wants to graduate this year, because he needs to get a job.
2. My birthday is the happiest day of my life because my family was there.
3. I couldn't sleep last night. Because it was hot.
4. I was an only child, I was often lonely.
5. Because the war, my parents had to leave their home.
6. We traveled a lot because of my father worked for the United Nations.
7. Since I didn't know English very well I can't understand anyone.
8. It has become easy to travel around the world, knowing a foreign language is more important than before.

12.4 Present and Past Real Conditionals

A

	main clause	conditional clause
1	He always feels better	if he goes swimming.

	condition	result
2	If I go to bed late,	(then) I can't get up early.

A conditional statement has a **main clause** and a **conditional clause**, as in **1**.

The adverb clause states a condition, and the main clause gives the result, as in **2**.

Notice: Conditional clauses usually begin with the word *if*. When the main clause comes second, it sometimes begins with the word *then*.

B

PRESENT REAL CONDITIONALS

3 If you live in a city, you **have** many job opportunities.

4 If you go to a shopping mall on the weekend, it's usually very crowded.

5 If I'm running late, I usually **take** the bus.

6 If I've done a lot of work, I **feel** good.

PAST REAL CONDITIONALS

7 If it rained, she always **took** the bus.

8 I always **did** the dishes if he cooked.

COMPARE *IF* AND *WHEN*

9a The alarm rings **if** someone opens the window.

9b The alarm rings **when** someone opens the window.

A present real conditional describes:
- a fact or general truth, as in **3 – 4**
- something that happens regularly and its result, as in **5 – 6**

A past real conditional describes something that happened regularly in the past and its result, as in **7 – 8**.

With present and past real conditionals, we can use *when* or *whenever* instead of *if* with very little difference in meaning, as in **9a – 9b**.

Notice that we use many different verb forms in present and past real conditional statements. Some common verb forms are:

	conditional clause	main clause
PRESENT REAL CONDITIONALS	simple present present progressive present perfect	simple present *should* + base form *can* + base form
PAST REAL CONDITIONALS	simple past past progressive	simple past *used to* + base form

GRAMMAR TERMS: Conditional clauses are also called **if- clauses**. Present and past real conditionals are also called **zero conditionals**.

21 | Noticing Conditional Clauses Put a slash (/) between the two clauses in these sentences. Write *C* above the conditional clause and *R* above the result clause. Then check (✓) *True* or *False* according to your experience. `12.4 A`

Getting Around

		TRUE	FALSE
1.	You save a lot of money /if you use public transportation instead of a car. (R above "You save a lot of money", C above "if you use public transportation")	☐	☐
2.	If you travel by train during rush hour⁸, your ticket usually costs less.	☐	☐
3.	You can't buy a car if you are younger than 21.	☐	☐
4.	It's fun to drive long distances if you have a comfortable car.	☐	☐
5.	You don't need a map if you have GPS⁹ in your car.	☐	☐
6.	If you drive and text at the same time, you are asking for an accident.	☐	☐
7.	You need to be careful if you ride a bike in a city.	☐	☐
8.	You couldn't go very far in the 1800s if you didn't have a horse.	☐	☐
9.	If you ride a motorcycle, you have to wear a helmet¹⁰.	☐	☐
10.	You need a special driver's license if you want to drive a motorcycle.	☐	☐
11.	If you traveled overseas in the 1800s, you probably went by plane.	☐	☐
12.	If you travel by boat today, it's very expensive.	☐	☐

Write about It Choose four of the conditional clauses above. Add a different result clause to them.

You can read or do work if you use public transportation instead of a car.

> **FYI**
> We sometimes use the word *you* in a real conditional sentence to refer to people in general.

22 | Understanding Conditional Clauses Read the sentences below and underline the conditional clauses. Then decide what each sentence describes. Choose the correct answer from the box. `12.4 B`

> a. a fact or general truth
> b. something that happens regularly
> c. something that happened regularly in the past

____b____ 1. Cell phones are very useful. <u>If you are waiting somewhere,</u> you can call a friend and have a nice chat.

_____ 2. Busy people eat out a lot. If they have children, they may go to fast-food restaurants.

_____ 3. New York is a nice place to live if you don't have a car.

_____ 4. I don't feel good if I don't do a good job on something.

_____ 5. If I'm feeling stressed, I like to go for a long walk.

⁸**rush hour:** a time when there is a lot of traffic because people are traveling to or from work

⁹**GPS:** Global Positioning System; a piece of equipment that shows your location and helps you get somewhere

¹⁰**helmet:** a hard hat that keeps your head safe

_____ 6. It's not fair if some students cheat[11] on a test.

_____ 7. My mother punished me if I misbehaved—not my father.

_____ 8. When I was a child, if there was a lot of snow, we didn't have class.

_____ 9. No country is really developed if it has money but no technology.

_____ 10. My brother always helped me if I was having trouble with something.

_____ 11. If my mother gets home from work and she's really tired, she usually takes a nap[12].

_____ 12. We always had a big meal if we had company for dinner.

Think about It What verb form does each speaker use in the main clause and the conditional clause in Activity 22? Complete this chart and then answer the question below.

Verb in main clause	Verb in conditional clause	Verb in main clause	Verb in conditional clause
1. _can call, have_	_are waiting_	7.	
2.		8.	
3.		9.	
4.		10.	
5.		11.	
6.		12.	

QUESTION

Which sentences in Activity 22 use the same time frame in both the main clause and the conditional clause?

23 | Using Conditional Clauses Complete these sentences with information about your habits now and in the past. `12.4 B`

PRESENT HABITS

1. If I don't get enough sleep, _____ I feel tired _____.

2. If I need to relax, _____.

3. If I don't eat breakfast, _____.

4. I _____ if I'm hungry between meals.

5. I _____
   if I'm tired.

> **F Y I**
>
> We sometimes use _will_ in a main clause to predict something that commonly happens.
>
> If you don't get enough sleep, you **will feel** tired.

PAST HABITS

6. If I helped my mother when I was a child, _____.

7. If I didn't like the food we were eating, _____.

8. If I wanted something, _____.

9. If I couldn't go to sleep, _____.

10. _____ if I felt sick.

---

[11] **cheat:** to do something that is not honest   [12] **nap:** a short sleep during the day

12.5 Future Real Conditionals

A

1 **If she doesn't want me there**, I'll leave.

2 **If you like movies with a good story**, you'll probably like *Sense and Sensibility*.

3 I'll buy it for you **if you really like it**.

4 **If you get an email from him**, can you send it to us?

5 You might feel better **if you take a nap**.

6 **If you're not doing anything tomorrow**, come over.

In a future real conditional statement, the **adverb clause** states a condition, and the main clause gives the likely results in the future.

We sometimes use a future real conditional when we make:

- a plan, as in **1**
- a prediction, as in **2**
- a promise, as in **3**
- a request, as in **4**
- a suggestion, as in **5 – 6**

B

PRESENT CONDITION / FUTURE RESULT

7 How **is she going to pay** the bills **if she's not working** now? (*be going to* + base form / present progressive)

8 You'll **figure** it **out if** you **haven't done** so already. (*will* + base form / present perfect)

PAST CONDITION / FUTURE RESULT

9 **If you did** all the homework last week, **you'll do** well on the test. (simple past / *will* + base form)

10 You **won't be** hungry later **if you ate** a good breakfast. (*will* + base form / simple past)

FUTURE CONDITION / FUTURE RESULT

11 **If I have** time tomorrow, **I might go** downtown. (simple present / *might* + base form)

12 **If you don't go** to work tomorrow, **call** me. (simple present / imperative)

In a future real conditional, we can use many different verb forms in the conditional clause and the main clause, as in **7 – 12**. Some common verb forms are:

conditional clause	main clause	
simple present	*will*	
present progressive	*might*	+ base form
present perfect	*should*	
can/can't + base form	*be going to*	
simple past	imperative	

WARNING! We don't normally use *will* in the conditional clause even when it refers to the future, as in **11 – 12**.

GRAMMAR TERM: The future real conditional is also called the **first conditional**.

 GO ONLINE

🔊 **24 | Listening for Conditional Clauses** Choose the correct conditional clause from the box to complete each conversation below. Listen and check your answers. Then practice with a partner. `12.5 A`

if we don't have any money	if you tell me
if you decide to visit again	if you want to read something
if you get lost	if you're late for dinner
if you keep bugging[13] me	if you've heard this before
if you need me	if you've really learned it

1. A: Don't be nervous about the exam. You've studied really hard.

   B: But I'm afraid I'm going to forget everything.

   A: Relax. _If you've really learned it_ _____, you won't forget it.

2. A: Where were you?

   B: Nowhere special.

   A: Come on. _____, I won't get mad. I promise.

[13] **bug:** to bother or worry someone

3. A: Are you really going to drive there alone?

   B: Sure. Why not?

   A: Well, what will you do _____?

   B: But I won't get lost.

4. A: Nice meeting you, Jean.

   B: Nice meeting you, too. _____, call me.

   A: Thanks. I will.

5. A: I'm leaving now. _____, just call me at home.

   B: OK. Get some rest.

6. A: Sorry to bother you again.

   B: Look, I'm not going to get any work done _____.

7. A: Where are you?

   B: I'm still at school.

   A: Well, you'd better hurry home. Your father will be mad _____.

8. A: It's still raining and I'm bored.

   B: Well, _____, here's a good book.

9. A: Have I told you about the time I lost my phone at the beach?

   B: I don't think so.

   A: Well, stop me _____.

10. A: How much money do we have?

    B: Zero. None.

    A: But _____, we won't be able to go anywhere next week.

    B: That's true.

Think about It Look again at the sentences in Activity 24 with future real conditionals. How is the sentence used? Write a use from this box next to each sentence. (More than one answer may be possible.)

a plan	a prediction	a promise	a request	a suggestion

25 | Identifying Verb Forms Look again at the future real conditionals in Activity 24. What verb form does the speaker use in the main clause and the conditional clause? Complete this chart. `12.5 B`

Verb in main clause	Verb in conditional clause	Verb in main clause	Verb in conditional clause
1. *won't forget*	*'ve learned*	6.	
2.		7.	
3.		8.	
4.		9.	
5.		10.	

Think about It For each sentence, how are the verb forms similar or different in the two clauses? In which sentences do both clauses refer to the same time frame? Discuss ideas with your classmates.

26 | Matching Conditions and Results Use the information in this chart to match each condition below with a possible result. `12.5 B`

How the Vitamins in Food Can Help You

Vitamin	Food sources	What it does
Vitamin A	Liver[14], eggs, milk, carrots, tomatoes, apricots, cantaloupe, fish	Promotes[15] good eyesight; helps form and maintain healthy skin; may reduce the risk of some cancers
Vitamin C	Citrus fruits, strawberries, tomatoes	Promotes healthy teeth; helps heal[16] cuts more quickly
Vitamin D	Milk, fish; also produced by the body in response to sunlight	Builds strong bones and teeth
Vitamin E	Nuts, vegetable oils, whole grains, olives, asparagus, spinach	Helps in the formation of red blood cells[17]
Vitamin B2	Nuts, dairy products, liver	Helps change food into energy

CONDITIONS

1. If you eat a lot of fruit, ____
2. If you want to have healthy skin, ____
3. If you eat a lot of nuts, ____
4. If you want to have good teeth, ____
5. If you work outdoors in the sun, ____
6. If you don't eat fruit, ____
7. If you eat liver once a week, ____
8. If you don't have a lot of energy, ____
9. If you want your cuts to heal faster, ____
10. If you eat a lot of whole grains, ____

POSSIBLE RESULTS

a. you'll get a lot of vitamins E and B2.
b. drink plenty of milk and eat lots of fish.
c. you'll get plenty of vitamin D.
d. you'll get a lot of vitamins C and A.
e. you won't get a lot of vitamin C.
f. you'll get vitamins A and B2.
g. your body can form red blood cells more easily.
h. eat more citrus fruits and strawberries.
i. eat plenty of fish, carrots, and tomatoes.
j. you should eat more nuts, dairy products, and liver.

27 | Using Conditional Clauses Complete these sentences with your own ideas. Use a modal (*should, will,* etc.) or an imperative in the result clause. `12.5 B`

THINGS PARENTS SAY TO THEIR CHILDREN

1. If you want to go out, _put on your shoes_____.
2. If you want to earn some money, _____.
3. If your grades don't improve, _____.
4. If you don't clean your room, _____.
5. If you say that word again, _____.

---

[14]**liver:** the part of the body that cleans the blood
[15]**promote:** to help be better

[16]**heal:** to make well again
[17]**cells:** the smallest parts of any living thing

6. If you are late to class one more time, _____.

7. If you don't work harder, _____.

8. If you need some extra help, _____.

9. If you have any questions, _____.

10. If you have finished the test, _____.

Think about It Read one of the sentences you wrote in Activity 27 to the class. Ask your classmates if your sentence identifies a plan, prediction, promise, request, or suggestion.

A: If you want to go out, please be back by dinnertime.
B: I think that's a request.

28 | Noticing Conditional Clauses in a Text Read this student essay and underline all the conditional clauses. Then answer the questions below.

Three Good Reasons Not to Be a Workaholic

A workaholic is a person who works all the time. My uncle Mario is an example of a workaholic. He starts working early in the morning, and he doesn't stop until late at night. He almost never takes a day off from work, and in 20 years, he has taken only a few weeks of vacation. Most workaholics say they like to work, but I don't think it's good to be a workaholic.

What is bad about being a workaholic? If you are a married workaholic, you probably aren't going to have a very good relationship with your spouse[18]. How could you? You are never around to do things together or to help out at home.

If you are a workaholic with children, the consequences are even worse. If you don't spend time with your children, they might do poorly in school or have emotional problems.

Being a workaholic isn't good for your health either. Most workaholics don't have time to eat properly, exercise regularly, or relax and have fun. And if you don't do these things, you probably won't live a very long life.

QUESTIONS

1. How many present real conditionals did you find? How many future real conditionals?
2. If you take out the conditional clauses, what happens to the piece of writing? How is it different?

[18] **spouse:** husband or wife

12.6 Using Adverb Clauses in Speaking

A	**1** A: How long have you known each other? B: **Since we were 12.** **2** A: Are you going to leave soon? B: **If I can.** **3** A: Why are you leaving? B: **Because I'm tired.**	In conversation, we sometimes answer a question with an **adverb clause alone**, as in **1 – 3**.
B	**4** Tell me the truth **if you can.** **5** Watch it again **if you want.** **6** I need some help **if you don't mind.**	We sometimes use a **conditional clause** to soften a suggestion, request, or command, as in **4 – 6**.
C	**7** A: How are you going to fix your computer? B: I'm just going to reinstall the software. A: **What if** it doesn't work? (= What are you going to do if it doesn't work?) B: Then I'll think of something else. **8** A: Where's my laptop? B: Bill has it. A: **What if** he forgets to bring it? (= What are we going to do if he forgets to bring it?) **9** A: When do you want to go? B: **What if** we leave in an hour? (= Is it OK if we leave in an hour?) A: That's fine with me.	In conversation, speakers sometimes ask a question with **what if**, as in **7 – 9**. *What if* can mean a number of different things. For example: What if = | What are you going to do if . . . ? Is it OK if . . . ? Do you mind if . . . ? What will happen if . . . ? How would it be if . . . ?

GO ONLINE

29 | Using Adverb Clauses in Conversation Complete these conversations with the correct form of the verb in parentheses. Use contractions where possible. Then listen and check your answers. `12.6 A`

1. A: Why didn't you follow my instructions?

   B: Because they _____*weren't*_____ clear to me. (not be)

2. A: When do you want to go?

   B: Whenever you _____ ready. (be)

3. A: Do you want to go out tonight?

   B: Sure, if it _____ you happy. (make)

4. A: Why are you being so quiet?

   B: Because I _____ tired. (be)

5. A: Can I speak to Bob?

   B: If he _____ still here. (be)

6. A: If Bill calls, tell him I'll be late.

   B: Sure, if he _____. (call)

7. A: How long will you be there?

   B: Until I _____ everything. (finish)

8. A: Are you coming with us?

   B: If you _____. (not mind)

9. A: When are we going to have dinner?

   B: As soon as your father _____ home. (get)

10. A: When do you want to look at my homework?

    B: After we _____ dinner. (eat)

11. A: Hurry up. You're going to be late.

    B: Not if I _____ right now. (leave)

12. A: Why didn't you stop at the store?

    B: Because I _____ time. (not have)

13. A: How long has your sister played soccer?

    B: Since she _____ in high school. (be)

14. A: When did Sarah clean up the kitchen?

    B: Before she _____ to work. (go)

Talk about It Practice the conversations in Activity 29 with a partner.

Write about It What is Speaker B really saying in each conversation in Activity 29? Write the complete sentence.

I didn't follow your instructions because they weren't clear to me.

30 | Softening a Suggestion, Request, or Command Add a conditional clause from the box to soften each statement below. (You will use some conditional clauses more than once. More than one answer is possible.) `12.6 B`

if you want to	if you can	if that makes sense to you
if you don't want to	if you don't mind	if you want my advice
if it's OK with you	if you have time	

1. You don't have to go _if you don't want to_____.

2. I think we should leave early tomorrow _____.

3. Could you help me with my homework tonight _____?

4. Please try to come home early _____.

5. _____, I'd like to eat out tonight.

6. Call me later _____.

7. _____, I think you should put the money in the bank.

8. I'd like to talk to you for a few minutes _____.

9. I'd like to stay home tonight _____.

10. I don't want to go away for the weekend _____.

Talk about It Work with a partner. Choose one of the sentences you wrote above, and use it to write a conversation. Present your conversation to the class.

A: Are you going out this evening?
B: Yeah, I have a meeting but I really don't want to go.
A: You don't have to go if you don't want to.
B: But it's important and I really should go.

◀))) 31 | Listening for Questions with *What If* Listen to these conversations and write the questions. Then practice with a partner. ▮12.6 C▮

1. A: Let's eat out tonight.

   B: With the baby? *What if she starts crying?* _____

   A: Then we'll leave.

2. A: I really don't want to go skiing.

   B: Oh, come on. You'll have fun.

   A: But _____

   B: Why do you worry about everything?

3. A: I've been thinking about our trip to L.A.

   B: And?

   A: Well, _____? We'll save a lot of time.

   B: That's fine with me.

4. A: Did you call the store?

   B: Yeah, but no one answered.

   A: Well, _____

   B: Then we'll go somewhere else.

5. A: What do you want to do tonight?

   B: I don't know. _____

   A: Fine with me.

6. A: Are you really going to invite Bill for dinner?

   B: Sure. Why not?

   A: Well, _____

   B: Well, so what?

7. A: What time do you want to get together?

   B: _____

   A: That works for me.

8. A: Where's Jim? He's awfully late.

   B: I know. _____

   A: Then you'll have to run the meeting.

9. A: Are you going to answer the phone?

   B: Do I have to?

   A: _____

   B: OK, OK.

10. A: What did you get Ann for her birthday?

    B: A pair of shoes.

    A: Shoes? Really? _____

    B: Well, she can exchange them.

Write about It What does each *what if* question in Activity 31 mean? Write your ideas.

What are we going to do if she starts crying?

12.7 Using Adverb Clauses in Writing

A	**GIVING BACKGROUND INFORMATION** **1** **When I was eight years old,** my father took a new job in Canada. My whole family . . . **2** **Before I learned to drive,** I went everywhere on my bicycle. Some days I rode for hours. . . . **3** **Because I love to travel,** I'm always packing my bags to go somewhere. Last year, . . .	We sometimes use an **adverb clause** at the beginning of a sentence or paragraph to set the scene or give background information, as in **1 – 3**.
B	**VARYING SENTENCES WITH ADVERB CLAUSES** **4a** In 2002, I was an architecture student. I had to present my final project to a committee. I prepared my presentation carefully. I practiced it many times. I was very nervous. I couldn't sleep the night before the presentation. . . . (no adverb clauses) **4b** **When I was an architecture student in 2002,** I had to present my final project to a committee. I prepared my presentation carefully, and I practiced it many times. **Because I was very nervous,** I couldn't sleep the night before the presentation. . . .	Writers sometimes use adverb clauses to vary the length and structure of the sentences in a paragraph, as in **4b**. This helps to make a piece of writing more interesting.
C	**SUPPORTING OPINIONS** **5** Stress can be a good thing. For example, **if students are feeling stressed,** they may study more. **6** It's not good to be a workaholic. **If you work long days,** you don't have time to do things with your friends and family. **7** Good bosses need to be good at their job. **If they aren't,** their employees won't respect them.	Writers often give their opinion in a piece of writing. They might then use a sentence with a **conditional clause** to give an example to support their opinion, as in **5 – 7**.

GO ONLINE

32 | Giving Background Information Complete these sentences with information about yourself. Then add a second sentence with more information. **12.7 A**

1. When I was a child, _____.
   _____

2. Before I started school, _____.
   _____

3. Because I like _____, I _____.
   _____

4. When I started studying English, _____.
   _____

5. I _____ because I enjoy _____.
   _____

6. When I was 16, _____.
   _____

7. Ten years ago, while I was living in _____, I _____.
   _____

8. Because I've studied _____, I _____.
   _____

Write about It Choose one of the sentences you wrote in Activity 32 as a topic sentence, and develop it into a paragraph.

33 | Adding Sentence Variety Rewrite these paragraphs. Make them more interesting by adding several adverb clauses. You can also make other changes. (Many different answers are possible.) `12.7 B`

A	**B**
The most important qualities of a good parent are patience, creativity, and a sense of humor. Having children can be very stressful. There are things that a good parent can do to make life less stressful. Children ask a lot of questions. Parents have to answer those questions. Children also need entertainment. Young children can get bored easily and have a shorter attention span[19] than adults.	There are two important skills you need to run your own business: organization and the ability to make decisions. You must be very organized. You need to keep track of many things. For people who work from home, it's especially important to be well organized. It's easy to mix up your personal papers and your business papers. Business owners must be intelligent, too. You have to make many decisions, often very quickly. You need to make those decisions intelligently.

Think about It Compare the paragraphs you wrote above with a partner. How did you rewrite them differently?

34 | Analyzing Conditional Clauses in Writing Read this text and underline the conditional clauses. Then answer the questions on page 399. `12.7 C`

What Is the Most Useful Invention of the Past 50 Years?

The most useful invention of the past 50 years is the cell phone because it has made long-distance communication much easier. The cell phone is an especially convenient tool at work. If you go out for a business appointment, your clients and co-workers can easily contact you by phone. And if you need to travel out of town, the cell phone makes it easy to stay in touch with the office.

The cell phone has also made it easier to stay in touch with friends and family. If you are out shopping, you can call someone and ask for advice. Or if you are just waiting somewhere, you can call a friend for a chat. It's also easier to make last-minute plans when you have a cell phone. In general, cell phones have made our daily lives much easier.

[19] **attention span:** the amount of time someone can look or listen carefully

1. Why do you think the writer uses the conditional clauses? What purpose do they serve?

2. What other adverb clauses does the writer use? Circle them.

Write about It Rewrite the text in Activity 34. For example, you might want to combine the information in different ways or use different examples with conditional clauses.

The most useful invention of the past 50 years is the cell phone. It is an especially convenient tool if you need to communicate over long distances quickly....

35 | Using Conditional Clauses to Support an Opinion Write a sentence with a conditional clause to support each opinion. 12.7 C

1. The most useful invention of the past 50 years is the cell phone. _____
_____

2. Computers have completely changed the way people work. _____
_____

3. Electric cars are a great idea. _____
_____

4. People should recycle. _____
_____

5. Quitting smoking is very important. _____
_____

6. Learning a new language is useful. _____
_____

7. Everyone should exercise every day. _____
_____

8. Eating vegetables is good for your health. _____
_____

Think about It Compare your answers above with your classmates. How many different ways did you find to support each opinion?

Write about It Choose one of the statements above, and develop your ideas into a cohesive paragraph.

The most useful invention of the past 50 years is the cell phone. If you have a cell phone, you can communicate with someone immediately. You can also get information online, send emails, or take pictures....

WRAP-UP Demonstrate Your Knowledge

A | WRITING Study this picture. Work with a partner and identify the parts of the machine using the words in the box. Then write sentences to explain how the machine works. Use time, reason, and conditional clauses. (Many different answers are possible.)

THE TURN ON A LIGHT BULB MACHINE

PARTS OF THE MACHINE
ax
birdcage
bowling ball
bowling pin
boxing glove
hammer
iron
jug
light bulb
pool ball
pulley
rope
scale
track

When the glove hits the bowling ball, the ball rolls down and hits the bowling pin. When the bowling pin falls, it pulls on the rope.

B | PERSONAL REFLECTION Choose one of these statements to agree or disagree with. Make some notes to support your opinion, and give examples from your experience. Then explain to your classmates why you agree or disagree with the statement.

STATEMENTS

1. Everyone should do some charity work.
2. Studying a language is essential.
3. Nothing is impossible.
4. Actions are better than words.
5. Confidence is all you need to be successful.
6. Traveling is the best kind of education.

"I agree with the second statement. If you don't learn English, you can't get a job so easily. When I was 12, I decided to learn both English and Spanish. I chose those languages because so many people speak them. Before you choose a language, you should think about the kind of life you want. For example, if you want to travel a lot, English is very useful. If you want to earn a lot of money, maybe it's better to choose a different language, like Chinese. One day, I want to learn Chinese because I want to be a translator."

C | MAKING SUGGESTIONS Choose a city you know well. What should someone do there? Think about the topics in the box, and write as many suggestions as possible. Use conditional clauses in your suggestions.

art	great view	music	shopping
famous sites	interesting buildings	parks	sports
food	museums	places to walk	

If you are interested in art, go to the Museum of Modern Art.
If you like good music, try the Poisson Rouge.
If you like good food, you'll probably enjoy my favorite restaurant. It's called . . .

12.8 Summary of Adverb Clauses

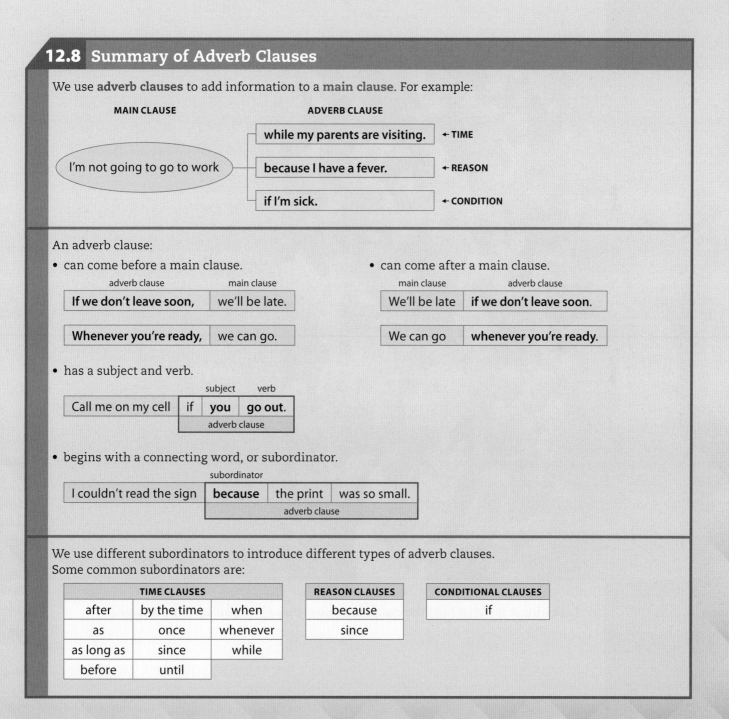

We use **adverb clauses** to add information to a **main clause**. For example:

MAIN CLAUSE — I'm not going to go to work

ADVERB CLAUSE:
- while my parents are visiting. ← TIME
- because I have a fever. ← REASON
- if I'm sick. ← CONDITION

An adverb clause:
- can come before a main clause.

adverb clause	main clause
If we don't leave soon,	we'll be late.

  | **Whenever you're ready,** | we can go. |

- can come after a main clause.

main clause	adverb clause
We'll be late	**if we don't leave soon.**

  | We can go | **whenever you're ready.** |

- has a subject and verb.

Call me on my cell	if	**you**	**go out.**
		subject	verb

  adverb clause

- begins with a connecting word, or subordinator.

I couldn't read the sign	**because**	the print	was so small.
	subordinator		

  adverb clause

We use different subordinators to introduce different types of adverb clauses.
Some common subordinators are:

TIME CLAUSES		
after	by the time	when
as	once	whenever
as long as	since	while
before	until	

REASON CLAUSES
because
since

CONDITIONAL CLAUSES
if

13 Comparisons

It's better to know some of the questions than all of the answers.

—JAMES THURBER,
CARTOONIST AND AUTHOR
(1894–1961)

Talk about It What does the quotation above mean? Do you agree or disagree?

WARM-UP

A | Read these sentences and check (✓) *True* or *False*. Then compare with your classmates. How many do you agree on?

Geography Trivia

	TRUE	FALSE
1. Africa is **larger than** Asia.	☐	☐
2. The Gobi Desert isn't **as hot as** the Sahara Desert.	☐	☐
3. The Nile is **the longest** river in the world.	☐	☐
4. Russia has **more trees than** Mexico.	☐	☐
5. Texas is almost **as big as** Chile.	☐	☐
6. A sea is **the same as** an ocean.	☐	☐
7. The Arctic has land all around it. Antarctica, **in contrast**, is surrounded by water.	☐	☐
8. The Amazon flows **faster than** most other rivers.	☐	☐

B | The phrases in blue in each sentence above are different ways we compare and contrast things. Based on the examples, answer these questions.

1. Which sentences describe things that are the same or similar?

2. Which sentences describe things that are different?

3. Which blue phrases include an adjective? Which ones include a noun? Which one includes an adverb?

4. Which sentence compares information with the sentence before it?

C | Look back at the quotation on page 402. Identify any comparisons.

13.1 Showing Similarities and Differences

We use many different forms and expressions to compare things. For example, comparisons can describe **similarities**, as in **1 – 9**, and **differences**, as in **10 – 18**.

A

SIMILARITIES	DIFFERENCES
DESCRIBING HOW THINGS ARE THE SAME	**DESCRIBING HOW THINGS ARE DIFFERENT**
1 I can throw **as far as** my coach can.	**10** The problem is **not as simple as** you think it is.
2 He doesn't run any **faster than** his brother.	**11** The streets are **narrower** in the old part of town.
3 My sister looks **like** my aunt.	**12** The knitting class is **less popular than** the cooking class.
4 The new program is very **similar to** the old one—they only changed a few things.	**13** Could you please speak **more slowly**?
5 **Both** children **and** adults will enjoy this story.	**14** My opinion is a bit **different from** yours.
DESCRIBING NO CHANGE OVER TIME	**DESCRIBING A CHANGE OVER TIME**
6 His hair is **as black as** it ever was.	**15** My niece has gotten a lot **taller**.
7 She's wearing **the same clothes** again.	**16** My job seems **more difficult** lately.
8 They **aren't playing** any **better** this year.	**17** He's working **more than** he used to.
9 We **don't** have **homework** this year.	**18** Grandma seems to have **less energy** these days.

1 | Identifying Similarities and Differences Do these sentences describe similarities or differences? Check (✓) your answer. `13.1 A`

COMPARING THINGS ON THE JOB	SIMILARITY	DIFFERENCE
1. I worked just as hard as he did.	☑	☐
2. Her ideas are very similar to mine.	☐	☐
3. This job isn't as difficult as my previous job.	☐	☐
4. I would like a bigger desk.	☐	☐
5. Both the manager and the assistant manager are on vacation today.	☐	☐
6. The two offices are almost the same.	☐	☐
7. Amanda comes to work on time and does everything that is required of her. However, some of her co-workers don't share that work ethic[1].	☐	☐
8. The new computer system is more powerful than the old one.	☐	☐
9. He does his work a little more enthusiastically[2] these days.	☐	☐
10. She sounds just like my old boss.	☐	☐
11. We've been getting a lot more customers lately.	☐	☐
12. That job certainly pays more than it used to.	☐	☐

Think about It Which sentences above compare the qualities of two things? Which sentences describe a change over time? What kinds of words tell us that a change is happening over time?

---

[1] **share that work ethic:** to have the same belief that hard work is important

[2] **enthusiastically:** with excitement and interest in something

A

adjective

1	Your bedroom is	as	**big**	as	my living room.
2	This restaurant isn't	as	**good**	as	it used to be.

adverb

3	She works	as	**hard**	as	the men do.
4	He doesn't play	as	**often**	as	his friend does.

much / many + noun

5	That fruit juice has	as	**much sugar**	as	a candy bar.
6	They don't have	as	**many bills**	as	we do.

We often use (**not**) **as . . . as** to say that things are the same or different. We can use (**not**) **as . . . as** with:

- an **adjective**, as in **1 – 2**

- an **adverb**, as in **3 – 4**

- **much** / **many** + a **noun**, as in **5 – 6**

B

COMPLETING (NOT) AS . . . AS

	first clause with as . . . as	noun phrase
7	I'm as tall as	**my father.**
8	This stove is as old as	**the house.**
9	Anna's hair is as long as	**Sarah's hair.**
10	Your guess is as good as	**mine.**

	first clause with as . . . as	noun phrase	verb
11	He **isn't** as tired as	I	am.
12	I've **been** there as many times as	she	has.
13	I can't **run** as fast as	my brother	can.
14	He **didn't sleep** as long as	the other boys	did.
15	He **visits** as often as	his sister	does.
16	She **talks** just as fast as	her mother	did.

We sometimes complete (**not**) **as . . . as** with a **noun phrase** alone, as in **7 – 10.**

We can also use a **noun phrase** and a **verb** to complete (**not**) **as . . . as**:

- For sentences with a helping verb or the main verb *be*, use a form of the helping verb or *be*, as in **11 – 14.**
- For sentences with no helping verb, use *do*, *does*, or *did*, as in **15 – 16.**

GO ONLINE

2 | Noticing (Not) As . . . As Underline the comparison in each sentence. Is (*not*) *as . . . as* used with an adjective, an adverb, or *much/many* + noun? Check (✓) your answers. **13.2 A**

TWO RESTAURANTS	ADJECTIVE	ADVERB	MUCH/MANY + NOUN
1. The Lunch Place isn't as expensive as Café Bravo.	✓	☐	☐
2. I think the food at The Lunch Place isn't quite as good as at Café Bravo.	☐	☐	☐
3. It seems that Café Bravo isn't as busy as The Lunch Place.	☐	☐	☐
4. Café Bravo has as many customers as The Lunch Place does.	☐	☐	☐
5. I like The Lunch Place, but not as much as I like Café Bravo.	☐	☐	☐
6. Café Bravo isn't as big as The Lunch Place, so it seems crowded.	☐	☐	☐
7. Café Bravo fills up at lunchtime, so get there as early as you can.	☐	☐	☐

	ADJECTIVE	ADVERB	MUCH/MANY + NOUN
8. The servers at Café Bravo aren't as friendly as the ones at The Lunch Place.	☐	☐	☐
9. Café Bravo doesn't have as many items on the menu.	☐	☐	☐
10. I don't go to The Lunch Place nearly as often as I go to Café Bravo.	☐	☐	☐

3 | Using *As* + Adjective + *As* Expressions that compare one thing to a very different thing are called similes. Many similes in English use *as . . . as*. Work with a partner. Match the beginnings of these similes with the endings. `13.2 A`

COMMON SIMILES WITH AS . . . AS

1. The twins are as alike as ___*i*___   a. A, B, C.

2. I've been as busy as ____   b. a bee.

3. The sound was as clear as ____   c. a pancake.

4. This room is as cold as ____   d. a bone.

5. The desert felt as dry as ____   e. the hills.

6. Don't worry—this recipe is as easy as ____   f. two peas in a pod.

7. I took the books out of my bag, and now it's

   as light as ____   g. snow.

                                          h. a bell.

8. That song is as old as ____   i. a tack.

9. Even though my grandmother is 80, she's still

   as sharp as ____   j. a bird.

                                          k. ice.

10. His face turned as white as ____   l. a feather.

11. There are no mountains here. The whole area is

    as flat as ____

12. Classes ended today and I feel as free as ____

peas in a pod

tack

feather

Talk about It What does each simile above mean? Share ideas with your classmates.

Talk about It There are many common expressions with *as . . . as* in English. What similar expressions do you have in your language? Tell them to a partner.

4 | Usage Note: Making (*Not*) *As . . . As* Stronger or Softer Read the note. Then do Activity 5.

We can use the adverbs **almost** and **just** in statements with **as . . . as**. We use *just* to make the statement stronger. We use *almost* to make the statement softer.

   1 Her car was **just as expensive as** mine. (emphasizes that things are the same)

   2 This table is **almost as old as** the house is. (Things are close to the same.)

We can use the adverbs **nearly** and **quite** in statements with **not as . . . as**. We use *nearly* to make the negative statement stronger. We use *quite* to make the statement softer.

   3 This class isn't **nearly as difficult as** the last one.

   4 He doesn't have **quite as much experience as** you do.

5 | Using *As* + Adjective/Adverb/Noun + *As* Complete these sentences using *as . . . as.* Use the words in parentheses and *much* or *many* if necessary. `13.2 A`

MY NEW NEIGHBORHOOD

1. My new neighborhood isn't _____*as expensive as*_____ my old one. (expensive)

2. It's just _____ the old one. (safe)

3. It doesn't have _____ the old one did. (trees)

4. It's almost _____ the old one was. (pretty)

5. I like living here _____ I liked living in my old neighborhood. (much)

6. My old neighbors weren't _____ the ones I have now. (friendly)

7. In the old neighborhood, people didn't spend _____ _____ they do here. (time outside)

8. That neighborhood wasn't nearly _____ this one is. (convenient)

9. I don't drive _____ I used to. (much)

10. This neighborhood isn't quite _____ the old one. (quiet)

my old neighborhood

my new neighborhood

Think about It Circle *almost, just, nearly,* and *quite* in the sentences above. Add one of those words to the sentences that don't include them. How does the meaning of the sentence change?

My new neighborhood isn't quite as expensive as my old one.

Write about It Write three sentences to compare two neighborhoods you know.

6 | Usage Note: *As Possible* and *As . . . Can* Read the note. Then do Activity 7.

> We often complete *as . . . as* with **possible** or a **noun phrase** + *can*.
>
> Please come **as soon as possible.** (= as quickly as you are able to)
> I got here **as early as possible.** (= as early as I was able to)
> I'm running **as fast as I can.** (= as fast as I am able to)
> She needs to earn **as much money as she can** before summer. (= as much money as she is able to)
> We tried to make our guests **as comfortable as possible.** (= as comfortable as we were able to)

🔊 7 | Listening for *As . . . As* Listen and complete these conversations. Then practice with a partner. `13.2 A`

1. A: Hurry up!

   B: I'll be there in a minute. I'm going _____*as fast as*_____ I can.

2. A: What do you think of the new clerk?

   B: He's pretty good. But he doesn't know _____ the last one.

3. A: Can you finish it tomorrow?

   B: I'm not sure. I'll finish it _____ possible.

4. A: What time do you need me here?

   B: _____ possible, please.

5. A: Toshi didn't do very well on the test.

   B: I don't think he studied _____ we did.

6. A: I'm sorry. I'm not quite ready yet.

   B: No worries. Take _____ you need.

7. A: Are you going to the gym again?

   B: Yeah. I go _____ I can.

8. A: Emma has a lot of energy.

   B: That's because she didn't work _____ we did.

9. A: Please fill this out _____ possible.

   B: Of course.

10. A: I'm a little nervous about learning the routine.

    B: Don't worry. We're going to make it _____ possible for you.

11. A: They didn't finish _____ the last group.

    B: They did a good job, though.

12. A: I'm trying _____ I can, but I just don't understand this.

    B: I know what you mean.

FYI
We sometimes abbreviate *as soon as possible* to *ASAP* in informal communication. Sometimes we even say "ASAP" (pronounced [ɛysæp]) rather than pronouncing the individual letters.

Think about It Which conversations in Activity 7 include *as possible* and *as . . . can*? Can you think of a different way to express the same idea?

I'm going as fast as I can. = I'm going as quickly as possible.

8 | Completing (*Not*) As . . . As Complete each sentence with a form of *be* or a helping verb. **13.2 B**

My Best Friend and I

1. My best friend is almost as tall as I _____*am*_____.

2. Her hair is as black as mine _____.

3. She likes to swim and run as much as I _____.

4. I don't have as many books as she _____.

5. I haven't traveled as much as she _____.

6. My house isn't as big as hers _____.

7. I'm almost as tall as she _____.

8. She hasn't lived here as long as I _____.

9. I like music as much as she _____.

10. I'm not quite as friendly as she _____.

FYI
Sometimes we complete (*not*) *as . . . as* with a longer clause.

He likes broccoli **as much as I like ice cream**.

Talk about It Tell a partner some things you have in common or don't have in common with a friend or family member. Use (*not*) *as . . . as.*

Write about It Write three of the facts you told your partner.

9 | Usage Note: (*Not*) *As . . . As* to Compare Times Read the note. Then do Activity 10.

> Sometimes we describe a change over time using (*not*) *as . . . as.* To help complete the comparison, we may use a **clause with *used to***, a **time clause**, or a **time expression**. Notice: We sometimes use a time expression by itself to complete the comparison.
>
> | **AS . . . AS WITH *USED TO*** | **AS . . . AS WITH A TIME CLAUSE OR TIME EXPRESSION** |
> |---|---|
> | I don't work as hard as **I used to.** | I don't work as hard as **I did when I was younger.** |
> | I don't have as much time as **I used to.** | I don't have as much free time **lately.** |
> | This place isn't as cheap as **it used to be.** | This place isn't as cheap **anymore.** |
> | I'm just as busy as **I used to be.** | I'm just as busy as **I was last year.** |

10 | Comparing Times with (*Not*) *As . . . As* Complete the descriptions below with the words from the box. (More than one answer is possible.) Then answer the questions that follow. `13.2 A–B`

difficult	fun	homework	shy	video games
friends	good	often	time	worried

THEN AND NOW

1. When I was younger, I didn't like to meet new people. Nowadays, I have just as many _____*friends*_____ as I used to, but I'm a lot more comfortable with strangers. I'm not as _____ anymore.

2. I don't like _____ as much as I did when I was younger. I used to play all day long. I still spend as much _____ on the Internet these days, though.

3. I think this school year is going to be just as _____ as last year. I don't have as much _____ this year, but I'm working more hours at my job.

4. I don't go to the movies as _____ as I used to. Theaters are so expensive, and watching movies at home on my big TV is just as much _____.

5. I used to get so nervous whenever I took a test, but I'm not as _____ anymore. Of course, I still do my work and I study, but now I try to relax and get a good night's sleep before exams. And my grades are just as _____ as they used to be.

QUESTIONS

1. Was each missing word an adjective, adverb, or noun?
2. Which comparisons include *used to*? A time expression? A time clause?
3. Which comparison does not have a second part? Why?

Write about It Write three sentences about ways that you have changed and one about how you have not changed since you were younger. Use (*not*) *as . . . as.* Share your sentences with a partner.

13.3 Using -er / More / Less with Adjectives and Adverbs

A

DESCRIBING DIFFERENCES WITH ADJECTIVES

1 The train is **faster** than the bus is.

2 I'm a lot **happier** than I used to be.

3 This new doctor seems a lot **friendlier** than my last one.

4 My life was **simpler** before I got promoted.

5 I decided to drop accounting and take biology. I think biology is **more interesting**.

6 The new rules are **less confusing**.

7 The chocolate ice cream is **better** than the vanilla.

We often use **adjectives** to describe differences. We can do this by adding:

* **-er** to most one-syllable and some two-syllable adjectives, as in **1 – 4**

* **more / less** before other adjectives with two or more syllables, as in **5 – 6** (*Less* is the opposite of *more*.)

Some adjectives have irregular comparative forms, as in **7**. These include:

bad – worse	far – farther / further	good – better

DESCRIBING DIFFERENCES WITH ADVERBS

8 Kate has always worked **harder** than I do.

9 Bob usually eats **more quickly** than his sister.

10 I see David a lot **less often** these days.

11 She sang the song **better** than her teacher did.

12 Thanks to online shopping, we can buy things **more easily** now. (NOT: ~~buy more easily things~~)

We describe differences with **adverbs** in a similar way as adjectives, as in **8 – 12**. Some adverbs have irregular comparative forms, as in **11**. These include:

badly – worse	far – farther / further	well – better

WARNING! We do not usually put an adverb between a verb and its object, as in **12**.

For information on the spelling of *-er* forms, see Activity 12, page 411.

B

COMPLETING -ER, MORE, AND LESS SENTENCES

13 The chocolate ice cream is **better than** the vanilla.

14 Bob usually eats **more quickly than** his sister.

15 Kate has always worked **harder than** I do.

16 The train is **faster than** the bus is.

17 I'm a lot **happier than** I used to be.

18 I see David a lot **less often** these days.

19 My life was **simpler** before I got promoted.

Often, we don't mention the second thing that we are comparing because it's obvious. If we do, we may use **than** with:

* a noun phrase, as in **13 – 14**

* a noun phrase + a main verb or helping verb, as in **15 – 16**

When we describe a change over time, we may use a clause with *used to*, a time expression, or a time clause to help complete the comparison, as in **17 – 19**.

 GO ONLINE

11 | Noticing -er/More/Less Forms Find the comparisons in this text. Circle the adjective forms and underline the adverb forms. Then answer the questions on page 411. **13.3 A**

My Dream Home

There are some major differences between my dream home and my real home. First of all, my

dream home is much (larger). My real home has two bedrooms, so I have to share one with my

brother. In my dream home, we each have our own huge bedroom. Of course, I'm older, so my

room should be a little bigger than his. And size isn't the only difference. My dream home is also newer and more modern than my real one. The air conditioner works better, and it has smarter

temperature controls. Also, my dream home is less noisy at night. Now we live on a big street, so

I can always hear the traffic. My dream home is right next to the beach, and the only thing I hear

at night is the waves.

QUESTIONS

1. How many comparisons use adjective forms? How many comparisons use adverb forms?
2. How many of the comparisons use *than* to say which two things are being compared? Why do you think most of the comparisons do not include *than*?

Talk about It How is your dream home different from your real home? Tell a partner. Use comparative adjectives and adverbs.

12 | Spelling Note: *-er* Adjectives and Adverbs Read the note. Then do Activity 13.

SPELLING RULES FOR ONE- AND TWO-SYLLABLE ADJECTIVES AND ADVERBS	EXAMPLES	
	adjective or adverb	*-er* form
1 For most one-syllable adjectives and adverbs, **add -er.** When a one-syllable adjective or adverb ends in *-e*, **add *-r*.**	fast high wide	**faster** **higher** **wider**
2 When a one-syllable adjective ends in a **c**onsonant + **v**owel + **c**onsonant (CVC), **double the final consonant and add -er.**	**big** **hot**	**bigger** **hotter**
3 When a two-syllable adjective ends in *-ow*, **add *-er*.** When a two-syllable adjective ends in *-le*, **add *-r*.**	nar•**row** sim•**ple**	**narrower** **simpler**
4 When a two-syllable adjective or adverb ends in *-y*, **change the -y to -i and add -er.**	ea•**sy** friend•**ly** an•**gry**	**easier** **friendlier** **angrier**

13 | Using *-er/More/Less* Forms Complete these sentences with the correct form of the adjectives and adverbs in parentheses. 13.3 A

Things Are Improving

1. My life is getting _____*better*_____ than it used to be. (good)
2. My job is a little _____, but it's also

   _____. (difficult/interesting)
3. My new co-workers are _____ than the ones

   I worked with before. (friendly)
4. I get home _____ now, which is really nice. (early)
5. My noisy roommate moved out, so my apartment is

   _____. (quiet)

FYI

We can use some two-syllable adjectives with either *-er* or *more*.

narrow**er**	**more** narrow
ang**rier**	**more** angry
simpl**er**	**more** simple

6. My new roommate works _____ than I do, so I have time alone in the apartment. (late)

7. I've been eating _____ so I'm feeling _____. (good/healthy)

8. I think I'm a little _____, too. (thin)

9. I also started exercising and I'm getting _____. (strong)

10. I'm feeling _____ and I fall asleep _____ at night. (relaxed/fast)

Talk about It Tell a partner about three things that have improved in your life.

14 | Completing Comparisons Match the beginnings of these sentences with the endings. Underline the two different things that are compared. (More than one answer is possible.) `13.3 B`

LIFE STAGES

1. <u>Teenagers</u> are more independent _*a*_   a. than <u>younger children</u>.

2. Parents are sometimes stricter[3] ____   b. than a 1-year-old.

3. A 20-year-old can usually run faster ____   c. than grandparents.

4. A teenager is often more emotional ____   d. than middle-aged people.

5. Small children usually cry louder ____   e. than an adult.

6. A college student often stays up later ____   f. than a 20-year-old.

7. Most elderly people walk more slowly ____   g. than older children.

8. Sometimes an older child will be more helpful ____   h. than a younger child.

9. A 60-year-old has had more experiences ____   i. than a 50-year-old.

10. A 3-year-old can speak more clearly ____   j. than a high school student.

Think about It Look at the second part of each sentence above. Add a verb after the noun phrase that matches the verb in the first part of the sentence.

Teenagers are more independent than younger children are.

Talk about It What are some things we expect of young people? What are some things we expect of older people? Why do we expect these things? Is it different in different cultures? Share ideas with your classmates.

Write about It Write one or two paragraphs about life stages. Try to use comparisons with adjectives and adverbs.

---

[3] **stricter:** more likely not to let people behave badly

15 | Usage Note: Making -er/More/Less Forms Stronger or Softer Read the note. Then do Activity 16.

We can use many expressions to make **-er**, **more**, and **less** forms stronger or weaker. They express "how much." We often use **a lot**, **even**, **much**, and **far** to express a greater difference. We often use **a bit** and **a little** to express a smaller difference.

EXAMPLES WITH ADJECTIVES	EXAMPLES WITH ADVERBS
My new computer is **a lot** faster.	They visit **much** more frequently than they used to.
The strawberries are great, but the raspberries are **even** more delicious.	His co-worker works **far** less often than he does.
The tests were almost the same, but the second one was **a bit** more difficult.	Things are changing **a little** faster than I expected.

WARNING! We do not use *very* to make *-er*, *more*, and *less* forms stronger or weaker.
(NOT: ~~My computer is very faster.~~)

16 | Using -er/More/Less Forms Complete the sentences below. Use the words from the box with -er, more, or less. (More than one answer is possible.) `13.3 A–B`

complicated	dangerous	efficient	often	powerful
convincing	easy	expensive	popular	smart

Technology—Now vs. Ten Years Ago

1. Computers are much ___*more powerful*___ now.

2. Cell phones are a lot _____ now. They used to just make calls and take pictures.

3. TV remotes are much _____ now. They used to just control the TV and the DVD player—now they control everything.

4. Free Wi-Fi is _____ to find now.

5. Ten years ago, cars didn't have as many airbags⁴ and they were _____.

6. There weren't as many hybrids⁵, and cars in general were _____ than they are now.

7. Large headphones are _____ now. It seems as if everyone is using them.

8. People were using the Internet a lot ten years ago, but we use it even _____ nowadays. Many of us use it all day long.

9. Good cameras are a little _____ than they used to be. And even the low-priced cameras take good pictures.

10. Special effects⁶ are far _____ than they used to be. Sometimes it's hard to tell what's real and what's not.

Think about It Circle *a lot*, *a little*, *even*, *much*, and *far* in the sentences above. Would you add any of these words to the sentences that don't have them? Which words would you use?

⁴ **airbags:** bags in the car that fill with air during an accident to protect the people inside
⁵ **hybrids:** cars that run on two sources of power, usually electricity and gasoline
⁶ **special effects:** parts of movies that are made on a computer

Write about It Write four sentences comparing technology today with the same technology ten years ago. Use at least one adverb to compare them. Share sentences with your classmates.

17 | Error Correction Correct any errors in these sentences. (Some sentences may not have any errors.)

1. My new sofa is much more comfortable that the one I used to have.
2. This car isn't as bigger as the other one.
3. I think this class is more hard this semester.
4. Matt isn't as experienced than his co-workers.
5. I'm much more happier now than I was last year.
6. Hassan works longer hours than John is.
7. The oranges are more good today.
8. This show is more bad than the last one we watched.
9. Mika comes here more often than her children does.
10. It seems as if this year's strawberries are more sweeter.

> **FYI**
>
> *Not as . . . as* has a similar meaning as *less* + an adjective/adverb.
>
> The movie is **not as interesting as** the book. (= The movie is **less interesting than** the book.)

13.4 Using *More* / *Less* / *Fewer* with Nouns and Verbs

A

DESCRIBING DIFFERENT AMOUNTS WITH NOUN PHRASES

		more + noun	*than*	
1	Matt takes	**more breaks**	than	I do.
2	The Lees have	**more money**	than	we do.

		less + noncount noun	*than*	
3	Jenni has	**less difficulty**	than	she used to.

		fewer + count noun	*than*	
4	This store has	**fewer workers**	than	the other one does.

5 I should eat **less sugar.**
6 It's nice to spend **more time** with my family.

We can use **more**, **less**, and *fewer* in **noun phrases** to describe different amounts. We can use:

- *more* with plural count nouns and noncount nouns, as in **1 – 2**
- *less* with noncount nouns, as in **3**
- *fewer* with plural count nouns, as in **4**

For more information on *more*, *fewer*, and *less*, see Unit 4, page 150.

When the meaning is clear, we sometimes use the noun phrase without *than* and the second part, as in **5 – 6**.

B

DESCRIBING DIFFERENCES WITH VERBS

	subject + verb (+ object)		*more* / *less*	*than*	
7	He talks		more	than	I do.
8	She weighs ten pounds		less	than	she weighed before.

9 I should really try to **eat less.** (= less than I do now)
10 I hope he **tells** us **more.** (= more than he told us before)

We can also use **more** and **less** by themselves after **verbs** to describe differences, as in **7 – 8**.

When the meaning is clear, we can omit *than* and the second part, as in **9 – 10**.

414

18 | Comparing Amounts Read this nutritional information. Write comparisons with *more/less/fewer* in the noun phrase. Use the words below in the order provided. `13.4 A`

Nutritional Information Per Serving

Small donut		Salmon (3 oz)		Medium fresh peach	
Protein	2.34 g	Protein	16.86 g	Protein	1.36 g
Fat	10.30 g	Fat	5.39 g	Fat	0.38 g
Fiber	0.7 g	Fiber	0	Fiber	2.2 g
Salt	181 mg	Salt	86 mg	Salt	0
Sugar	11 g	Sugar	0	Sugar	12.58 g
Calories	192	Calories	121	Calories	58

Slice of wheat bread		Steak (3 oz)		Canned peach in syrup	
Protein	3.01 g	Protein	16.67 g	Protein	0.76 g
Fat	1 g	Fat	15.44 g	Fat	0.26 g
Fiber	1.2 g	Fiber	0	Fiber	1.8 g
Salt	151 mg	Salt	42 mg	Salt	9 mg
Sugar	1.76 g	Sugar	0	Sugar	21.40 g
Calories	78	Calories	210	Calories	105

1. a donut/calories/a slice of wheat bread   *A donut has more calories than a slice of wheat bread.*
2. a slice of wheat bread/fat/a donut   _____
3. a donut/fiber/a slice of wheat bread   _____
4. salmon/calories/steak   _____
5. salmon/protein/steak   _____
6. a canned peach/salt/a fresh peach   _____
7. a fresh peach/calories/a canned peach   _____
8. a canned peach/sugar/a donut   _____
9. a donut/protein/a fresh peach   _____
10. a slice of wheat bread/fiber/a fresh peach   _____

Talk about It Tell your classmates the foods you should or would like to eat more, less, or fewer of.

"I should eat more fish."   *"I'd like to eat more dessert!"*

19 | *More/Less* with Nouns and Verbs Find the comparisons in these conversations. Circle noun phrases with *more/less/fewer*. Underline *more/less* by itself after a verb. Then practice with a partner. `13.4 A–B`

1. A: Could you get me (more cough syrup)?
   B: Yes, of course. I'll be right back.

2. A: This car has more power than my old one.
   B: It probably uses more gas, too.

3. A: These light bulbs use less energy than those.

B: I know, but they cost a lot more.

4. A: Did you injure your back?

B: Yeah. I'm afraid the exercises did more harm than good[7].

5. A: He got in another car accident?

B: Yep. Fortunately there was less damage[8] this time.

6. A: How's the new job?

B: It's great, but I have a lot less free time than I used to.

7. A: You're giving her more credit than she deserves.

B: I don't think so. She worked hard on this project.

8. A: Do you think Rob will help us?

B: Probably. He has more time than money right now.

9. A: Your piano playing has really improved.

B: Well, I'm practicing more.

10. A: Was the meeting helpful?

B: Not really. I still have more questions than answers.

Think about It Look at each comparison you circled in Activity 19. Is *more/less* used in a noun phrase or by itself after a verb? Write *NP* (noun phrase) or *AV* (after a verb) next to each one.

20 | Using *More/Less/Fewer* with Nouns and Verbs Complete these questions. Use the words in parentheses and *more*, *less*, or *fewer*. (More than one answer is possible.) 13.4 A–B

LIFESTYLE

1. Do you _____*exercise more*_____ than you did last year? (exercise)

2. Do you _____ on Monday than on Friday? (study)

3. Do you _____ than you did when you were younger? (take naps)

4. Do you _____ now than you did last year? (go out to eat often)

5. Do you _____ now than you did two years ago? (do homework)

6. Do you _____ than you used to? (eat healthy food)

7. Do you _____ than you used to? (work hours)

8. Do you _____ than you had three years ago? (have friends)

9. Do you _____ on the weekends than on the weekdays? (sleep)

10. Do you _____ than you used to? (own books)

> **F Y I**
>
> Sometimes you will hear people use *less . . . than* (instead of *fewer . . . than*) with plural count nouns.
>
> There are a lot **less cars** on the road today.

Talk about It Ask and answer the questions you completed above with a partner. Use complete sentences. For negative answers, use *less* or *fewer*.

A: *Do you exercise more than you did last year?*
B: *No. I exercise less.*

Think about It Which of the questions you completed above use *more*, *less*, or *fewer* in a noun phrase? Which use *more*, *less*, or *fewer* after a verb?

---

[7] **do more harm than good:** to have a bad result instead of being helpful

[8] **damage:** physical harm that is done to something

13.5 Repeated Comparisons and Double Comparisons

<table>
<tr><td>A</td><td>

REPEATED COMPARISONS

1 She's getting **thinner and thinner.**

2 The salespeople here are getting **more and more aggressive.**

3 I think these pills are **less and less effective.**

4 These problems are occurring **more and more frequently.**

5 The bus has been coming **less and less often.**

6 More and more applications are coming in every week.

7 I see **fewer and fewer people** smoking.

</td><td>

We sometimes repeat an **-er**, **more**, or **less form** to show that something is continuing to change over time, as in **1 – 5**.

We can repeat comparisons with:

- adjectives, as in **1 – 3**

- adverbs, as in **4 – 5**

- nouns, as in **6 – 7**

</td></tr>
<tr><td>B</td><td>

DOUBLE COMPARISONS

8 The more you practice, **the better** you get.

(If you practice more, you get better than you used to be.)

9 The older I get, **the less** I understand about people.

(As I get older, I understand less about people than I did before.)

</td><td>

We can use **double comparisons** to show that one change causes another change, as in **8 – 9**. To do this, we use *the* + *more*, *less*, or an *-er form* in both clauses.

</td></tr>
</table>

21 | Using Repeated Comparisons Describe each situation with a repeated comparison. (More than one answer may be possible.) Then share your sentences with a partner. `13.5 A`

ONGOING CHANGES

1. There was a tiny crack in the window. A few days ago it was two inches long. Now it's four inches long.

   It's getting longer and longer.

2. The first test in your class was easy. The second was harder. The last one was very difficult.

3. Your uncle used to weigh 170 pounds. Two years ago, he weighed 185. Now he weighs 200 pounds.

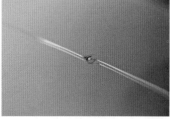

crack

4. First, one new student came to class. Then three more came. Last week, five new students came to class.

5. He traveled abroad twice a couple of years ago. Last year, he traveled abroad four times. This year, he is traveling abroad eight times.

6. The first show was OK. The second show was pretty good. The most recent show was fantastic.

7. Grandfather used to walk at a normal pace. Then he started walking more slowly. Now he walks very slowly.

8. A few people used to eat dinner at that restaurant. Last year, more people started eating there. Now there are a lot of people there every night.

9. In her 20s, she was very interested in politics. In her 30s, she wasn't as interested in politics. Now she's not very interested in politics at all.

10. Two years ago, his aunt and uncle gave him some money. Last year, they gave him more money. This year, they gave him even more money.

Think about It Do the sentences you wrote above use repeated comparisons with adjectives, adverbs, or nouns?

Write about It Write three sentences about continuing changes in your life. Use repeated comparisons.

22 | Using Double Comparisons Complete each double comparison with your own ideas. Then share your sentences with a partner. 13.5 B

LIFE LESSONS

1. The older you get, *the less sleep you need* .

2. The harder you work, _____ .

3. The more you practice your English, _____ .

4. The more money you save now, _____ .

5. The more you exercise, _____ .

6. The later you stay up at night, _____ .

7. The closer you get to graduation, _____ .

8. The more often you go out to eat, _____ .

9. The more new friends you make, _____ .

10. The more time you spend on computer games, _____ .

13.6 Other Ways of Comparing

THE SAME, SIMILAR, AND DIFFERENT

	subject	verb (+ adverb)	noun phrase with *the same / similar / different*
1	My father and my brother	have	the same name.
2	My two co-workers	have	similar ideas.
3	These	are	different problems.
4	My friends and I	like totally	different kinds of music.

We sometimes use *the same*, *similar*, and *different* to compare. We can use them:

• in a noun phrase, as in **1 – 4**

A

	subject	linking verb (+ adverb)	*the same / similar / different*
5	Our names	aren't	the same.
6	Their ideas	are	similar.
7	These problems	seem completely	different.

• after *be* or other linking verbs, as in **5 – 7**

	subject	linking verb (+ adverb)	*the same as / similar to / different from*	noun phrase
8	Your shoes	are	the same as	mine. (my shoes)
9	This laptop	looks	similar to	the one at school.
10	This painting	isn't really	different from	the others.

We also use *the same as*, *similar to*, and *different from* to compare, as in **8 – 10**.

LIKE AND ALIKE

	subject	verb	*like*	noun phrase	
11	She	is		a sister	to me.
12	Your phone	sounds	like	a bird.	
13	That house	looks		a castle.	
14	That boy	speaks		an adult.	

We can use *like* to say that two things are similar (or act in a similar way), as in **11 – 14**. In these sentences, we are comparing qualities of one thing with another.

B

	subject	verb (+ adverb)	*alike*
15	My brother and I	look	
16	We	aren't at all	alike.
17	You and I	think a lot	

We also use *alike* after a verb to compare the qualities of two things, as in **15 – 17**.

23 | Using *The Same/Similar/Different* Look at the picture and complete these sentences. (More than one answer may be possible.) `13.6 A`

SIMILARITIES AND DIFFERENCES

1. Carlos and Toshi are wearing _____*the same*_____ hat.
2. Their shirts are _____.
3. They have _____ watches.
4. Their bags are _____.
5. They are waiting at _____ bus stop.
6. They aren't _____ age.
7. Their pants are _____.
8. Their shoes look _____.
9. They have _____ phones.
10. They are doing _____ thing—using their phones.

Write about It Rewrite five of the sentences above in a different way.

Their hats are the same.

Talk about It Work with a partner. Compare two classmates in the room. Talk about how they are the same, similar, or different.

24 | Usage Note: Making *The Same, Similar,* and *Different* Stronger or Softer Read the note. Then do Activity 25.

We can use many expressions to make *the same* (*as*), *similar* (*to*), and *different* (*from*) stronger or softer.

EXAMPLES WITH *THE SAME* (*AS*)
Sam and I are **about** the same age.
That blouse is **almost** the same color as your eyes.
They walked in at **more or less** the same time.

Venus and Earth are **nearly** the same size.
Those pictures look **exactly** the same.
The chairs look similar, but they aren't **quite** the same.

EXAMPLES WITH *SIMILAR* (*TO*)
A peach and a nectarine are **very** similar.
You don't look **very** similar to your mother.
Those girls aren't related, but they look **quite** similar.

EXAMPLES WITH *DIFFERENT* (*FROM*)
My opinion is **a bit** different from yours.
Something looks **a little** different, but I'm not sure what.
The new model isn't **very** different from last year's.
College is **completely** different from what I expected.

25 | Using *The Same As/Similar To/Different From* Complete these conversations. Choose the correct words and phrases in parentheses. Listen and check your answers. Then practice with a partner. `13.6 A`

SHOPPING

1. A: This shampoo is _____*exactly the same as*_____ that one, but it's much cheaper.

   B: Well, it's not _____*quite the same*_____. It doesn't smell as good.

   (exactly / quite / the same as / the same)

2. A: Do you think these shoes look _____ those?

   B: Not at all! The color is _____, but the style is _____.

   (completely/the same as/similar/different)

3. A: This belt is _____ the one I already have.

   B: How about this one instead? It's _____.

   (totally/almost/the same as/different)

4. A: These sandals are _____ those.

   B: Yeah, they are. But they're _____.

   (very/a bit/similar to/different)

5. A: These jeans are _____ the ones they used to have.

   B: Actually, I'd say they're _____!

   (a little/totally/different/different from)

6. A: Which shirt would look better on me?

   B: I don't know. They're _____.

   A: I know, but they're _____.

   (about/a little/different/the same)

7. A: We came here at _____ time yesterday, and it wasn't this busy!

   B: That's because yesterday was Sunday. It's _____ on the weekends.

   (completely/more or less/the same/different)

8. A: Do these colors match?

   B: I don't think so. They're _____, but they're not _____.

   (exactly/quite/similar/the same)

26 | Using *Like* Expressions that compare one thing to a very different thing are called similes. Many similes in English use *like*. Match the beginnings of these similes with the endings. 13.6 B

COMMON SIMILES USING *LIKE*

1. She swims like *b*   a. a horse.

2. This suit fits like ____   b. a fish.

3. He's sleeping like ____   c. a glove.

4. This school runs like ____   d. the back of my hand.

glove

5. He eats like ____   e. a baby.

6. Your words cut like ____   f. a chicken with its head cut off.

7. I want to fly like ____   g. a well-oiled[9] machine.

8. Please hurry. Run like ____   h. a knife.

9. I know this city like ____   i. an eagle.

10. She's running around like ____   j. the wind.

eagle

Talk about It What does each simile above mean? Share ideas with your classmates.

Talk about It There are many common expressions with *like* in English. What similar expressions do you have in your language? Tell them to a partner.

[9] **a well-oiled machine:** a machine that runs smoothly because its parts have been oiled

27 | Usage Note: Making *Like* and *Alike* Stronger or Softer Read the note. Then do Activity 28.

We can use many expressions to make **like** and **alike** stronger or softer.

EXAMPLES WITH *LIKE*

It smells **a little** like gas in here.

He's not **a bit** like my old boss.

The new store is **somewhat** like the old.

The leaves tasted **a lot** like spinach.

Her voice sounds **exactly** like my mother's.

Your car looks **just** like mine. I can't even tell them apart.

She doesn't look **very much** like her aunt.

EXAMPLES WITH *ALIKE*

I think Mary and her sister look **a bit** alike.

We're **a lot** alike in some ways.

David and James talk **just** alike. It's amazing.

I don't think John and Matt look alike **at all**!

28 | Using *Like* and *Alike* Unscramble the words to make sentences about family similarities. `13.6 B`

FAMILY SIMILARITIES

1. My son and my father are both very athletic and they both love sports.

   They are very much alike. _____ (are/much/they/alike/very)

2. My son and my husband are both tall with curly back hair.

   _____ (like/looks/my son/a lot/my husband)

3. One of my sisters is tall and the other is short.

   _____ (don't/they/alike/at all/look)

4. When he answers the phone, I always think he is his father.

   _____ (sound/they/alike/exactly)

5. My daughter is outgoing and friendly, but my son is shy and quiet.

   _____ (a bit/they/are/not/alike)

6. My uncle likes to sing and tell jokes and so does my father sometimes.

   _____ (like/acts/my uncle/my father)

7. Both my mother and my grandmother like to read, but they are very different otherwise.

   _____ (a little/is/my mother/my grandmother/like)

8. My cousins Rob and Sam are twins.

   _____ (like/looks/Rob/just/Sam)

9. My sister and I like similar things, but our personalities are very different.

   _____ (I/my sister/are/and/alike/somewhat)

10. If you look at her mouth and chin, you can see they are similar to her mother's.

    _____ (her mother/she/a little/looks/like)

Write about It Choose five of the sentences above and write different sentences with a similar meaning.

My son is a lot like my father.

Talk about It Tell a partner about the family resemblances in your family or in another family you know. Use *like* and *alike.*

29 | Error Correction Correct any errors in these sentences. (Some sentences may not have any errors.)

1. My niece looks alike my grandmother.
2. Those two books are exactly like.
3. My uncle and my brother have same name.
4. Your bag is very similar as mine.
5. This class is very different to my old one.
6. My car is the same almost as yours.
7. I think my problem is different a little from yours.
8. Those two movies have very similar story.
9. This room isn't look like the one we had last year.
10. Mittens and gloves are similar to.

13.7 Using *the + -est / Most / Least* Forms of Adjectives and Adverbs

We use *the + -est / most / least* forms of **adjectives** and **adverbs** to compare one thing to **the other members of a group it belongs to**, as in **1 – 3**.

1 I'm **the shortest person in my family.** (group = my family)

2 Hassan always finishes his work **the fastest of everyone in class.** (group = the class)

3 This is **the most interesting trip we've ever taken.** (group = all of the trips we've taken)

GRAMMAR TERM: We call expressions using *-est / most / least* the **superlative forms**.

A

4 I'm not sure which color I want. Just give me **the lightest one.**

5 Everyone did a good job, but Sara worked **the hardest.**

6 **The simplest explanation** is usually right.

7 Matt gets up **the earliest,** so he can make coffee in the morning.

8 What's **the most delicious thing** on the menu?

9 That shipment arrived **the most recently.**

10 I bought the white shirt because it was **the least expensive.**

11 He speaks **the least fluently** of everyone in the class.

12 That place serves **the best breakfast** in town.

13 I sang **the worst** of all.

- With most one-syllable and some two-syllable adjectives and adverbs, we add *-est*, as in **4 – 7**.

- With most other adjectives and adverbs with two or more syllables, we use *most / least*, as in **8 – 11**.

- Some adjectives and short adverbs have irregular *-est* forms, as in **12 – 13**. These include:

bad – worst	far – farthest / furthest	good – best
badly – worst	far – farthest / furthest	well – best

For information on the spelling of *-est* forms, see Activity 31, page 423.

B

COMPLETING *-EST, MOST,* AND *LEAST* SENTENCES

14 Julie is **the most reliable of my employees.**

15 Amanda works **the fastest of all the students.**

16 Mika is **the shortest student in the school.**

17 She works **the hardest in her family.**

18 He is **the nicest person (that) I know.**

19 This is **the best fish (that) I've ever tasted.**

Often, we don't mention the group of people or things that we are comparing because it's obvious. If we do, we often use a **prepositional phrase** with

- *of* to describe a group that something or someone belongs to, as in **14 – 15**

- *in / on / at,* etc., to describe a group or a place, as in **16 – 17**

We also use **adjective clauses** in sentences with *-est / most / least* forms, as in **18**. These adjective clauses often have present perfect verbs, as in **19**.

GO ONLINE

30 | Noticing *the* + *-est/Most/Least* Forms Read these sentences and underline the uses of *-est/most/least* forms. `13.7 A`

Hotel Reviews

RATING	COMMENT
★★★★	1. The room wasn't very big, but it had <u>the most comfortable</u> bed I've ever slept in.
★★★★★	2. They served the tastiest[10] appetizers[11] before dinner, and the dinner was delicious, too.
★	3. I ended up paying a lot less than the lowest online price, but it still wasn't worth it.
★★	4. I heard that the West Tower was the newest, so I booked my room there. But when I got there I discovered that it is also the farthest from the beach.
★★★★★	5. The hotel staff has some of the kindest, most generous people you'll ever meet.
★★★★	6. The hotel is one of the largest in the world, so don't be surprised if you get lost!
★★★	7. Bring your GPS[12]—this is not the easiest place to find.
★★★★★	8. We chose this hotel because it was the least expensive one on the beach, so we were surprised at how nice it was.
★★★	9. My biggest complaint is that the free Wi-Fi was really weak.
★★★★	10. Our group was staying in three different rooms. I liked my room because it had the best view of the ocean.

Think about It Are the forms you underlined above adjectives or adverbs?

Think about It Which *-est/most/least* forms are part of noun phrases? Which come after a form of *be*?

> **F Y I**
>
> Sometimes we use a possessive determiner before an *-est/most/least* form instead of *the*.
>
> She spent **her** happiest years in that house.

31 | Spelling Note: *-est* Adjectives and Adverbs Read the note. Then do Activities 32–33.

SPELLING RULES FOR ONE- AND TWO-SYLLABLE ADJECTIVES AND ADVERBS	EXAMPLES	
	adjective or adverb	*-est* form
1 For most one-syllable adjectives and adverbs, **add -*est*.** When a one-syllable adjective or adverb ends in *-e*, **add -*st*.**	fast high wide	**fastest** **highest** **widest**
2 When a one-syllable adjective ends in a **c**onsonant + **v**owel + **c**onsonant (CVC), **double the final consonant and add -*est*.**	**big** **hot**	**biggest** **hottest**
3 When a two-syllable adjective ends in *-ow*, **add -*est*.** When a two-syllable adjective ends in *-le*, **add -*st*.**	nar•**row** sim•**ple**	**narrowest** **simplest**
4 When a two-syllable adjective or adverb ends in *-y*, **change the -*y* to -*i* and add -*est*.**	ea•**sy** friend•**ly**	**easiest** **friendliest**

[10] **tastiest:** most delicious; best to eat
[11] **appetizers:** small amounts of food that you eat as the first part of a meal

[12] **GPS:** Global Positioning System, a piece of equipment that tells your location and helps you get somewhere

32 | Using *the* + *-est/Most* Forms with Prepositional Phrases Complete the beginning of each sentence with *the* + the *-est/most* form of the adjective in parentheses. Then match it with the correct prepositional phrase. `13.7 A–B`

Geography Facts

1. The Step Pyramid of Djoser is _____ *the oldest* _____ ___j___
   (old)
                                   a. in recorded history.
2. Mount McKinley is _____ mountain ___   b. in the United States.
   (tall)
                                   c. of the world's oceans.
3. São Paulo is _____ city ___   d. in South America.
   (large)
                                   e. on earth.
4. The Great Wall is _____ landmark[13] ___   f. in China.
   (famous)
                                   g. of all the continents.
5. Oymyakon, Siberia is one of _____ ___   h. in Japan.
   (remote)
                                   i. in France.
       places   j. of the pyramids in Egypt.
6. The eruption of Krakatoa was _____ ___
   (big)
       explosion
7. The Eiffel Tower is one of _____ ___
   (popular)
       tourist destinations
8. The Atlantic is _____ ___
   (salty)
9. With an average elevation of 330 meters, Australia is
   _____ ___
   (low)
10. Mount Fuji is one of _____ places ___
    (recognizable)

Step Pyramid of Djoser

Write about It Look online to find more information about the places and things above. Can you write any other sentences using *the* + the *-est/most* forms of adjectives?

> **FYI**
>
> We often use *one of the* before an *-est/most/least* adjective + plural noun.
>
> That is **one of the oldest buildings** in the city.

33 | Using *the* + *-est/Most/Least* Forms of Adverbs Add *the* + the *-est/most/least* form of the adverb in parentheses to these questions. (More than one answer may be possible.) `13.7 A`

IN YOUR CLASS
               the earliest
1. Who usually gets to class? (early)
                   ∧
2. Who travels to get to school? (far)
3. Who is late to class? (frequently)
4. Who do you remember being absent from class? (recently)
5. Who gives the right answer? (often)
6. Who speaks English? (fluently)

---

[13] **landmark:** a big building or another thing that you can see easily from far away

7. Who finishes their homework? (fast)

8. Who does their homework? (carefully)

9. Who do you think works? (hard)

10. Who writes? (neatly)

11. Who can draw? (good)

12. Who talks? (loud)

13. Who talks? (quietly)

14. Who laughs? (easily)

15. Who dresses? (fashionably)

Talk about It Take turns asking and answering the questions in Activity 33 with a partner. Make notes of your answers. Then compare with your classmates. How many answers do you agree on?

A: Who usually gets to class the earliest?
B: Uh . . . probably Sarah.

34 | Using *the* + *-est/Most* Forms with Adjective Clauses Match the first part of each sentence with the correct adjective clause. Then complete each sentence with information about yourself, and share with a partner. 13.7 B

MY EXPERIENCES

1. _____ was the most expensive thing __*b*__   a. I know.
   (thing)
2. _____ is the most delicious thing ____   b. I bought this year.
   (food)
3. _____ miles is the farthest ____   c. I've ever walked.
   (number)
4. _____ is the most generous employer ____   d. I've ever eaten.
   (person or company)
5. _____ hours is about the longest ____   e. I've ever stayed awake.
   (number)
6. _____ is the most beautiful place ____   f. I've ever visited.
   (place)
7. _____ is the funniest person ____   g. I've ever been.
   (person)
8. _____ was the scariest experience ____   h. I've studied.
   (something that happened)
9. _____ is the most difficult subject ____   i. I've ever had.
   (school subject)
10. _____ is the most interesting city ____   j. I've ever worked for.
    (city name)

Think about It Which sentences above can you rewrite using *one of the* + a plural noun? Which ones can you not restate? Why not?

My new computer was one of the most expensive things I bought this year.

Write about It Choose four of the adjective clauses above, and write new sentences with *the* + *-est/most*. Use *one of the* if necessary.

35 | Usage Note: *-est/Most/Least* vs. *-er/More/Less* Read the note. Then do Activity 36.

We use *the + -est / most / least* forms of adjectives and adverbs when we compare something to the rest of a group it belongs to. We usually describe the group with a prepositional phrase or an adjective clause.	We use *-er / more / less* forms of adjectives and adverbs when we compare one thing to another. We often introduce the second thing with *than*.
COMPARE	
1a He's **the tallest** student in the classroom.	**1b** He's **taller** than the other students in the class.
2a He's **the nicest** person that I've ever met.	**2b** He's **nicer** than most other people.
3a She talks **the loudest** of all of us.	**3b** She talks **louder** than the rest of us do.

36 | Using *-est/Most/Least* and *-er/More/Less* Use the correct form to complete each sentence. (More than one answer may be possible.) `13.7 A–B`

Vacations

1. I think the beach is _____*the best*_____ place to take a vacation. (good)

2. Lying on the beach is _____ than sightseeing. (relaxing)

3. _____ vacation that I ever had was a trip with my family. (stressful)

4. Exploring a place on my own is _____ than taking a tour. (exciting)

5. I'd love to visit all _____ places in the world. (beautiful)

6. My parents think going to museums is _____ than lying on the beach. (interesting)

7. For me, visiting museums and looking at buildings is _____ way to spend a vacation. (bad)

8. _____ I've ever traveled is about 2,000 miles. (far)

9. Someday when I have more money, I'll travel _____. (often)

10. Small towns are much _____ than big cities, and they can be very interesting, too. (cheap)

Talk about It Do you agree or disagree with each statement above? Tell a partner.

Think about It How did you know whether to use *-est/most* or *-er/more* in the sentences above?

37 | Error Correction Correct any errors in these sentences. (Some sentences may not have any errors.)

1. His computer is fastest than mine.
2. Old Town is the more interesting part of this city.
3. My mom makes best cookies.
4. Traffic today is the most slowest that it has been in a long time.

5. It was the most large turtle that I had ever seen.

6. All three books are pretty good, but I liked that one the less.

7. For the interview, she wore her nicer dress.

8. City Hall is the tallest building of my city.

9. This is the bigger meal that I've ever eaten.

10. I'm having the most difficulty with this job than the last one.

13.8 Using *the + Most / Least / Fewest* with Nouns and Verbs

<table>
<tr><td rowspan="11">A</td><td colspan="4" align="center">*the most / least / fewest*
with nouns</td><td rowspan="5">We can use *the most*, *the least*, and *the fewest* in **noun phrases**. We can use:
• *the most* with plural count nouns and noncount nouns, as in **1 – 2**
• *the least* with noncount nouns, as in **3**
• *the fewest* with plural count nouns, as in **4**</td></tr>
<tr><td>1</td><td>Matt takes</td><td>the most breaks</td><td>at work.</td></tr>
<tr><td>2</td><td>Whoever has</td><td>the most money</td><td>should pay!</td></tr>
<tr><td>3</td><td>He puts</td><td>the least effort</td><td>into his job.</td></tr>
<tr><td>4</td><td>This group has</td><td>the fewest problems.</td><td></td></tr>
<tr><td colspan="4">subject + verb (+ object) *the most / least*</td></tr>
<tr><td>5</td><td>She talks to me</td><td>the most</td><td>of all.</td><td rowspan="2">We can also use *the most / the least* by themselves after **verbs**, as in **5 – 6**.</td></tr>
<tr><td>6</td><td>I probably work</td><td>the least</td><td>in my family.</td></tr>
</table>

38 | Using *the + Most/Least/Fewest* with Nouns and Verbs Complete these sentences with *the most*, *the least*, or *the fewest*. Compare your answers with a partner. 13.8 A

A RESTAURANT HOST

1. I spend _____ the most _____ time figuring out where to seat people.

2. The part of the job I like _____ is talking to rude customers.

3. We usually get _____ customers on weekday mornings.

4. The servers with _____ experience sometimes get promoted to host.

5. Customers like the window seats _____.

6. They like the seats next to the kitchen _____.

7. It seems as if large parties always come in when we have _____ tables available.

8. Teenagers usually make _____ noise and older people make _____.

9. The servers share their tips with me, so I make _____ money when we're busy.

Think about It In each sentence above, is *the most/the least/the fewest* used in a noun phrase or by itself after a verb? Write *NP* (noun phrase) or *AV* (after a verb) next to each one.

Talk about It Tell a partner four things about your job or about school. Use *the least*, *the most*, and *the fewest* with a noun or verb.

13.9 Using Comparisons in Speaking

A

COMPARE

1a She's as old as **I am.**
1b She's as old as **me.**

2a He has the same job as **I do.**
2b He has the same job as **me.**

3a I'm older than **she is.**
3b I'm older than **her.**

4a I have more experience than **he does.**
4b I have more experience than **him.**

5a He has lived longer than **we have.**
5b He has lived longer than **us.**

When speakers make comparisons in informal conversation, they sometimes use an **object pronoun** instead of a **subject** + **verb**, as in **1 – 5**.

People do this because it is a shorter way to compare two things. Many people consider this incorrect in written English.

B

6 A: I don't like the new model.
   B: Why not? It's just **as good.** (= as good as the old model)

7 A: Do you want to go to the park?
   B: Let's go tomorrow. It's not quite **as crowded** on Mondays. (= not as crowded as it is on other days)

8 A: This looks a lot like the other apartment, doesn't it?
   B: It's **bigger.** (= bigger than the other apartment)

9 A: How are you feeling?
   B: **Better.** (= better than I was feeling before)

When we can understand the context from a conversation, we often use **unfinished comparisons**.

With *as . . . as* comparisons, we may not include the second part of the *as* form, as in **6 – 7**.

With *-er/more/less*, we often omit *than* and the information that follows, as in **8**.

We can even use a single comparative adjective as a response if the context is clear, as in **9**.

ONLINE

39 | Noticing Object Pronouns in Comparisons Listen and complete each conversation with a comparison using an object pronoun. Then practice with a partner. **13.9 A**

1. A: I can't reach the top shelf.
   B: Sure you can. You're just
   _____*as tall as me*_____.

2. A: How can they afford that car?
   B: Well, they have a lot
   _____.

3. A: I heard Kate got a raise.
   B: I don't know why. We work
   _____.

4. A: John's playing is getting a lot better.
   B: I know. I should practice
   _____.

5. A: Why are they leaving already?
   B: They got here _____.

6. A: How long have you worked here?
   B: Two years. Not _____!

7. A: My sister is a lot _____.
   B: Don't be silly. You're just as pretty as she is.

8. A: How many years has she lived here?
   B: Five or so. About _____.

9. A: Are you _____?
   B: No, we're about the same height.

10. A: David can go out, but you need to stay home.
    B: Why? I'm almost _____.

Think about It Rewrite each comparison above using subject + verb. Then practice the conversations again using your new comparisons.

A: I can't reach the top shelf.
B: Sure you can. You're just as tall as I am.

40 | Noticing Unfinished Comparisons Use the comparisons in the box to complete the conversations below. Listen and check your answers. Then practice with a partner. `13.9 B`

as big	better	harder	more interesting	more talented	shorter
as funny	better	more difficult	more often	older	taller
as weak					

1. A: He grew three inches this year.

    B: I thought he looked _____ *taller* _____!

2. A: Remember how you used to stay up all night?

    B: Well, I'm _____ now and I know _____.

3. A: How's the new class?

    B: It's _____, but also _____.

4. A: How's your mom feeling?

    B: A lot _____. Not _____.

5. A: How's the new apartment?

    B: It's not _____, but it's nice.

6. A: What does she look like now?

    B: Pretty much the same. Her hair is _____.

7. A: So, are you still working as hard as you used to?

    B: _____

8. A: Do you think she's as talented as her sister?

    B: Possibly _____.

9. A: How was the new show?

    B: It was OK. It wasn't _____.

10. A: Boy, Anna really knows her way around this place.

    B: Well, she comes here _____.

Think about It How could you complete each comparison above? Why do you think we don't usually use the complete forms in speaking?

41 | Using Unfinished Comparisons Ask and answer these questions with different classmates. Use short, unfinished comparisons with *-er/more* and *not as . . . as*. Try not to use the same adjective twice. `13.9 B`

CHANGES

1. How is this school different from your last school?

    A: How is this school different from your last school?
    B: It's bigger. And there are more students.

2. How is your current home different from a place where you used to live?

3. How is the weather today different from the weather three months ago?

4. How is our teacher different from your last teacher?

5. How is this grammar book different from your last grammar book?

6. How is this classroom different from your living room?

7. How is fast food different from home-cooked food?

8. How is your life different this year compared to last year?

13.10 Using Comparisons in Writing

A

USING LINKING EXPRESSIONS

1 If you go to Mayfield Park in the morning, you'll see lots of moms with babies, small children in the playground, and maybe a few adults jogging or exercising. **On the other hand**, if you visit at night, you'll probably only see teenagers in the park.

2 Many companies charge hundreds of dollars for this service. **In contrast**, our services are far less expensive.

3 The old system caused a lot of problems for our staff. The new system, **however**, has been working well ever since we installed it.

4 The employees complained about the night manager. **Similarly**, they criticized the general manager for not acting sooner.

5 You know that we must invest money in our future. **In the same way**, we must invest our time.

When we compare ideas in a paragraph, we often use linking expressions to show differences and similarities. For example:

- *On the other hand*, *in contrast*, and *however* introduce differences, as in **1 – 3**.
- *Similarly* and *in the same way* express similarities, as in **4 – 5**.

We usually use linking expressions like these at the beginning of a clause or sentence, as in **1 – 2** and **4 – 5**. However, we can also sometimes use them between the subject and the verb, as in **3**.

B

BOTH (OF) AND NEITHER (OF)

My two grandfathers have a lot in common:

6 **Both men** grew up on farms.

7 **Both of them** moved to a big city.

My two grandmothers are very different, but they have a few things in common:

8 **Neither woman** was born in this country.

9 **Neither of them** learned English as a child.

plural noun
10 **Both chairs** are broken.

singular noun
11 **Neither child** is at school today.

	plural noun phrase or plural pronoun	
12 Both of	the chairs/them	are fine.
13 Neither of	the children/us	likes tomatoes.

We often use *both* or *both of* for a positive similarity between two things, as in **6 – 7**, and *neither* or *neither of* for a negative similarity, as in **8 – 9**. Although we can use these words in conversation, they are more common in written English.

We use:

- *both* + a plural noun phrase, as in **10**
- *neither* + a singular noun phrase, as in **11**
- *both of / neither of* + a plural noun phrase or plural pronoun, as in **12 – 13**

We usually use *both* or *both of* + a noun phrase with a **plural verb**, as in **10** and **12**, and *neither* or *neither of* with a **singular verb**, as in **11** and **13**.

C

BOTH . . . AND / NEITHER . . . NOR

14 **Both the government and the corporations** are responsible for the current situation.

15 **Neither the customer inside nor the people** waiting outside were able to hear the announcement.

In more formal writing, we *sometimes* use *both . . . and . . .* and *neither . . . nor . . .* to say that two things are similar or perform (or do not perform) the same action.

- *Both . . . and* uses a plural verb, as in **14**.
- *Neither . . . nor* uses a verb that agrees with the subject closest to it, as in **15**.

430

42 | Noticing Comparisons Circle the words and expressions in this passage that show contrast and similarity. **13.10 A**

The Internet

The Internet has changed the way people communicate. Communication across cities, states, and countries has never been easier, and an average person can now instantly connect with friends, family, and strangers. (On the other hand), people now spend less time on face-to-face communication. So the question is this: does the Internet bring us closer together or push us further apart?

It is unfortunate that we don't communicate in person as much as we used to, but new technology provides many social benefits. First, we can communicate with a far greater number of people because of the Internet. When it was necessary to see people in person, write letters, or talk on the telephone, most of us couldn't communicate with very many people every day. Most people would see or speak to a few friends and family members. Similarly, we saw only a few co-workers and couldn't work with large numbers of people.

Second, the Internet becomes a more powerful social tool every year. Both friends and family can stay in closer contact because of online video telephoning and chatting. In the same way, people who meet each other briefly in person can get to know each other better online. Some people have become more isolated because they interact online instead of going out. However, in general, the Internet has brought us closer together.

F Y I
We don't usually use linking expressions more than once in the same paragraph; we usually use them in longer pieces of writing.

Think about It Underline the other types of comparisons used in the passage above.

43 | Using Linking Expressions for Similarity and Contrast Add the linking expressions in parentheses to these paragraphs. 13.10 A

Student Paragraphs

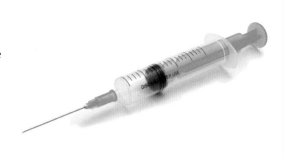

1. (in contrast) Years ago, diseases like measles[14] and polio[15] were common. Children often got them, and if you grew up in that time, you probably knew someone who got one of them. People nowadays are often not even aware of these diseases. They get vaccinated as children, and they may go their whole lives without meeting someone who has had measles or polio.

2. (on the other hand) I like to eat in restaurants. It's nice to sit down while someone serves me a meal. I like eating dishes that I never make at home. I am a pretty good cook. Sometimes I enjoy spending hours in the kitchen preparing a great meal.

3. (similarly) It's easier to eat healthy food if you cook at home. You can choose the ingredients that you want to cook with. You can control how much salt and sugar are added to your food.

4. (in contrast) Bicycles are a safe, fun, and economical form of transportation. When you ride a bicycle, you don't have to spend money on gas. You can also get a good workout from riding a bicycle. Cars use a lot of expensive fuel, and driving everywhere doesn't give you any of the benefits of exercise.

5. (however) Online classes are very convenient. You can study when you want to for as long as you want to. I sometimes prefer a traditional class.

6. (in the same way) Sometimes when I'm doing homework, I get distracted by the Internet. Instead of studying, I go online to see what my friends are doing or to watch a movie. I can get distracted during an online class.

7. (on the other hand) Small schools are nice because you get to know all of the students. When you start a new class, you see a lot of the same people, so you feel comfortable and relaxed. Big schools have more programs and more opportunities for study.

8. (similarly) If you have lived in a small town, you know that it can get boring. Sometimes you want to see new things and meet new people. A small school can seem boring after a while.

Write about It Choose one of the comparisons above. Write your own short paragraph comparing the two things. Use a linking expression to show contrast or similarity.

---

[14] **measles:** an illness that makes small red spots appear on your skin

[15] **polio:** a serious disease that makes a person unable to move certain muscles

44 | Using *Both (of)* and *Neither (of)* Complete these sentences with *both, neither, both of,* or *neither of.*

`13.10 B`

Barcelona and Los Angeles

1. _Both of_ the cities are near the coast.
2. _____ one gets very cold in the winter.
3. _____ them have a lot of traffic.
4. _____ are quite crowded.
5. _____ city is the capital of its country.
6. _____ Barcelona and Los Angeles have large, diverse[16] populations.
7. _____ them have a lot of good restaurants.
8. _____ Barcelona nor Los Angeles has a lot of green space.
9. _____ the cities have hosted the Summer Olympics.
10. _____ the cities has hosted the Winter Olympics.

Barcelona

Los Angeles

Write about It Write four sentences about two places that you know. Use *both, neither, both of,* and *neither of* to describe what they have in common.

45 | Using *Both . . . And* and *Neither . . . Nor* Write a single sentence about each situation. Use *both . . . and . . .* or *neither . . . nor . . . .* Pay careful attention to whether the verb you use is singular or plural. `13.10 C`

Playing Games

1. Chess is difficult to play well.
   Go is difficult to play well.

   Both chess and go are difficult to play well.

2. Board games can be a great way for people to socialize.
   Sports can be a great way for people to socialize.
3. Tennis provides a good workout.
   Swimming provides a good workout.
4. Computer games are not good for physical fitness.
   Board games are not good for physical fitness.
5. Soccer is a fast-moving sport.
   Basketball is a fast-moving sport.
6. Soccer doesn't require a lot of equipment.
   Basketball doesn't require a lot of equipment.
7. Adults like to play games.
   Children like to play games.
8. Card games can be fun for the family.
   Board games can be fun for the family.
9. Chess isn't a game for small children.
   Bridge isn't a game for small children.

chess

go

bridge

[16]**diverse:** very different from each other

46 | Error Correction Correct any errors in these sentences. (Some sentences may not have any errors.)

1. Both my school and my job is on Cuesta Avenue.
2. Neither of brothers is married.
3. Nor my high school teacher nor my college teacher told me about this rule.
4. Both parent told me to study tonight.
5. Neither the movies we saw was very good.
6. Both my sister love that song.
7. Neither the strawberries nor the lemons is ripe yet.
8. Both of computers have been having problems lately.
9. Neither the classes is very difficult.
10. Neither the printer nor the scanner are working.

WRAP-UP Demonstrate Your Knowledge

A | GROUP DISCUSSION Work in a group. Take turns discussing these topics. Talk about each topic one at a time. Use expressions from the box below to make comparisons about the topic. When everyone has spoken about the topic, go on to the next topic.

"An SUV is not as much fun as a sports car."
"A sports car goes faster than an SUV."

TOPICS

1. a sports car vs. an SUV
2. a school cafeteria vs. a restaurant
3. taking a bus vs. driving a car
4. a supermarket vs. a small grocery store
5. running vs. swimming
6. reading a book vs. watching a movie
7. a university vs. a high school
8. one famous person vs. another (your choice)

EXPRESSIONS		
(not) as . . . as	different (from)	neither
-er than	like	neither of
more than	alike	both . . . and . . .
the same (as)	both	neither . . . nor . . .
similar (to)	both of	

B | SURVEY Work with a small group. Follow these instructions to complete a group survey.

1. Work together to complete these survey questions. As a group, write three more questions to add to the survey.

2. Use the survey questions to interview several classmates who are not in your group. Write short answers.

3. Return to your group and report back on your classmates' answers.

"The most interesting place Isabel has ever visited is Malaysia."

Questions	Answers
1. What's the most interesting _____ you have ever _____?	
2. What's the best _____ you have ever _____?	
3. Who is the _____ person you know?	
4. What is the _____ place you have ever _____?	
5. What is the most difficult _____ you have ever _____?	
6. What is the worst _____ you have ever _____?	
7. What is one of your least favorite _____?	
8.	
9.	
10.	

C | WEB SEARCH Look online for descriptions of two similar products or places; for example, two tourist destinations, hotels, restaurants, cars, or phones. Write sentences to compare the two things.

○ ○ ○

Museums of Mexico

MEXICO CITY

MONTERREY

The National Museum of Anthropology was established in 1964. It gets about two million visitors a year. The museum has 23 rooms and many outdoor gardens. The exhibits include thousands of items that show the history of Mexico.

Open Tues.–Sun. from 9 a.m. to 7 p.m.

General admission: $57 MN[17]

The Museum of Contemporary Art was established in 1991. It has 11 rooms and covers 5,000 square meters, with a large central garden. It gets thousands of visitors a year. The exhibits include paintings from contemporary Latin American artists.

Open Tues. and Thurs.–Sun. from 10 a.m. to 6 p.m., Wed. from 10 a.m. to 8 p.m.

General admission: $70 MN

The two museums are not in the same city.
The Museum of Contemporary Art is newer.
The National Museum of Anthropology is bigger and gets more visitors.
The Museum of Contemporary Art isn't open as many hours.

D | WRITING Choose one of the topics from this box or another topic, and write a paragraph about it. Use some of the language for expressing comparisons that you learned in this unit.

> **TOPICS**
> two ways of losing weight
> a good boss and a bad boss
> this decade and another decade
> two famous stories or movies
> driving a car vs. taking public transportation
> a warm-weather vacation vs. a cold-weather vacation
> working as a server in a restaurant vs. working as a flight attendant

Some people try to lose weight by eating <u>fewer</u> calories, and some people try to lose weight by exercising. Exercise is important because it helps you build muscle, and muscles burn calories <u>faster</u> than fat does. Exercise also makes you feel good, so you are <u>less likely</u> to go off your diet. <u>However</u>, most overweight people need to change their diets, too. You don't need to count every calorie. If you choose <u>healthier</u> food and eat <u>smaller</u> servings, you will lose weight. <u>Both</u> exercise <u>and</u> diet are important for losing weight.

[17] **MN:** national money of Mexico

DESCRIBING SIMILARITIES	*as* + adjective / adverb + *as* *as* + *much / many* + noun + *as*	His hair is just **as black as** it used to be. I can run **as fast as** you can. I have **as much time as** you need.
	the same (as)	This picture is **the same as** that one. These pictures are **the same**.
	similar (to)	Your idea is **similar to** mine. Our ideas are **similar**.
	like	The clouds look **like** a herd of white elephants.
	alike	Their stories are very much **alike**.
	similarly	They finished the highway very quickly last year. **Similarly**, the bridge is going to be finished early this year.
	in the same way	Your teachers give you exams to learn your progress. **In the same way**, your employers will do evaluations of your work.
	both / both of	**Both** cars are very old. But **both of them** run quite well.
	neither / neither of	**Neither** book is very interesting. Fortunately, **neither of them** is required for this class.
	both . . . and	**Both** Spain **and** Portugal are located on the Iberian Peninsula.
	neither . . . nor	**Neither** this school **nor** my old one has a cafeteria.
DESCRIBING DIFFERENCES	*not as* + adjective / adverb + *as* *not as much* + noncount noun / *many* + count noun + *as*	I'm **not as energetic as** my sister. I can't run **as fast as** you can. I don't have **as much time as** I used to.
	-er / more / less forms of adjectives and adverbs	This view is even **lovelier than** the last one. She talks **louder than** I do. He's running **less often** these days.
	more / less / fewer + noun	Coffee has **more caffeine than** soda. They're making soy sauce with **less salt** in it now.
	verb + *more / less*	He **calls more** than he should. They **are eating less** than they used to.
	different (from)	Her left shoe is **different from** her right shoe. They like **different** kinds of food.
	in contrast	Our public transportation is fast, efficient, and cheap. **In contrast**, private cars get stuck in traffic and use expensive gasoline.
	on the other hand	He is very smart and does excellent work. **On the other hand**, he doesn't get along with his co-workers very well.
	however	It sounds like a good idea. **However**, I don't know all of the details yet, so I might be wrong.
-EST / MOST / LEAST ADJECTIVES AND ADVERBS	*the* + *-est / most / least* forms of adjectives and adverbs	That's **the yellowest rose** I've ever seen. Khalid runs **the fastest** of all of us. That is **the least attractive** option.
	the most / least / fewest + noun	Could you give me the one with **the least sugar**? John has **the most experience** with these things.

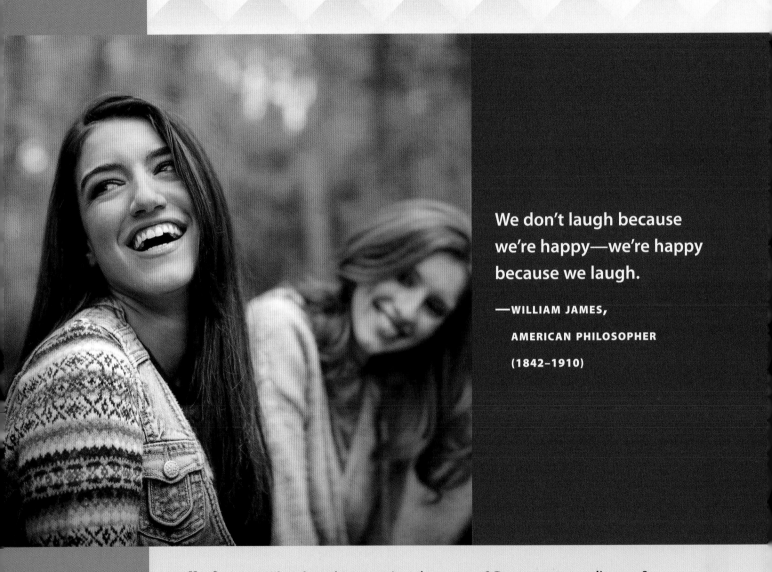

14 Sentence Patterns

We don't laugh because we're happy—we're happy because we laugh.

—WILLIAM JAMES,
AMERICAN PHILOSOPHER
(1842–1910)

Talk about It What does the quotation above mean? Do you agree or disagree?

WARM-UP

A | Match the beginnings of these proverbs with the endings. What does each proverb mean? Is there a similar one from your culture? Share your ideas with the class.

PROVERBS FROM AROUND THE WORLD

1. Make money, ____
2. It is the grass that suffers[1] ____
3. Men learn little from success, ____
4. Hope is a great breakfast, ____
5. Don't count your chickens ____
6. Wait until night ____

a. when elephants fight. (*African*)
b. but it is a poor dinner. (*Czech*)
c. before you say it has been a fine day. (*French*)
d. but they can learn much from failure. (*Arabian*)
e. but don't let money make you. (*Danish*)
f. before they hatch[2]. (*Greek*)

B | Answer these questions about the sentences above.
1. Circle the verbs in each sentence. Do all the sentences have verbs in both halves?
2. Underline the subjects in each sentence. Do all the sentences have subjects in both halves?
3. What words connect the two parts of each sentence?
4. Could the part on the left be a complete sentence? Could the part on the right be a complete sentence? If not, why not?
5. Which verbs (besides *be*) are followed by a noun or noun phrase?

C | Look back at the quotation on page 438. Identify all the verbs and any connecting words.

---

[1] **suffer:** to experience something bad   [2] **hatch:** to come out of an egg

14.1 Sentences, Clauses, and Phrases

A

SIMPLE SENTENCES WITH ONE CLAUSE

subject (noun phrase)	predicate (the verb and everything after it)
1 My uncle	is going to go to the store.
2 My friend	had never ridden a bicycle before today.

SENTENCES WITH TWO CLAUSES

subject	predicate	subject	predicate
3 The flight arrived early		but there wasn't a gate for the plane.	

subject	predicate	subject	predicate
4 He couldn't sleep last night		because the rain was so loud.	

Most sentences contain one or more **clauses**. Every clause has two main parts, as in **1 – 2**:

- a **subject**—a noun phrase near the beginning of the clause
- a **predicate**—one (or more than one) verb and everything that comes after it

Many sentences contain more than one clause, as in **3 – 4**. See Chart 14.8 for more information about these kinds of sentences.

B

PHRASES

noun phrase	verb	noun phrase and other phrase types
5 A child		**a big responsibility.** (noun phrase)
6 She	is	**really happy.** (adjective phrase)
7 Your mother		**on the phone.** (prepositional phrase)
8 My grandmother	walks	**very slowly.** (adverb phrase)

Within clauses, we use words together in natural groups called **phrases**. Examples of some phrase types are shown in **5 – 8**.

WARNING! A phrase is not a complete sentence.

GRAMMAR TERMS: A complete clause is also called a **main** or **independent clause**.

 GO ONLINE

1 | Identifying Subjects and Predicates Underline the subject of each clause. Circle the predicate.

`14.1 A`

HIGHLAND UNIVERSITY

Office of Admissions

Dear Amanda:

Congratulations! You have been accepted to Highland University!

Highland University has a lot to offer you. Our faculty can provide you with an excellent education, and we have many exciting student organizations. We offer small classes, active learning, and many opportunities for international study.

The registration form is enclosed[3]. If you would like a place in our fall class, you must mail this form to us no later than May 1.

Our Spring Orientation programs begin in April. I hope to see you on campus then.

Sincerely,

Michaela Turner

Michaela Turner
Director of Admissions

Think about It Which sentences above have one clause? Which have two clauses?

[3] **enclosed:** in the envelope

2 | Identifying Phrases and Clauses Label the phrases *P* and the clauses *C*. Add a capital letter and final punctuation to each complete sentence. `14.1 A`

SUMMER FUN

_P_ 1. my favorite time of year

____ 2. to the beach for the day

____ 3. I love to swim in the ocean

____ 4. the community swimming pool

____ 5. the water is a nice escape[4] from the heat

____ 6. my family sometimes eats dinner in the backyard

____ 7. on warm July evenings

____ 8. the long days pass quickly

____ 9. delicious summer fruit

____ 10. six weeks of vacation

Write about It Write complete sentences using the phrases above.

1. Summer is my favorite time of year.

Think about It What did you add to each phrase above to make it a complete sentence? Did you add a subject? A predicate? Something else?

3 | Identifying Kinds of Phrases Study the information in the box. Then label the highlighted phrases below as noun phrases (*NP*), prepositional phrases (*PP*), adjective phrases (*AdjP*), and adverb phrases (*AdvP*). `14.1 B`

> **Noun phrase** = (determiner) + (adjective) + noun + (prepositional phrase/adjective clause): *the young men in my class*
> **Prepositional phrase** = preposition + noun phrase: *at the bank*
> **Adjective phrase** = (adverb) + adjective: *extremely difficult*
> **Adverb phrase** = (adverb) + adverb: *very slowly*

Albert Einstein

PP

1. Albert Einstein was born in Germany   in 1879.

2. When he was a child, his head was unusually large.

3. His parents were quite worried about him.

4. In addition, he began speaking fairly late.

5. But his parents didn't worry for very long.

6. When he was a young boy, he was very interested in his father's compass[5].

7. He learned advanced mathematics very quickly.

8. He always got excellent scores on physics and math tests.

9. Before World War II, Einstein moved to the United States.

10. Most people consider him   one of the world's most brilliant scientists.

---

[4] **escape:** a way of getting away from a place or situation

[5] **compass:** a thing for finding directions, with a needle that always points north

A

	subject	verb	direct object
1	Sarah	found	**a key.** (Found what?)
2	He	is holding	**the baby.** (Holding what?)

	subject	verb	indirect object	direct object
3	Tom	got	**his son** (For whom?)	**a computer.**
4	She	is making	**them** (For whom?)	**lunch.**

	subject	verb	direct object	indirect object
5	Ron	brought	**presents**	**for the children.**
6	They	gave	**the check**	**to us.**

To give a complete meaning, some verbs need a **direct object** (usually a kind of noun phrase), as in **1 – 2**. We call these **transitive** verbs.

We can use some transitive verbs with two objects—direct and indirect. An **indirect object** answers the question *to or for whom or what*.

- We usually place indirect objects before direct objects in a sentence, as in **3 – 4**.
- Sometimes we put an indirect object after a direct object using **to** or **for**, as in **5 – 6**.

EXAMPLES OF VERBS THAT ARE USED TRANSITIVELY

VERBS THAT CAN USE A DIRECT OBJECT				
carry	find	know	put	see
catch	forgive	like	raise	take
create	get	lose	receive	use
enjoy	hold	need	remember	want
expect	keep	push	say	watch

VERBS THAT CAN USE BOTH A DIRECT AND AN INDIRECT OBJECT		
buy	give	promise
bring	hand	sell
cook	make	teach
get	offer	throw

4 | Identifying Direct and Indirect Objects Underline the direct objects and circle the indirect objects in this article. `14.2 A`

Salt

Salt has been very important in human history. We need <u>salt</u> to live, and we also preserve[6] food with salt. Long ago, people followed animals to find salt, and when they ate a lot of meat, they got all the salt they needed. However, when people began farming, they needed more salt and it became very valuable.

People traded[7] salt around the world. In some places, traders exchanged gold for an equal amount of salt. Egyptian ships brought salt to the Greeks. In Abyssinia, people used rock salt as money. The Romans gave salt to their soldiers as part of their pay. The English word *salary* comes from this ancient use of salt.

Nowadays, of course, many people eat too much salt. We put it on almost everything we eat.

[6] **preserve:** to keep something in good condition   [7] **trade:** to buy and sell

Think about It What kinds of verbs use indirect objects? Do you notice any similar meaning or pattern among them?

5 | Using Indirect Objects Complete these sentences with direct and indirect objects and your own ideas. `14.2 A`

THINGS I'VE NEVER DONE

1. I've never taught _____my classmates_____ _____a Chinese song_____ .
2. I've never made _____ _____ .
3. I've never cooked _____ for _____ .
4. I've never thrown _____ _____ .
5. I've never brought _____ for _____ .
6. I've never bought _____ for _____ .
7. I've never offered _____ _____ .
8. I've never given _____ to _____ .

Talk about It Share your sentences above with a partner. Tell your partner if you would like to do any of the things you wrote about.

"I'd like to teach my classmates a Chinese song."

Write about It Rewrite each sentence above, changing the order of the direct and indirect object. Add a preposition if necessary.

1. I've never taught a Chinese song to my classmates.

6 | Using Direct and Indirect Objects Complete the chart below. Write sentences about things that have happened recently. Use the verbs in the box. (Some sentences will not have an indirect object.) `14.2 A`

ask	enjoy	give	hand	leave	offer	remember	send	tell

IN THE LAST WEEK				
Subject	**Verb**	**Indirect object**	**Object**	**Rest of sentence**
1. *My teacher*	*handed*	*me*	*my last test*	*yesterday.*
2.				
3.				
4.				
5.				
6.				
7.				
8.				
9.				

7 | Error Correction Correct any errors in these sentences. (Some sentences may not have any errors.)

1. It remembered me my last day of school.
2. My uncle is teaching to me the family business.
3. We bought that software because we really needed.
4. He says me, "Good morning" every day.
5. He brought to her a chocolate cake.
6. No, thanks. I don't want.
7. Thank you so much for giving it us.
8. We enjoyed very much the dinner.

14.3 Intransitive Verbs

A

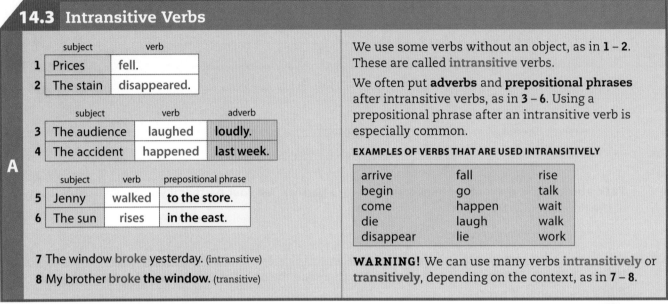

	subject	verb
1	Prices	fell.
2	The stain	disappeared.

	subject	verb	adverb
3	The audience	laughed	**loudly.**
4	The accident	happened	**last week.**

	subject	verb	prepositional phrase
5	Jenny	walked	**to the store.**
6	The sun	rises	**in the east.**

7 The window **broke** yesterday. (intransitive)
8 My brother **broke** the window. (transitive)

We use some verbs without an object, as in **1 – 2**. These are called **intransitive** verbs.

We often put **adverbs** and **prepositional phrases** after intransitive verbs, as in **3 – 6**. Using a prepositional phrase after an intransitive verb is especially common.

EXAMPLES OF VERBS THAT ARE USED INTRANSITIVELY

arrive	fall	rise
begin	go	talk
come	happen	wait
die	laugh	walk
disappear	lie	work

WARNING! We can use many verbs **intransitively** or **transitively**, depending on the context, as in **7 – 8**.

8 | Identifying Transitive and Intransitive Verbs Read this article. Write *I* above the **bold** intransitive verbs and *T* above the **bold** transitive verbs as they are used in the article. `14.3 A`

The Invisible Gorilla

It is a simple test: **watch** a video of people playing basketball.

Some players **are wearing** white shirts and some are wearing black

shirts. **Count** the passes of the players in white shirts.

Christopher Chabris and Daniel Simons first **gave** people this

test in 1999. Participants counted the passes without any problem.

But something unusual **happened** during the game: a man in a gorilla

suit **walked** by. About half of the test participants didn't see him.

Since that time, Chabris and Simons have the given "the invisible

gorilla" test hundreds of times. The same thing always **happens**.

When the gorilla **arrives**, almost half of the people don't **notice** him

because they are concentrating on something else. In one version of

the experiment, participants **talked** on a cell phone while they counted

the passes. About 90 percent of these people **did not see** the gorilla.

Because "the invisible gorilla" became world-famous, Simons decided to try again in 2010 with a different test. This time, people knew about the gorilla test, so they **expected** something unusual to happen. In the new video, a gorilla **appears** in the middle of a basketball game and **stands** in front, so everyone **sees** him. However, two other unexpected things also happen: one of the players **disappears** and the curtain behind them changes color. When Simons gave this test, only 17 percent of the people **noticed** these two things. This shows that even when we are **prepared** for them, we are not good at noticing unusual events.

Think about It Find the intransitive verbs in Activity 8 that are followed by prepositional phrases. Circle the prepositional phrases.

9 | Using Intransitive Verbs Write complete answers to these questions. Then ask and answer the questions with a partner. 14.3 A

GETTING TO KNOW YOU

1. When was the last time you laughed a lot? What were you laughing at?

   I laughed a lot on Saturday night. I was laughing at a TV show.

2. Who was the last person you talked to? What did you talk about?
3. Where would you like to work someday?
4. How often do you cook? Who do you cook for?
5. Besides the people you live with, who do you talk to the most? How do you communicate? (For example, in person, online, or on the phone?)
6. Have you ever fallen and hurt yourself? What happened?
7. Where do you go during your free time?
8. What do you really hate to wait for?
9. How often do you sing? Where do you sing?

> **STUDY STRATEGY**
>
> Most dictionaries label verbs with [I] and/or [T] for *intransitive* and *transitive*. When you learn a new verb, if you write I or T (or I/T) next to it in your notes, that will help you use it correctly.

Think about It Underline the verbs in the answers you wrote above. How many did you follow with a prepositional phrase? What is after the other verbs?

Think about It Which of the verbs above can you use transitively? Write a sentence using the verb transitively if possible.

10 | Error Correction Correct any errors in these sentences. (Some sentences may not have any errors.)

1. The teacher handed my test.
2. The accident happened us yesterday.
3. She was very angry at her parents, but she finally forgave.
4. Someone disappeared the car!
5. He arrived school early this morning.
6. I saw to her in the bus station last night.
7. My boss promised to me a raise.
8. He waited me for a long time yesterday.
9. I used to have a bicycle, but someone stole.
10. The teacher talked us about the schedule.

14.4 Linking Verbs

A

LINKING VERB + ADJECTIVE COMPLEMENT

1 She **seems** **tired**.

2 Your job **sounds** **really exciting**.

3 Marty **looks** **upset**. I wonder what's **wrong**.

4 After two years, he **became** **very ill**.

5 When I told her what happened, she **got** **really mad**.

LINKING VERB + OTHER COMPLEMENTS

6 My sister **became** **a doctor** after many years of study*.

7 He **is** **a very nice man**.

8 The dishes **are** **in the cabinet**.

9 I **am** **certain** about this. (NOT: I am certainly about this.)

Linking verbs are a special type of intransitive verb. However, like transitive verbs, they need something else to make them complete—called a **complement**.

For all linking verbs, we can use an adjective complement, as in **1 – 5**.

EXAMPLES OF COMMON LINKING VERBS

be	feel	look	smell
become	get	seem	sound

We can also use *become* and *be* with other forms:

- *become* + noun phrase*, as in **6**
- *be* + noun phrase*, as in **7**
- *be* + prepositional phrase, as in **8**

*Notice that a noun phrase after *be* or *become* is not a direct object—it tells more about the subject. It does not receive the action of the verb.

WARNING! We do not use an adverb as a complement for a linking verb, as in **9**.

 GO ONLINE

11 | Identifying Linking Verbs Underline the linking verbs in these conversations. Then practice with a partner. `14.4 A`

CONVERSATIONS ON CAMPUS

1. A: Your friend <u>seems</u> really nice.
   B: She is. We should all have lunch sometime.
   A: Sounds good!

2. A: I was looking for you yesterday.
   B: I wasn't on campus. I was at work, actually.
   A: Oh, you got a job? Congratulations!

3. A: Your lunch smells delicious! What is it?
   B: Noodle soup. My mom made it.

4. A: Do you know that guy?
   B: Yeah, I do. He's in my business class.
   A: He looks very excited about something.
   B: He is. He just won the student council[8] election.

5. A: I haven't seen Joseph lately.
   B: I know. He got sick last week and hasn't come back yet.

6. A: I can't find my phone. I've looked everywhere!
   B: Did you try Lost and Found? It's in the main office.

7. A: Did you hear they're going to put in a new engineering building?
   B: No, where?
   A: Right behind the old one. It's going to be very nice.
   B: Well, I hope they finish it before I graduate!

8. A: Have you heard about the new economics professor?
   B: Yeah. Everyone is talking about him. His classes sound very interesting.

[8] **student council:** student government

> **WARNING!**
>
> We can use some verbs as both **linking** verbs and **transitive** verbs.
>
> That pot roast really **smells delicious**! (linking verb)
>
> I can really **smell the flowers** at this time of year. (transitive verb)

9. A: Marco is in really good shape.

   B: He spends a lot of time at the gym. I think he wants to become a personal trainer.

Think about It Circle the complement of each linking verb in Activity 11. Is it an adjective phrase, a prepositional phrase, or a noun phrase? Which linking verbs do not include the complement? Why?

Talk about It Talk with a partner about your impressions of people and things at school. Use *be, seem, become, feel, look, sound,* and *smell.*

12 | Error Correction Correct any errors in these sentences. Use the same verb. You may need to write a new complement. (Some sentences may not have any errors.)

1. This class seems a lot of difficulty.
2. Your father sounds a nice man.
3. Sora had no one to talk to at the picnic. She felt out of place.
4. That chair looks really comfortably.
5. Did I cook this too long? It smells burning.

6. Why does Matilda look so seriously? Did something happen?
7. Sang isn't here. He got too much anger and walked out.
8. She became very famously, but she was still unhappy.

14.5 Questions

A

YES/NO QUESTIONS

—	first helping verb or *be*	subject	rest of the sentence
1	Are	they	going?
2	Has	he	ever been there?
3	Do	you	have a dollar?

MOST *WH-* QUESTIONS

	wh- word	first helping verb	subject	rest of the sentence
4	What time	does	he	leave tonight?
5	Where	did	you	go on vacation?
6	What	are	they	doing?
7	Why	have	they	left so early?

WH- QUESTIONS ABOUT THE SUBJECT

	wh- word (subject)	helping and main verbs	—	rest of the sentence
8	Who	has been		here before?
9	What	is going on		downtown?
10	What	happened		yesterday?
11	Who	comes		to these meetings?

In *yes/no* questions and most *wh-* questions, the first helping verb (or *be*) comes before the subject, as in **1 – 7**.

In some *wh-* questions, the *wh-* word is the subject. We put the *wh-* question word first, followed by the rest of the sentence, as in **8 – 11**.

WARNING! Simple present and simple past questions about the subject do not need a helping verb, as in **10 – 11**.

B

NEGATIVE *YES/NO* QUESTIONS

12 A: Isn't Anna **coming** home for dinner? I expected her at 5.
B: Yeah, she is. She'll be here in a few minutes.

13 A: Doesn't Alan **like** the food?
B: No, he doesn't.
A: I'm surprised. I thought he loved this dish.

We sometimes use **negative yes/no questions** to confirm an expectation, as in **12 – 13**. We ask the question with a negative because something didn't happen (or isn't happening) in the way we expected.

13 | Forming Questions Write questions about activities. Use your own ideas. Then, for each question, circle the first helping verb (or the main verb *be*), and underline the subject. `14.5 A`

Activity Survey

1. What _____ (are) you doing _____ tomorrow?

2. What _____ yesterday?

3. Have you ever _____ ?

4. Are you going to _____ next week?

5. Did you _____ last week?

6. Where does _____ ?

7. Where is _____ ?

8. How often _____ ?

9. Are you _____ ?

10. Where do you _____ ?

11. Were you _____ ?

12. Does _____ ?

Talk about It Compare your questions above with a partner. How did you complete them differently? Then ask and answer the questions.

A: *What are you doing tomorrow?*
B: *Well, I have class and then I have to work.*

14 | Identifying *Wh-* Questions about the Subject Circle the *wh-* questions about the subject in this conversation. (Not every numbered item has a *wh-* question about the subject.) `14.5 A`

THE NEXT DAY

1. A: So who came to the dinner?

   B: Carlos, Amy, Kevin, Rita . . . the usual people.

2. A: Did you see Lisa?

   B: Yeah, she was there. She got into an argument with Rita.

   A: Really? What happened?

   B: Someone told Lisa that Rita was talking about her.

3. A: Who told her that?

   B: I have no idea. But Lisa was mad! Rita denied[9] it, though.

4. A: Did Lisa believe her?

   B: I think so. Rita is a nice person. . . . So where did you go last night?

5. A: I went to work. Someone called in sick, so I worked some extra hours.

   B: Who called in sick?

   A: Matt.

   B: Oh, really? That's funny. Matt was at dinner with us!

[9] **deny:** to say something isn't true or didn't happen

15 | Writing *Wh-* Questions Read this article about the explorers. Then complete the questions below about each explorer. 14.5 A

EXPLORERS

1. The Vikings were early explorers from Northern Europe. They built long wooden boats and explored great distances. From the eighth to the twelfth centuries, they explored as far east as Constantinople and as far west as Newfoundland.

2. Later, there was a lot of exploration from Southern Europe. Ferdinand Magellan sailed from the Atlantic to the Pacific Ocean and then across the Pacific. His expedition[10] was the first one to travel around the globe. Magellan didn't make the whole voyage[11], though, because he died in battle in the Philippines.

3. Hernán Cortéz traveled from Spain to the Americas about the same time as Magellan. He led the expedition that caused the Aztec empire to fall.

4. Francisco Pizarro was also from Spain. He was a distant cousin of Hernán Cortéz. He conquered the Inca empire in Peru.

5. Europeans were not the only explorers. Ahmad ibn Fadlan was an Arab explorer in the tenth century who traveled to what is now Central Russia. He described the people he saw there. Today many scholars believe these are the earliest descriptions of the Vikings.

6. Zheng He was a Chinese explorer who led voyages to Southeast Asia, the Middle East, and East Africa. He lived from 1371 to 1433.

QUESTIONS

1. Question: _Who built_____ long wooden boats for exploration?

   Answer: The Vikings.

   Question: Where _____?

   Answer: Northern Europe.

2. Question: _____ an expedition that

   traveled around the globe?

   Answer: Magellan.

   Question: _____ the whole voyage?

   Answer: Because he died in the Philippines.

3. Question: _____ travel?

   Answer: About the same time as Magellan.

   Question: _____ his expedition do?

   Answer: It caused the fall of the Aztec empire.

4. Question: _____ a distant cousin of Cortéz?

   Answer: Pizarro.

   Question: _____ conquer?

   Answer: The Inca empire in Peru.

> **STUDY STRATEGY**
> Writing questions about the material you're studying can help you prepare for tests.

[10] **expedition:** a long trip for a special purpose   [11] **voyage:** a long trip by ship or in space

5. Question: _____ to Central Russia

in the tenth century?

Answer: Ahmad ibn Fadlan.

Question: _____

Answer: The people he saw there. (Possibly the Vikings.)

6. Question: _____ to Southeast Asia,

the Middle East, and East Africa?

Answer: Zheng He.

Question: _____

Answer: From 1371 to 1433.

Talk about It Ask and answer the questions in Activity 15 with a partner. Try to answer from memory.

16 | Usage Note: Answering Negative Questions Read the note. Then do Activity 17.

> Answer **negative questions** the same way you would answer **positive questions**. In other words, answer them according to the truth of the situation.
>
> **TRUTH: MARIA GOT HERE AT 9:00.**
>
> A: **Did** Maria get here at 9?   A: **Didn't** Maria get here at 9?
> B: **Yes, she did.**   ⟶   B: **Yes, she did.**
>
> A: **Did** Maria get here at 8?   A: **Didn't** Maria get here at 8?
> B: **No. She got here at 9.** ⟶ B: **No. She got here at 9.**

17 | Asking Negative Questions Complete these conversations. Write negative questions using the verbs in parentheses. (Many different questions are possible.) Then practice with a partner. `14.5 B`

1. A: All I see are sandals and tennis shoes. *Don't you sell boots?* _____ (sell)

   B: I'm sorry. We only sell boots in the fall and winter.

2. A: Why do we need to have a conference? _____ (be)

   B: Oh, yes. Kate's a wonderful student. I'm making appointments with all of the parents.

3. A: It's so crowded here already! _____ (open)

   B: Yes, we just opened last weekend. Our food has been getting great reviews.

4. A: Those are all so big! _____ (have)

   B: No, I'm sorry. This is the smallest soda we have.

5. A: I can't believe she doesn't want any! _____ (like)

   B: Yeah, she likes ice cream, but she just ate. She's full.

6. A: It's cold out here! _____ (need)

   B: I left my sweatshirt in the car. But I'll be OK once we start running.

7. A: He doesn't seem to understand me. _____ (speak)

   B: Yes, he can speak English. You just talk really fast.

8. A: You're going out tonight. _____ (study)

   B: Yeah, I should. But I don't feel like it.

Talk about It For each conversation in Activity 17, where do you think the people are? Who do you think is speaking?

Talk about It Choose one of the situations in Activity 17 and add three or four more lines. Try to use one more negative question.

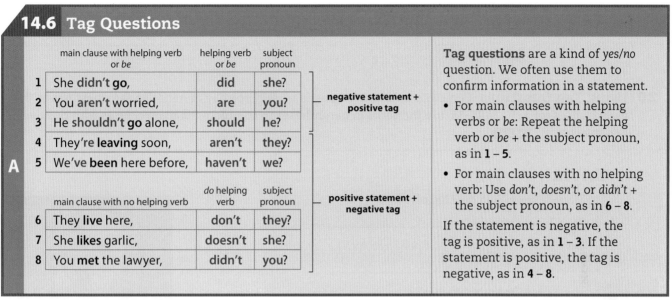

14.6 Tag Questions

A

	main clause with helping verb or *be*	helping verb or *be*	subject pronoun	
1	She **didn't go**,	did	she?	negative statement + positive tag
2	You **aren't** worried,	are	you?	
3	He **shouldn't go** alone,	should	he?	
4	They're **leaving** soon,	aren't	they?	positive statement + negative tag
5	We've **been** here before,	haven't	we?	

	main clause with no helping verb	*do* helping verb	subject pronoun
6	They **live** here,	don't	they?
7	She **likes** garlic,	doesn't	she?
8	You **met** the lawyer,	didn't	you?

Tag questions are a kind of *yes/no* question. We often use them to confirm information in a statement.

- For main clauses with helping verbs or *be*: Repeat the helping verb or *be* + the subject pronoun, as in **1 – 5**.
- For main clauses with no helping verb: Use *don't*, *doesn't*, or *didn't* + the subject pronoun, as in **6 – 8**.

If the statement is negative, the tag is positive, as in **1 – 3**. If the statement is positive, the tag is negative, as in **4 – 8**.

18 | Pronunciation Note: Tag Questions Listen to the note. Then do Activity 19.

When we don't know if a statement we've made is true, we use a tag with rising intonation.

LESS CERTAIN STATEMENTS + TAG WITH RISING INTONATION

1 A: You live near here, **don't you?**
B: Yes. Just a few blocks away.

2 A: He isn't sick, **is he?**
B: No, I don't think so.

When we are fairly sure a statement we've made is true, we use a tag with falling intonation.

MORE CERTAIN STATEMENTS + TAG WITH FALLING INTONATION

3 A: You told her the answer, **didn't you?**
B: Yes, I did. Sorry.

4 A: You've been here before, **haven't you?**
B: Yes. A couple of times.

19 | Identifying Tag Question Intonation Listen to the questions. Draw a rising ↗ or falling ↘ intonation line over each tag. Then practice with a partner. **14.6 A**

1. A: You're staying for dinner, aren't you?
   B: I can't. I've got too much work to do.

2. A: You wanted coffee, didn't you?
   B: That's OK. Tea is fine.

3. A: He's visiting his sister, isn't he?
   B: I think he's on a business trip.

4. A: She isn't sick, is she?
   B: Nope. I just saw her at the mall.

5. A: You don't like cherries, do you?

   B: I like them. I just can't eat them—I'm allergic.

6. A: He's already taken this class, hasn't he?

   B: Yep. He took it last year.

7. A: The neighbors weren't home last night, were they?

   B: I didn't see them.

8. A: You'll call tomorrow, won't you?

   B: I promise.

20 | Using Tag Questions Complete these trivia questions. Add positive or negative tag questions to the main clauses for 1–10. In 11–18, use the verbs in parentheses to complete the main clauses with positive or negative forms. `14.6 A`

Trivia

1. Mount Everest is in the Himalayas, _____*isn't it*_____?

2. The Chinese invented paper, _____?

3. Jonas Salk developed the first polio vaccine[12], _____?

4. India doesn't border Russia, _____?

5. The Nile is the longest river, _____?

6. Humans can't see ultraviolet light, _____?

7. Delhi has a large population, _____?

8. Thomas Edison didn't invent the telephone, _____?

9. Switzerland doesn't have a coastline, _____?

10. Humans have walked on the moon, _____?

11. The Aztecs _____*lived*_____ in Mexico, didn't they? (live)

12. Sweden _____ an Olympics, hasn't it? (hold)

13. Cleopatra _____ Egypt, didn't she? (rule)

14. Shakespeare _____ English novels, did he? (write)

15. Benjamin Franklin never _____ as U.S. president, did he? (serve)

16. The world population _____ a lot, hasn't it? (increase)

17. Nelson Mandela _____ the president of South Africa, wasn't he? (be)

18. In the 1400s, many people _____ from the Black Plague[13], didn't they? (die)

Thomas Edison

Nelson Mandela

Talk about It Ask and answer the questions above with a partner. How many statements are true?

A: Mount Everest is in the Himalayas, isn't it?
B: Yes, it is.

Write about It Work with a partner. Write four trivia tag questions. Write two correct questions and two incorrect questions. Find a new partner and ask each other your questions.

---

[12]**polio vaccine:** a substance that protects against the disease polio

[13]**Black Plague:** a disease that spread quickly and killed many people

21 | Using Questions Complete these conversations. Write positive tag questions, negative questions, or questions about the subject for the responses. (Many different questions are possible.) If necessary, look back at Charts 14.5–14.6 for information on a question form.

1. A: Have you seen Tony today?

   B: _No. Isn't he at work?_

   A: Oh, you're right. I guess I'll see him later.

2. A: Here are the groceries.

   B: _____

   A: Oh, I forgot! I'll have to go back.

3. A: I think we're out of rice.

   B: _____

   A: No, we don't. I used it yesterday.

4. A: I don't think Sarah has finished the project.

   B: _____

   A: I don't know. I'll ask her.

5. A: We can't afford a new car.

   B: _____

   A: Yes, but we need to save that money for tuition.

6. A: It seems as if Ted is not talking to Alan.

   B: _____

   A: I don't know. I didn't hear about that.

7. A: I'm starving[14]!

   B: _____

   A: Maybe. I'll look.

8. A: I didn't get all the reading done.

   B: _____

   A: I don't know. I hope that's true!

9. A: Someone stole my bike last night.

   B: _____

   A: I thought I did. Maybe I forgot.

10. A: Paul still isn't here.

    B: _____

    A: Yes, but he isn't answering his phone.

Talk about It Compare the questions you wrote above with a partner. How did you complete the conversations differently? Then practice with your partner.

Think about It How can you rewrite each of your questions above using a different form? Does the meaning of the question change in any way? How?

1. He's at work, isn't he?   OR   Is he at work?

[14] **starving:** very hungry

14.7 Multi-word Verbs

A

1 Do you want to **try on** this shirt?

2 Did you **fill out** all the forms?

3 You need to **calm down**.

4 **Watch out!** The floor is slippery.
(watch out = be careful)

5 I **came across** an interesting article online.
(came across = found)

6 You really can't **do without** a car here.
(do without = manage not having)

We use some verbs together with a small word like *on*, *out*, *across*, and *down*, as in **1 – 3**. We call these verbs **multi-word verbs**.

Multi-word verbs function as a single word. They often have a meaning that is different from the meanings of the individual words, as in **4 – 6**.

GRAMMAR TERMS: Phrasal verbs and **prepositional verbs** are two kinds of **multi-word verbs**.

B

TRANSITIVE MULTI-WORD VERBS

7 Please **put away** your books.

8 Don't forget to **hand in** your homework.

9a She **turned down** a good job.

9b She **turned** a good job **down**.

9c She **turned down** a really good job at an entertainment company.

9d She **turned** it **down**.

We can use many multi-word verbs transitively (with an **object**), as in **7 – 8**.

One group of multi-word verbs are separable; the object can come in two places:

• directly after the multi-word verb, as in **9a**

• between the verb and the small word, as in **9b**

When the object is a long noun phrase, it usually comes directly after the multi-word verb, as in **9c**.

When the object is a pronoun, it usually comes between the verb and the small word, as in **9d**.

For a list of common transitive multi-word verbs, see the Resources, page R-6.

C

INTRANSITIVE MULTI-WORD VERBS

10 She isn't **coming back**.

11 My parents **dropped by** yesterday.

12 **Wake up!** It's already 10 o'clock.

We can use some multi-word verbs intransitively (without an object), as in **10 – 11**.

Notice that we often use intransitive multi-word verbs as imperatives, as in **12**.

For a list of common intransitive multi-word verbs, see the Resources, page R-7.

GO ONLINE

22 | Understanding Multi-Word Verbs Complete each set of questions with the correct form of a multi-word verb from the box. **14.7 A**

1. How do you feel when you _____*get back*_____ from a long trip?

2. When do you usually _____ on the weekend?

3. Do you and your best friend always _____?

4. What is one good way to _____ in your career?

get ahead = become more successful in something
get along = have a friendly relationship
get back = return
get up = get out of bed

5. Do you _____ your mother or your father?

6. Is there a sport you would like to _____ someday?

7. Why do some people _____ more work than they can possibly do?

8. Do you usually _____ notes during class?

9. How carefully do you _____ your homework before you hand it in?

10. When did you last _____ a word in a dictionary?

11. Why do people _____ holidays?

12. Who _____ you when you were a child?

> **take after** = be or look like an older member of your family
> **take down** = write down something that is said
> **take on** = accept or decide to do something
> **take up** = start doing something regularly (for example, as a hobby)

> **look after** = be responsible for or take care of someone or something
> **look forward to** = wait for something with pleasure (because you expect to enjoy it)
> **look over** = read something to see how good, interesting, etc., it is
> **look up** = search for information—usually in a book

Talk about It Ask and answer the questions in Activity 22 with a partner.

A: *How do you feel when you get back from a long trip?*
B: *I'm usually pretty happy to be home.*

Talk about It Join another pair. Tell them three things you learned about your partner.

23 | Using Transitive Multi-Word Verbs Underline each multi-word verb in these conversations and circle the object. Then match each multi-word verb with a definition on the right. **14.7 B**

1. A: I can't <u>figure out</u> (this remote).
   B: Yeah, it's really confusing. Did you try turning off the TV?
   A: Yes, but it didn't work.
   B: I have the manual if you want to look up the instructions.
   A: OK.

   a. _____ = move the switch on a machine, etc., to stop it from working
   b. _____ = search for information
   c. ___*figure out*___ = understand; find the answer to

2. A: I hear Tomas Garcia is taking over the accounting department.
   B: That's good news. He'll do a good job.

3. A: My brother turned down the job at the movie theater.
   B: How come?
   A: He got a better job at a restaurant.

   d. _____ = cancel
   e. _____ = say no to something
   f. _____ = take control or responsibility for something

4. A: Where is everyone?
   B: Maria called off the meeting. Didn't you hear?
   A: No, no one told me.

5. A: Are you going to try on that shirt?

   B: Nah. I can't afford it anyway.

   A: I can lend you the money if you want.

   B: Really? Thanks. I'll pay back every cent.

6. A: You need to fill out this application today.

   B: Can't I do it tomorrow?

   A: You know, you really shouldn't put off

   something so important.

g. _____ = complete a printed form

h. _____ = delay doing something

i. _____ = give money back to the
   person you borrowed it from

j. _____ = put on clothing to see if it fits
   you and how it looks

Talk about It Practice the conversations in Activity 23 with a partner. Then practice them again and move the object between the verb and the small word.

*A: I can't fig̲u̲r̲e̲ **this remote** o̲u̲t̲.*
*B: Yeah, it's really confusing. Did you try t̲u̲r̲n̲i̲n̲g̲ **the TV** o̲f̲f̲?*

24 | Using Separable Multi-Word Verbs Work with a partner. Take turns reading a sentence aloud. The other person responds with a multi-word verb and *I've already . . . (pronoun) . . .* 14.7 B

1. Don't forget to take out the trash.

   A: Don't forget to take out the trash.
   B: I've already taken it out.
   A: Thanks.

2. Don't forget to check over your homework.
3. Don't forget to fill out the form.
4. Don't forget to clean out the refrigerator.
5. Remember to turn down the heat before you go.

6. Don't turn the job down yet.
7. Remember. You promised to clean off the table.
8. Could you open up the windows for me?
9. Don't forget to put away the dishes.
10. Remember to shut off the lights upstairs.
11. Please don't throw out your drawings.
12. Remember to write down the directions.
13. Don't forget to pay back your sister.

Think about It Why does person B above answer with a pronoun instead of a noun phrase?

> **STUDY STRATEGY**
>
> To learn separable multi-word verbs, practice saying them in three different ways:
>
> **hand in** my paper / **hand** my paper **in** / **hand** it **in**

25 | Transitive or Intransitive? Is the writer using the **bold** multi-word verb transitively or intransitively? Write *T* (transitively) or *INT* (intransitively) above the verb. 14.7 C

                                           T
1. The best way to **work out** your problems is to talk about them.

2. When I spend a lot of time exercising, I sleep better at night.

   Then I feel more energetic when I **wake up** in the morning.

3. In 2011, Reza Pakravan **set out** on a 1,200-mile trip across the

   Sahara desert.

4. When I was ten years old, my parents gave me a special gold ring

   for my birthday. I wore it every day and never **took** it **off**.

> **FYI**
>
> Some multi-word verbs have a transitive meaning in one context and an intransitive meaning in another.
>
> **pay off** (something) = pay all the money that you owe for something
> **pay off** = be successful

5. After I **pay off** my school loans, my credit will get even better.

6. I **grew up** as a middle child. I have an older sister and younger brother.

7. When I feel stressed, I try to **slow down** my breathing, quiet my thoughts, and relax my muscles.

8. With my pale skin, green eyes, and red hair I definitely **stood out**.

9. On my first job I had to **show up** at 7:00 in the morning. The owner needed me to be there at that time and no later.

10. A good businessperson has to be able to make a plan for a successful business and then be able to work hard to **carry out** the plan. If your plan is a good one, then your hard work will **pay off** in the end. If you are not dedicated enough, then you may **give up** before your business has a chance to be successful.

Think about It What do you think each **bold** verb in Activity 25 means? Compare ideas with your classmates. Then check your answers by looking the verbs up in a dictionary.

Write about It Use each of the multi-word verbs in Activity 25 in a sentence of your own.

14.8 Compound and Complex Sentences

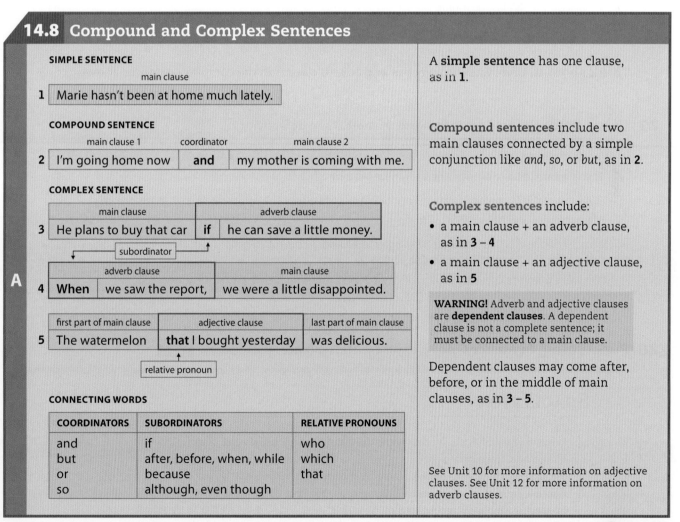

A

SIMPLE SENTENCE

main clause

1 | Marie hasn't been at home much lately. |

A **simple sentence** has one clause, as in **1**.

COMPOUND SENTENCE

main clause 1 | coordinator | main clause 2

2 | I'm going home now | **and** | my mother is coming with me. |

Compound sentences include two main clauses connected by a simple conjunction like *and, so,* or *but,* as in **2**.

COMPLEX SENTENCE

main clause | adverb clause

3 | He plans to buy that car | **if** | he can save a little money. |

subordinator

adverb clause | main clause

4 | **When** | we saw the report, | we were a little disappointed. |

first part of main clause | adjective clause | last part of main clause

5 | The watermelon | **that** I bought yesterday | was delicious. |

relative pronoun

Complex sentences include:
- a main clause + an adverb clause, as in **3 – 4**
- a main clause + an adjective clause, as in **5**

WARNING! Adverb and adjective clauses are **dependent clauses**. A dependent clause is not a complete sentence; it must be connected to a main clause.

Dependent clauses may come after, before, or in the middle of main clauses, as in **3 – 5**.

CONNECTING WORDS

COORDINATORS	SUBORDINATORS	RELATIVE PRONOUNS
and	if	who
but	after, before, when, while	which
or	because	that
so	although, even though	

See Unit 10 for more information on adjective clauses. See Unit 12 for more information on adverb clauses.

26 | Identifying Simple, Compound, and Complex Sentences Label each sentence as simple (*S*), compound (*CD*), or complex (*CX*). `14.8 A`

Travel Advice: Rio de Janeiro

1. We took two tours, and they were both great. _CD_

   The guides[15] who showed us around were very helpful. ____

2. If you haven't been to Sugar Loaf mountain, you really should go. ____

   The views from the top are amazing. ____

3. I recommend the hang-gliding tour. ____

   It's an incredible experience and it's not too expensive. ____

4. You can see some local art in the Centro Cultural Banco do Brasil. ____

   There are also a library and a cinema inside, so it's easy to spend a

   day there. ____

5. At Tijuca National Park, you can explore a tropical[16] forest right in the

   middle of the city. ____

   I recommend taking a tour because you can really see the less-visited

   places. ____ It's just beautiful. ____

Think about It Underline the adjective and adverb clauses in the complex sentences above.

27 | Usage Note: Using Commas Read the note. Then do Activity 28.

> We use a comma after an adverb clause when it comes before the main clause.
> **If she wants to have dinner,** she should be here by 6:00.
>
> We usually do not use a comma before coordinators when they join two short main clauses.
> He lives here **and** he works in Milton.
>
> However, if the clauses are long, we sometimes add a comma. The comma shows where one main clause ends and the next one begins.
> We were going to come by after work, **but John's meeting didn't end until almost 8:00.**

28 | Punctuating Sentences Add a comma to the sentences if necessary. `14.8 A`

SHACKLETON

1. Ernest Henry Shackleton first went to Antarctica in 1901, but he became ill and had to go home.
2. He wanted to explore Antarctica so he returned there in 1907.
3. Because he went farther south than anyone else had the king of England honored him when he returned.

---

[15] **guides:** people who show places to tourists   [16] **tropical:** coming from the hottest, wettest parts of the world

4. Although he got close Shackleton was not the first person to reach the South Pole.
5. Roald Amundsen got to the South Pole first but Shackleton went back to Antarctica later for more exploration.
6. While his ship was approaching Antarctica it became trapped in the ice.
7. Shackleton hoped the ship would be able to escape when the warmer weather came in the spring.
8. The ship was destroyed and Shackleton and his men had to stay on the ice for almost 500 days. They all survived.

Think about It Look at the sentences above where you added a comma. How does having a comma help you understand the sentence better?

29 | Using Complex Sentences Rewrite these compound sentences as complex sentences with adverb clauses. Use the word in parentheses. Add a comma if necessary. `14.8 A`

City News

1. A new store opened in the mall yesterday, and traffic was terrible on Third Street. (because)

   Because a new store opened in the mall yesterday, traffic was terrible on Third Street.

2. The electricity went out, and a lot of people went to the park to keep cool. (when)
3. The city tore down some historical buildings and people are angry. (because)
4. The town opened a new library, but the old one is still crowded. (although)
5. They were putting in the new highway, and they discovered some ancient artifacts[17]. (while)
6. Some people are finding work, but unemployment is still high. (even though)
7. There was a third robbery at the gas station, and the police installed new security cameras. (after)
8. They cut a lot of trees down and they repaired the sidewalks[18]. (before)

Think about It Which of the sentences above sound better with a subordinator? Why?

30 | Using Complex Sentences Rewrite each compound sentence as a complex sentence with an adjective clause. `14.8 A`

SCHOOL DAYS

1. The students took the train today and they were late to class.

   The students who took the train today were late to class.

2. The teacher assigned a new book and it was really hard.
3. The counselor visited class last week and she spoke really fast.
4. We watched a video and I had seen it before.
5. The group presented first and they talked about Chile.

---

[17] **artifacts:** objects of historical interest

[18] **sidewalks:** raised surfaces on the side of a street for people to walk on

6. I spoke to a new student and she's from Morocco.

7. I bought a notebook for class and it was not the right size.

8. The teacher gave a lecture, and it really helped me understand the chapter.

31 | Combining Sentences Rewrite the sentences. Use the correct connecting word in parentheses. `14.8 A`

Restaurant Reviews

1. Try the delicious lobster. Stay away from the meat dishes. (although/but)

   Try the delicious lobster but stay away from the meat dishes.

2. Order any of their popular dishes. You'll be happy with your meal. (if/or)

3. I had a bowl of soup. It was the best I've ever tasted. (but/that)

4. The service at the Bamboo Restaurant was bad. They were very busy. (because/who)

5. The server was unfriendly. He brought our lunch. (and/who)

6. I've been to lots of steakhouses. I've never found a better one than Nico's. (because/but)

7. We were waiting for a table. They gave us a free cup of coffee. (if/while)

8. I heard that this was the best sushi place in town. I really wanted to try it. (after/so)

14.9 Introduction to the Passive

A

ACTIVE SENTENCES

	subject (agent)	verb	object (receiver)	
1	The custodian	**cleaned**	the floor	yesterday.

PASSIVE SENTENCES

	subject (receiver)	be + past participle	
2	The floor	**hasn't been cleaned.**	
3	Twelve people	**were injured**	in the storm.

	subject (receiver)	be + past participle	by + agent
4	This book	**was written**	**by** my professor.
5	The food	**is donated**	**by** local charities.

Most English sentences are **active**. In active sentences, we focus on the person or thing that causes or does the action—the **agent**, as in **1**.

Sometimes we want to focus on the **receiver** of the action instead of the agent—the person or thing that the action happens to. In this case, we use a **passive** verb form, as in **2 – 3**.

We use **be** + the **past participle of a main verb** (-*ed* / -*en* form) to form the passive. See Chart 14.12 for more examples.

We mention the agent only when it is important information. Then we often do it in a prepositional phrase with **by** + a noun phrase, as in **4 – 5**.

WARNING! We can only use transitive verbs in passive sentences (verbs with an object).

32 | Identifying Passive Verbs Circle the passive verb forms in these sentences. `14.9 A`

EARTHQUAKES

1. Earthquakes are caused by movements in the earth's crust[19].
2. Small earthquakes happen every day around the world.
3. They are measured using instruments called seismometers.
4. Most people don't notice earthquakes of magnitude[20] 2 and lower.
5. On the other hand, magnitude 7 earthquakes can cause a lot of damage.
6. Some earthquakes are deep and some are shallow.
7. The worst damage is usually caused by shallow earthquakes.
8. Other geological events[21], like tsunamis and volcanic eruptions, are sometimes caused by earthquakes.

Think about It How many of the sentences above have *by* phrases? In each case, can you explain why the *by* phrase was included?

33 | Using the Passive Circle the verbs in these sentences. Then rewrite each sentence in the passive. Do not include the agent. `14.9 A`

CRIME AND PREVENTION

1. Someone (took) a girl's bicycle.

   A girl's bicycle was taken.

2. Someone robbed the jewelry store three times.
3. Robbers stole money and jewelry from the safe.
4. Men guard both entrances to the bank.
5. An employee takes the money to the bank every day.
6. Cameras videotape the customers in the store.
7. The store owners always prosecute[22] shoplifters[23].
8. Police caught the thief in the park.
9. The police arrested the thief.
10. People steal things from supermarkets every day.

Think about It Why was the *by* phrase not necessary in the sentences above?

---

[19] **crust:** a hard layer on the surface of something
[20] **magnitude:** the power of an earthquake
[21] **geological events:** things that affect the land in a particular area

[22] **prosecute:** to officially charge someone with a crime in court
[23] **shoplifters:** people who steal from a store while pretending to be customers

34 | Using the Passive with *By* Phrases Complete the sentences below with the things and people in the boxes. You can look online for help if necessary. `14.9 A`

CREATIONS, INVENTIONS, AND DISCOVERIES

the Eiffel Tower

Marie Curie

THINGS	
Don Quixote	the *Mona Lisa*
radium	the Olympics
the Eiffel Tower	the printing press
the Great Pyramid	*Titanic*

PEOPLE	
Gustave Eiffel	Marie Curie
James Cameron	Miguel de Cervantes
Johannes Gutenberg	the ancient Egyptians
Leonardo da Vinci	the ancient Greeks

1. _Radium_____ was discovered by _____Marie Curie_____.
2. _____ was written by _____.
3. _____ was invented by _____.
4. _____ was directed by _____.
5. _____ was built by _____.
6. _____ was painted by _____.
7. _____ were started by _____.
8. _____ was designed by _____.

Write about It Choose three of the passive verbs + *by* phrases above. Complete the sentences using other discoveries, inventions, or creations. Share your sentences with a partner.

35 | Using the Present Passive Rewrite the sentences that you think would sound better in the passive. Include the *by* phrase only if it seems important. Then compare your choices with classmates. `14.9 A`

JOB ORIENTATION

1. The receptionists answer the phones.
2. You won't need to worry about the phone calls.
3. Someone opens the doors at 7 a.m.
4. Saul and Remy do most of the filing.
5. People store the office supplies in that cabinet.
6. You can call me if you need any help.
7. Someone picks up the mail in the afternoon.
8. Someone sets the alarm every evening.

14.10 Using Clauses and Phrases in Speaking

A	**STRINGING TOGETHER SEVERAL CLAUSES** **1** A: I went to the bank yesterday **and** I ran into Jeff, **and** he is doing great these days, **but** we didn't have too much time to talk **'cuz** I had to go to school, **but** I'm definitely going to call him soon and catch up more. B: Well, say hi for me.	In speaking, we often string together several clauses or phrases using **connecting words**, as in **1**. The most common connecting words in speaking are *and*, *but*, *or*, *so*, and *because* (often pronounced /cos/ or /cuz/).
B	**2** A: Why didn't you come with us last night? B: **Because I just didn't have enough time.** **3** A: I sold my guitar yesterday. . . . B: **Which is a good thing.** You needed the money. A: I know. Gonna miss it, though.	We often use just a **phrase** or a **dependent clause** alone as a response to a question or statement, as in **2 – 3**. **WARNING!** We do not use dependent clauses alone in writing.
C	**4** You can't wear that because of the dress code. **5** We have coffee, tea, and orange juice. **6** I stayed up late last night watching TV, / so I'm really tired today. **7** He's at home. / At least, / I think he is.	We use intonation and pauses to make our speech easier to understand. • We often use falling intonation at the end of a clause or a series of words, as in **4 – 5**. • We also sometimes put short pauses (/) after phrases and clauses. When you read aloud, punctuation can help you know when to pause, as in **6 – 7**.
D	**USING *DO* / *DOES* / *DID* TO EMPHASIZE INFORMATION** **8** A: Too bad you didn't go to the concert. It was great. B: I **DID** go! I was in the back, so you didn't see me. **9** A: Tom doesn't want to stay here, does he? B: He **DOES** want to stay. He's just not feeling well. **10** A: Did you live in Paris? B: Well, I didn't live in Paris, but I **DID** live in France for a while. **11** A: Didn't she take out the trash? B: She **did NOT** take out the trash. I took it out.	When we want to emphasize a contrast or unexpected information, we sometimes use the helping verbs *do* / ***does*** and ***did*** in positive statements, as in **8 – 10**. We **stress** the helping verb in these sentences. We often do this to show emphasis or to disagree with another speaker's statement. For negative statements, we sometimes use the full, uncontracted form for emphasis, as in **11**. In these sentences, we stress ***not***.

GO ONLINE

36 | Identifying Connecting Words in Speaking Listen to the story about James Holman. Check (✓) the correct box each time you hear a connecting word. `14.10 A`

And	But	Or	So	Because ('cuz)

Think about It Which connecting word above is not used? Why do you think this is?

Talk about It Listen to the story again. Then retell the story to a partner. When you listen to your partner tell the story, note how many times he or she uses *and*, *but*, *or*, *so*, and *because*.

37 | Identifying Dependent Clauses and Phrases in Speaking Listen and write the responses to complete these conversations. Then practice with a partner. 14.10 B

MAKING PLANS

1. A: Let's go for a walk. I need to wake up.

   B: *After I finish my essay.*_____

   A: OK. But how long will that take?

   B: _____

2. A: Let's invite Rosa.

   B: _____

   A: Yeah, her.

3. A: Why are you taking next week off?

   B: _____

   A: Nice! Post some pictures.

   B: _____

4. A: When are you going on vacation?

   B: _____

   A: I know what you mean.

5. A: Are you going to the show on Friday?

   B: _____

   A: Wow! You're really a fan.

6. A: Are you going to fold the laundry?

   B: Yeah. _____

   A: OK.

7. A: I hear you're leaving town for a few days.

   B: Yep. _____. Why not?

   A: Have fun.

8. A: When should we have dinner?

   B: _____. I'm starving.

38 | Using Phrases and Clauses in Speaking Complete each conversation with a clause. Use the connecting word provided and your own ideas. 14.10 B

1. A: I love that game. It's so much fun.

   B: And _____.

   A: Yeah, that's true, too.

2. A: I fell asleep at 7 yesterday.

   B: Because _____?

   A: Well, maybe.

3. A: When should I make the rice?

   B: While _____?

   A: That's a good idea.

4. A: I kind of want to stay home tonight.

   B: But _____?

   A: Exactly.

5. A: Will you finish the reading on time?

   B: If _____.

6. A: When did you go to the restaurant?

   B: After _____.

7. A: When should we buy the cake?

   B: Before _____.

8. A: Why did you turn your phone off?

   B: Because _____.

Talk about It Compare the answers you wrote in Activity 38 with a partner. How did you complete the conversations differently? Then practice the conversations.

39 | Identifying Pauses Listen to the article. Mark every pause with a /. `14.10 C`

Shark Attack

A teenager was attacked by a shark on Saturday. / Matt Adama and a few

friends were surfing when he fell off his board and felt a pain in his foot.

At first he thought the pain was from stepping on a rock, but then he

realized it was something much worse. He swam back to the shore, where

a man helped him. The man, who had military training, tied something

around Adama's leg to stop the bleeding. When paramedics[24] carried him off the beach, the teen was

surprisingly cheerful, even smiling for the cameras. The wound[25] required 40 stitches[26], and doctors say

it will take six weeks to recover. Adama says that he'll be back on his surfboard as soon as possible.

Talk about It Compare your answers above with a partner. Then take turns reading the story aloud. Remember to use falling intonation at the end of each sentence.

40 | Using Emphatic *Do* Ask and answer these questions with a partner. Give answers that describe your own life. Use emphatic responses, and provide an additional explanation or contrasting statement. `14.10 D`

EMPHASIZING CONTRASTING INFORMATION

1. You didn't wake up on time this morning, did you?

   "I DID wake up on time. I woke up as soon as my alarm rang."
   OR   *"You're right. I didn't wake up on time. I woke up an hour late."*

2. Didn't you work today?

---

[24] **paramedics:** people who have special training in helping sick or injured people but are not doctors
[25] **wound:** an injury, especially a cut

[26] **stitches:** short pieces of thread that doctors use to sew the edges of a cut together

3. You didn't use your computer last night, did you?

4. You don't really like school, do you?

5. Doesn't your best friend live in this city?

6. Didn't you eat breakfast this morning?

7. You don't study very much, do you?

8. You didn't watch TV last night, did you?

> **F Y I**
>
> In sentences that use *be* as a main verb or have a helping verb (such as *be*, *have*, or *can*), we often show emphasis by using the uncontracted form.
>
> A: You're not a student here.
> B: I AM a student! Look—here's my ID.

14.11 Using Linking Expressions and Sentence Variety in Writing

A

USING LINKING EXPRESSIONS

1 We are selling very few of that model lately, and the prices have gone up. **As a result,** we're not going to order any more for next year.

2 She couldn't find the type of sugar she normally used in the cake recipe. **Instead,** she used regular brown sugar, and the cake was not as good as usual.

3 You need to watch the plants carefully and take care of any problems immediately. **For instance,** if the leaves begin to turn brown, you may need to water more often.

4 Technologies in food growing may end hunger in this century. **In addition,** as we learn how to cure more diseases, more people will live longer.

In addition to coordinators and subordinators, writers sometimes use **linking expressions** to connect ideas. Linking expressions include single adverbs, prepositional phrases, and other forms.

The most common way we use linking expressions is at the beginning of the second clause or sentence, followed by a comma, as in **1 – 4**. Linking expressions signal what comes next. For example:

- *as a result*: a result or consequence
- *instead*: The next sentence contrasts with an earlier statement.
- *for instance*: An example is coming next.
- *in addition*: We are adding new information.

See Unit 11, Chart 11.9, for more linking expressions.

B

USING SENTENCE VARIETY

5 Many forms of exercise are good for you, **and** it's important to choose an enjoyable one. **For instance,** I love to play volleyball with friends. Volleyball gets you running and jumping. It also exercises your arms **as** you reach up to hit the ball. Stress is one of the worst things for your health, **but** enjoying yourself in a game helps to relieve stress. **While** you are playing, you forget about any problems or responsibilities you face.

In good writing, it is important to use a variety of sentence patterns. This makes our writing more interesting. The paragraph in **5** contains simple, compound, and complex sentences and a variety of connecting words.

 GO ONLINE

41 | Identifying Linking Expressions Underline the linking expressions in this text. Then write *result*, *contrast*, *example*, or *new information*. `14.11 A`

Health

1. Your mental health is just as important as your physical health. Take time to do things that relieve stress and make you feel good. <u>For instance,</u> make sure that you spend some time with friends and family every day. _____*example*_____

2. Some people believe that it's not necessary to spend a lot of time exercising. Instead, they say, you should exercise hard for half an hour every day. _____

3. In many countries, fast food is becoming more and more popular, and people are exercising less. As a result, more people are overweight. _____

4. Heavily processed foods like packaged food, frozen food, or white bread often don't have enough nutrients and fiber. In addition, many processed foods have a lot of salt. _____

5. Many people feel that they don't have enough time to exercise, but you don't need to spend an hour at the gym every day. Instead, take a fast walk around your neighborhood in the evenings. _____

6. Processed carbohydrates like white bread quickly turn into sugar when you eat them. As a result, blood sugar rises quickly and then falls. This makes you feel hungry again sooner. _____

7. Different kinds of fruits and vegetables provide different vitamins, so you should eat a variety every day. For instance, you could eat berries with breakfast, an orange for a snack, and both a green and a yellow vegetable with dinner. _____

8. Eating a wide variety of fruits and vegetables helps you get all of the vitamins you need. In addition, if you eat a variety of foods, you are less likely to become bored with your diet. _____

processed foods

foods with many nutrients and fiber

42 | Using a Variety of Connecting Words Use the connecting words in the box to complete this essay. 14.11 A–B

Food Preparation: Then and Now

People are better off now than in the past _____*because*_____ they don't have to spend so

much time preparing food. In the old days, people had more free time, _____

life is very busy now. People don't want to spend all day in the kitchen.

   Now, anyone can make a delicious meal in 30 minutes. _____, people

have more time to do other things, like work or spend time with family. Even kids don't

have to wait for their mom or dad to prepare food anymore. _____, they can

heat up a frozen pizza or make a quick sandwich _____ they get hungry.

Kids are busy, too!

   People can still spend hours in the kitchen making a big meal _____ they

want to, but they don't have to anymore, _____ that's why easier preparation

is an improvement. Now there is a choice.

| and |
| as a result |
| because |
| but |
| if |
| instead |
| when |

43 | Using Linking Expressions Connect the ideas in the paragraphs below using the words and phrases in the box. `14.11 A`

as a result	instead	for instance	in addition

SPORTS

1. American football players wear a lot of protection so that they don't get injured during the game. All players wear helmets and padding[27] to protect their bodies. _____, some players wear special collars to protect their necks.

2. English rugby is a very physical game, but the players rarely wear any kind of padding or protection. _____, they play in jerseys[28] and shorts, with only a mouth guard to protect their teeth.

3. Ping-Pong is a very popular sport in China, and many people begin playing at a young age. _____, it's not surprising that many of the world's best players are Chinese.

4. Soccer is the most popular sport in the world. It is played in over 200 countries by more than 250 million people. Many people say that soccer became so popular because it doesn't require any expensive equipment except a ball. _____, it doesn't require a special field and can be played in any open space.

5. In soccer, players pass the ball with their feet, but in American football, players don't kick the ball that often. _____, for most of the game, they hand or throw the ball to each other.

6. In the past, very few women participated in the Olympics. _____, in the 1952 Summer Olympics, fewer than 12 percent of the athletes were women. At the 2012 Summer Olympics, over 40 percent of the athletes were women.

7. When most people think of golf, they imagine players walking slowly on a grassy field. It seems as if golf players wouldn't get injured very often. But golf players use the same arm movements many times during every game. _____, injuries to the elbow, back, and shoulders are quite common.

American football

rugby

Ping-Pong

golf

---

[27] **padding:** soft material used for protection

[28] **jerseys:** shirts that are part of a sports uniform

44 | Identifying Sentence Variety Read this paragraph. Write *simple*, *compound*, or *complex* above each sentence. `14.11 B`

THE TURTLE AND THE RABBIT

complex
There once was a rabbit who passed by a turtle walking slowly down the road. The rabbit stopped and laughed because the turtle was so very slow. The rabbit said, "I'll race you to the top of the hill." The turtle agreed. The rabbit laughed again, and he ran quickly to the bottom of the hill. When he looked back, the turtle was very far behind. The rabbit didn't think he needed to hurry. Instead, he decided to sleep for a while. "I'll wait until he gets here. Then I'll run up the hill," he thought. When the turtle got to the bottom of the hill, he saw the rabbit sleeping.  He kept walking. He walked all the way to the top of the hill. Finally the rabbit woke up. When he ran to the top of the hill, he discovered that the turtle was already there.

45 | Using Sentence Variety Study this chart. Then rewrite the paragraph below. Change some of the simple sentences to compound and complex sentences. Add connecting words if necessary. `14.11 B`

Connecting words		
Coordinators connect two equal main clauses.	**Subordinators** connect a main clause and a dependent clause.	**Linking expressions** usually come at the beginning of a sentence or clause and connect it to the ideas that came before.
and, but, or, so	if after, before, when, while because although, even though	as a result instead for instance in addition

Listening

Listening is an important skill. It can help you become a success in the world. I listen to my parents. I find out important information. I find out what time we'll have dinner! I listen to my teachers. I learn when my homework is due. I listen to my friends. I discover what is going on with their lives. Sometimes they are having a hard time. Just listening to them will make them feel better. Business owners need to listen to their customers. They want to know what products customers want. Politicians need to listen to the people. They can take care of the people's needs. Teachers should listen to their students. They'll know what students need to learn. By listening we make life better for ourselves and for others.

Listening is an important skill, and it can help you become a success in the world. . . .

Talk about It Share the paragraph you rewrote above with a partner. What different choices did you make to rewrite the paragraph?

A | GAME Work with a group. Share information about your past.

a. Use ten index cards or pieces of paper. On each card or piece of paper, write one of the following: *but, or, so, that, which, because,* and three linking expressions.

b. Stack the cards upside down. Take turns picking up a card and answering the first question below. Use the word on the card and two clauses in your answer. Once everyone has answered, move on to the next question. When all the cards have been used, shuffle them and put them back in a pile. Continue until everyone has answered all eight questions.

c. Choose one group member to write down each sentence. Work as a group to check that each one is correct.

QUESTIONS

1. What did you do in the summers when you were younger?

   It's very hot in my town, so I went swimming a lot.

   SO

2. What was your favorite free-time activity when you were a child?
3. What was your favorite school subject when you were young?
4. What was your hometown like?
5. What did you want to be when you grew up?
6. What was difficult for you when you were a child?
7. What was easy for you?
8. Who was one of your favorite people?

B | CONFIRMING INFORMATION What do you know about your classmates? Write negative and tag questions about ten different classmates to confirm things that you think you know.

1. *You work at a restaurant, don't you?*
2. *Doesn't your brother go to this school?*

Ask each person his or her question. Tell the class how many you got right.

C | RECORDING A STORY Follow these instructions to record a story on an audio recording device.

1. Record yourself telling a short story about someone you know. It can be a friend, a family member, or a famous person. Spend a minute or two preparing, but don't write down what you are going to say.

2. Play the recording for a group. Listen to each person's story twice. Write down every use of *and, but, or, so,* and *because.* Talk about the story. Was it easy to follow? Were the relationships between ideas clear?

D | TELLING A STORY Work with a partner. Write a short story that you are both familiar with. It can be a fairy tale (like "Cinderella"), a traditional story, or a story from a movie. Use at least one simple, one complex, and one compound sentence and one linking expression. Meet with another pair and share your stories.

14.12 Summary of Sentence Patterns

CLAUSES AND SIMPLE SENTENCES

SUBJECT	PREDICATE		
subject	intransitive verb	adverb or prepositional phrase	
My grandfather	walks	slowly.	
		to the store.	

subject	linking verb	complement	
That recipe	sounds/looks	delicious.	← adjective
Bill	seems	a little worried.	← adjective phrase
Sasha	is becoming	a lawyer.	← noun phrase *only with be or become*
My sister	is	in Chicago.	← prepositional phrase *only with be*

subject	transitive verb	direct object
Hiro	sold	the house.

subject	transitive verb	indirect object	direct object
The lecture	gave	me	an interesting idea.

subject	transitive verb	direct object	*to/for* phrase (indirect object)
Rolando	brought	presents	for the children.

PASSIVE SENTENCES

subject	passive verb		
The trash	is picked up	at 6:00.	← simple present
His house	was damaged	in the storm.	← simple past
The street	hasn't been cleaned	yet.	← present perfect
You	will be taken care of	as soon as possible.	← future with *will*
Broccoli	can be eaten	cooked or raw.	← modal
Plans	are being made	to improve the city.	← present progressive

LINKING EXPRESSIONS

SENTENCE	LINKING EXPRESSION + CLAUSE
He lost his job and had no savings.	**As a result**, he couldn't pay his rent.
Many of her hobbies seem very dangerous to me.	**For instance**, she likes to go mountain climbing alone.

COMPOUND SENTENCES

MAIN/INDEPENDENT CLAUSE	COORDINATOR	MAIN/INDEPENDENT CLAUSE
They came early,	so	they got the best seats.
He lost his wallet,	but	someone returned it.

COMPLEX SENTENCES

ADVERB/DEPENDENT CLAUSE	MAIN/INDEPENDENT CLAUSE
Before you decide,	look at all the facts.
If you want more dessert,	just help yourself.

MAIN/INDEPENDENT CLAUSE	DEPENDENT CLAUSE
You can watch TV	**if** you get home early.

BEGINNING OF MAIN CLAUSE	ADJECTIVE/DEPENDENT CLAUSE	END OF MAIN CLAUSE
The woman	**that** Maria introduced us to	was really smart.

Resources

I. Non-Action Verbs

agree	consist of	fear	include	mind	recognize	think
appear	contain	feel	involve	need	remember	understand
appreciate	cost	fit	know	owe	see	want
be	dislike	hate	like	own	seem	weigh
believe	doubt	have	look	possess	smell	wish
belong	envy	hear	love	prefer	suppose	
conclude	equal	imagine	mean	realize	taste	

Remember:

- A non-action verb describes a state (an unchanging condition).
- Non-action verbs are also called **stative verbs**.
- Some verbs have more than one meaning. They can function as a non-action verb in one context and an action verb in another.

II. Linking Verbs

appear	become	get*	look	seem	sound	turn*
be	feel	grow*	remain	smell	taste	

* with a meaning of *become*

Remember: A linking verb can have an adjective as a complement.

III. Irregular Verbs

BASE FORM	SIMPLE PAST	PAST PARTICIPLE		BASE FORM	SIMPLE PAST	PAST PARTICIPLE
beat	beat	beaten		lose	lost	lost
become	became	become		make	made	made
begin	began	begun		mean	meant	meant
bend	bent	bent		meet	met	met
bet	bet	bet		pay	paid	paid
bite	bit	bitten		put	put	put
bleed	bled	bled		quit	quit	quit
break	broke	broken		read	read	read
bring	brought	brought		ride	rode	ridden
build	built	built		ring	rang	rung
buy	bought	bought		rise	rose	risen
catch	caught	caught		run	ran	run
choose	chose	chosen		say	said	said
come	came	come		see	saw	seen
cost	cost	cost		sell	sold	sold
cut	cut	cut		send	sent	sent
dig	dug	dug		set	set	set
draw	drew	drawn		sew	sewed	sewn
drink	drank	drunk		shake	shook	shaken
drive	drove	driven		shoot	shot	shot
eat	ate	eaten		show	showed	shown
fall	fell	fallen		shut	shut	shut
feed	fed	fed		sing	sang	sung
feel	felt	felt		sink	sank	sunk
fight	fought	fought		sit	sat	sat
find	found	found		sleep	slept	slept
fly	flew	flown		speak	spoke	spoken
forbid	forbade	forbidden		speed	sped	sped
forget	forgot	forgotten		spend	spent	spent
forgive	forgave	forgiven		spread	spread	spread
freeze	froze	frozen		stand	stood	stood
get	got	gotten		steal	stole	stolen
give	gave	given		swear	swore	sworn
go	went	gone		sweep	swept	swept
grow	grew	grown		swim	swam	swum
hear	heard	heard		take	took	taken
hide	hid	hidden		teach	taught	taught
hit	hit	hit		tear	tore	torn
hold	held	held		tell	told	told
hurt	hurt	hurt		think	thought	thought
keep	kept	kept		throw	threw	thrown
know	knew	known		understand	understood	understood
lay	laid	laid		wake	woke	woken
lead	led	led		wear	wore	worn
leave	left	left		win	won	won
lend	lent	lent		write	wrote	written
let	let	let				

IV. Spelling Rules for the -s/-es Form of Verbs

To form the third-person singular *(he/she/it)* for the simple present:

1 Add -es to verbs that end in -sh, -ch, -ss, -s, -x, or -z.

| finish | finishes | touch | touches | pass | passes | relax | relaxes |

2 For verbs ending in a consonant + -y, change the -y to -i and add -es.

| study | studies | worry | worries | deny | denies | fly | flies |

3 Three verbs have a special spelling:

| go | goes | do | does | have | has |

4 For all other verbs, add -s.

| like | likes | buy | buys | see | sees | speak | speaks |

V. Spelling Rules for the -ing Form of Verbs

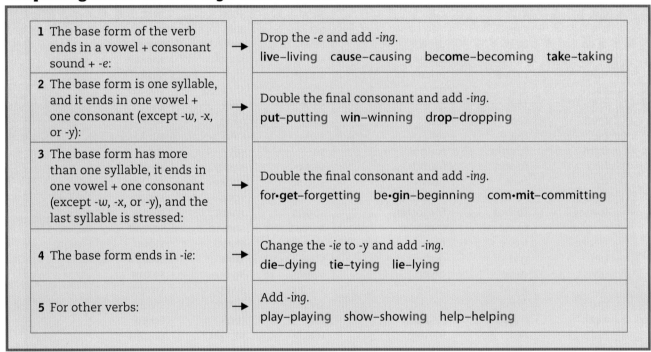

1 The base form of the verb ends in a vowel + consonant sound + -e:	→	Drop the -e and add -ing. live–living cause–causing become–becoming take–taking
2 The base form is one syllable, and it ends in one vowel + one consonant (except -w, -x, or -y):	→	Double the final consonant and add -ing. put–putting win–winning drop–dropping
3 The base form has more than one syllable, it ends in one vowel + one consonant (except -w, -x, or -y), and the last syllable is stressed:	→	Double the final consonant and add -ing. for•get–forgetting be•gin–beginning com•mit–committing
4 The base form ends in -ie:	→	Change the -ie to -y and add -ing. die–dying tie–tying lie–lying
5 For other verbs:	→	Add -ing. play–playing show–showing help–helping

VI. Spelling Rules for the -*ed* Form of Verbs

SPELLING RULES	base form	simple past
When the base form of a regular verb ends in -*e*, **add -*d*.**	close refuse	closed refused
When the base form ends in a consonant + -*y*, **change the -*y* to -*i* and add -*ed*.**	study worry identify	studied worried identified
When the base form has one syllable and ends in a **c**onsonant + **v**owel + **c**onsonant (CVC), **double the final consonant and add -*ed*.** (Warning! Do not double a final *w*, *x*, or *y*: *play / played, wax / waxed, row / rowed*.)	plan jog drop	planned jogged dropped
When the base form of a two-syllable verb ends in a **c**onsonant + **v**owel + **c**onsonant (CVC) and the last syllable is stressed, **double the final consonant and add -*ed*.**	re·fer re·gret	referred regretted
For all other regular verbs, **add -*ed*.**	open destroy	opened destroyed

VII. Common Transitive Verbs

VERB + DIRECT OBJECT

Examples: *begin the day; believe everything; bring a sweater*

allow	close*	end*	include	love	raise	show	visit*
ask*	complete	enjoy	intend	make	read*	speak*	want
attempt	consider	expect	introduce	mean	receive	start*	wash*
begin*	create	feel*	invent	meet*	recognize	study*	watch*
believe*	cut*	find	involve	move*	refuse	surround	win*
bring	describe	follow*	keep*	need	remember*	take	write*
build	design	forgive	know*	pass*	save	teach	
buy	destroy	hear*	leave*	pay*	say	tell	
call*	develop	help*	lend	produce	see*	think*	
carry	discover	hold*	like	provide	send	throw	
cause	do	identify	lose*	put	serve	use	

* verbs that we can also use intransitively (without a direct object)

Remember: Transitive verbs need an object (a noun phrase or pronoun) to complete their meaning.

VERB + INDIRECT OBJECT + DIRECT OBJECT

Examples: *ask the teacher a question; bring your sister a sweater*

ask	forgive	lend*	pay	save	teach*
bring	give*	make	promise*	send*	tell*
buy	hand*	offer*	read*	serve*	throw*
find	leave*	owe*	refuse	show*	wish*

* The indirect object can come before or after the direct object.

VIII. Common Intransitive Verbs

Examples: *The movie begins at 8:00. She doesn't hear very well.*

agree	cough	freeze*	lie	remember*	stop*
appear	cut*	go	live	ring*	study*
arrive	decrease*	happen	look	rise	swim
begin*	die	hear*	lose*	see*	visit*
belong	disappear	help*	matter	shake*	wait
bleed	dream*	hide*	meet*	sit	walk*
break*	drown	hurt*	move*	sleep	wash*
burn*	end*	increase*	pass*	sneeze	watch*
call*	fall	laugh	rain	snow	win*
close*	follow*	leave*	read*	start*	work
come					

* verbs that we can also use transitively (with a direct object)

Remember: Intransitive verbs make sense without an object.

IX. Common Transitive Multi-Word Verbs

act out	clear out	finish off	keep out	pay off	set aside	think of
blow away	close down	finish up	laugh off	pick out	set down	think over
blow up	come across	flag down	lay aside	pick up	shake up	think up
break down	cover up	get across	lay down	pin down	shave off	throw away
break off	cut off	get along with	leave out	play back	shut down	throw down
bring out	cut out	get into	let down	point out	shut off	throw out
bring up	dig out	get off	let out	pour out	sign up	try on
call off	dig up	get on	lock up	put aside	slow down	turn back
call on	do away with	get over	look after	put away	sort out	turn down
call up	do over	give away	look down on	put down	stretch out	turn off
carry on	do without	give out	look forward to	put off	sweep away	use up
carry out	drop off	give up	look over	put on	take after	wake up
check into	dry off	hand in	look up	put up with	take back	wash off
check off	dry out	hand out	look up to	read back	take down	wash out
check out	eat up	heat up	make up	read over	take off	wear down
check over	empty out	help out	mix up	ring up	take on	wear out
cheer up	figure out	hold off	move out	round off	take out	work out
chop down	fill out	hold up	open up	run over	take over	write down
clean off	fill up	hunt down	pass over	save up	take up	write off
clean up	find out	jot down	pay back	see through	tell off	

Remember: Transitive multi-word verbs need an object (a noun phrase or pronoun) to complete their meaning.

Some multi-word verbs have more than one meaning. We can use them transitively in one context and intransitively in another.

Examples: They **broke down** the door to get inside. (transitive)

My car **broke down** on the bridge. (intransitive)

You can't **turn back** the clock. (transitive)

Let's **turn back** now. (intransitive)

X. Common Intransitive Multi-Word Verbs

back up	cry out	get up	keep out	pull up	sign off	start off
blow out	dig in	go off	melt away	quiet down	sit up	take off
break down	drive off	grow back	move in	rest up	slow down	turn over
calm down	eat out	grow up	move out	roll over	slow up	turn up
carry on	end up	hang on	pass by	run away	speak up	wake up
catch on	fade away	heat up	pass on	set off	speed up	wear down
catch up	fall over	hurry up	pass out	show off	split up	wear off
cool off	get back	join in	pull through	shut up	stand up	

Remember: An intransitive multi-word verb = a multi-word verb that can be used without an object.

Some multi-word verbs have more than one meaning. We can use them transitively in one context and intransitively in another.

Examples: You need to **cheer up**. (intransitive)

I tried everything, but I couldn't **cheer her up**. (transitive)

Don't **give up**! You can do it. (intransitive)

I **gave up soda** and lost five pounds. (transitive)

XI. Common Verbs Followed by Gerunds

VERB + GERUND

Examples: *appreciate having; avoid getting; denied knowing*

admit	continue*	enjoy	love*	prefer*	risk
advise	defend	finish	mean**	quit	start*
appreciate	delay	forget**	mention	recall	stop**
avoid	deny	hate*	mind	recommend	suggest
begin*	detest	imagine	miss	regret**	tolerate
can't help	discuss	involve	need**	remember**	try**
can't stand*	dislike	keep	postpone	resist	
consider	dread*	like*	practice	resume	

* can also be followed by a *to-* infinitive   ** can be followed by a *to-* infinitive but with a change in meaning

VERB + OBJECT + GERUND

Examples: *hear him talking; saw my friends leaving; found them sitting*

discover	feel	find	hear	notice	see	watch	

XII. Common Verbs + Prepositions Followed by Gerunds

Examples: *argue about going; apologize for being; cope with losing; dream of becoming*

VERB + *ABOUT*	VERB + *AT*	VERB + *FOR*	VERB + *IN*	VERB + *INTO*
argue about care about complain about forget about talk about think about worry about	aim at work at	apologize for blame for care for forgive for thank for use for	believe in result in specialize in succeed in	look into

VERB + *LIKE*	VERB + *OF*	VERB + *ON*	VERB + *TO*	VERB + *WITH*
feel like	accuse of approve of dream of hear of think of	concentrate on depend on go on insist on keep on plan on work on	admit to confess to object to	cope with deal with

XIII. Common Adjectives + Prepositions Followed by Gerunds

Examples: *afraid of being; bad at making; excited about going*

ADJECTIVE + *OF* + GERUND	ADJECTIVE + *AT* + GERUND	ADJECTIVE + *ABOUT* + GERUND
afraid of aware of capable of fond of incapable of proud of tired of	bad at better at effective at good at great at successful at upset at	bad about concerned about enthusiastic about excited about happy about nervous about serious about sorry about worried about

ADJECTIVE + *FROM* + GERUND	ADJECTIVE + *IN* + GERUND	ADJECTIVE + *FOR* + GERUND
different from evident from exempt from free from obvious from safe from tired from	crucial in effective in important in interested in involved in useful in	available for crucial for famous for important for necessary for responsible for sorry for suitable for useful for

XIV. Common Verbs Followed by *To-* Infinitives

VERB + *TO-* INFINITIVE

Examples: *agree to go; asked to leave; decide to stay*

afford	can't stand*	desire	hope	plan	remember**	threaten
agree	claim	dread*	intend	prefer*	request	try**
aim	consent	fall	learn	prepare	say	volunteer
appear	continue*	forbid	like*	pretend	seek	vow
ask	dare	forget**	love*	proceed	seem	wait
attempt	decide	get	manage	promise	start*	want
beg	decline	hate*	mean**	prove	stop**	wish
begin*	demand	help	need**	refuse	struggle	
bother	deserve	hesitate	offer	regret**	tend	

* can also be followed by a gerund   ** can be followed by a gerund but with a change in meaning

VERB + OBJECT + *TO-* INFINITIVE

Examples: *advised me to go; reminded me to call; helped them to move*

advise**	beg*	encourage**	hate*	know**	permit**	teach**
allow**	believe**	expect*	help*	like*	persuade**	tell**
appoint**	challenge**	forbid**	imagine**	love*	prefer*	urge**
ask*	choose*	force**	instruct**	need*	promise*	want*
assume**	consider**	get*	judge**	order**	remind**	warn**

* object is optional   ** object is required

XV. Common Verbs Followed by Gerunds or *To-* Infinitives

Examples: *begin working / begin to understand; continue talking / continue to work*

begin	forget*	love	prefer	start
can't stand	hate	mean*	regret*	stop*
continue	like	need*	remember*	try*

* with a change in meaning

XVI. Examples of Differences in Meaning Between Gerunds and *To-* Infinitives

VERB	GERUND	*TO-* INFINITIVE
forget	I'll never **forget watching** her win the race. (= I'll never forget the time I watched her win the race.)	I **forgot to watch** the race on TV. (= The race was on TV but I didn't watch it.)
mean	Being an adult **means having** responsibilities. (= involves/necessitates responsibilities)	I **meant to call** but I didn't have time. (= intended/planned to call)
remember	I **remembered seeing** his picture in the newspaper. (= First I saw his picture; later I remembered it.)	I **remembered to call** him. (= First I remembered and then I called him.)
stop	She finally **stopped talking**. (= She was talking and then she stopped.)	She **stopped to talk** to me. (= She stopped first so she could talk to me.)
try	I **tried calling** but no one was at home. (= I made the phone call but no one answered.)	I **tried to call** but my phone wasn't working. (= I made the effort but I couldn't call.)

XVII. Common Noncount Nouns

advice	coffee*	flour	homework	medicine*	peace	snow
air	confidence	fruit*	information	milk	physics	soap
baggage	courage	fun	glass*	money	progress	spaghetti
beauty	economics	furniture	heat	music	rain	sugar
behavior*	electricity	gasoline	jewelry	news	research	traffic
blood	entertainment	grammar	knowledge	noise*	rice	truth*
bread	equipment	hair*	literature	organization*	safety	violence
cash	evidence	happiness	luck	oxygen	salt	water
chemistry	excitement	health	luggage	paint*	sand	weather
clothing	experience*	help	mathematics	patience	smoke	work*

* often has a count meaning or a noncount meaning

XVIII. Common Noun Suffixes

SUFFIX	EXAMPLES	SUFFIX	EXAMPLES	SUFFIX	EXAMPLES
-age	shortage storage	-er	painter singer	-ity	inequality purity
-ance -ence -ancy -ency	appearance existence vacancy frequency	-hood	brotherhood childhood neighborhood sisterhood	-ment	announcement development excitement resentment
-ant -ent	assistant consultant president student	-ian	comedian historian librarian	-ness	gentleness kindness loneliness sadness
-ation	examination organization	-ics	athletics physics	-ology	biology ecology psychology
-cracy	autocracy democracy	-ion	action connection	-or	actor conductor inventor
-ee	employee trainee	-ist	artist capitalist scientist	-ship	citizenship friendship

XIX. Common Noun + Noun Combinations

family	+	business / friend / history / life / member / room / support / values
government	+	agency / employee / official / policy / program / regulation / spending
police	+	car / chief / department / force / interview / officer / station
world	+	bank / championship / cup / economy / leader / record / trade / view / war
business	+	administration / community / leader / owner / people / plan / school / world
car	+	accident / company / crash / door / keys / radio / seat / wash / window
city	+	center / council / government / hall / limits / manager / official / police / street
health	+	benefits / care / insurance / officials / problems / professionals / services
labor	+	costs / day / force / market / movement / party / relations / statistics / union
TV	+	ad / camera / commercial / guide / movie / news / series / set / show / station

XX. Common Adjectives

These are the 100 most common adjectives in English in order of frequency.

other	little	human	full	current	serious	religious
new*	important	local	special	wrong*	ready	cold
good*	political	late	easy	private	simple	final
high	bad	hard*	clear	past	left	main
old*	white*	major	recent	foreign	physical	green
great	real	better	certain	fine	general	nice*
big*	best	economic	personal	common	environmental	huge
American	right*	strong	open	poor	financial	popular
small	social	possible	red	natural	blue	traditional
large	only	whole*	difficult*	significant	democratic	cultural
national	public	free	available	similar	dark	
young	sure*	military	likely	hot	various	
different*	low	true*	short	dead*	entire	
black*	early	federal	single	central	close	
long*	able*	international	medical	happy*	legal	

* common in conversation

XXI. Common Adjective Suffixes

SUFFIX	MEANING	EXAMPLE		SUFFIX	MEANING	EXAMPLE
-able -ible -ble	possible to	acceptable noticeable divisible		-ing	producing a particular state or effect	exciting interesting
-al	connected with	environmental experimental		-ish	describing nationality or language	English Spanish
-ant -ent	having a particular quality	different		-ive	having a particular quality	attractive effective
-centric	concerned with or interested in	egocentric		-less	not having something	fearless hopeless
-ed	having a particular state or quality	bored patterned		-like	similar to	childlike
-ese	from a place	Chinese Japanese		-looking	having the appearance	good-looking odd-looking
-free	without the thing mentioned	fat-free tax-free		-most	the furthest	southernmost topmost
-ful	having a particular quality	helpful useful		-ous	having a particular quality	dangerous religious
-ial	typical of	dictatorial		-proof	to protect against the thing mentioned	soundproof waterproof
-ical	connected with	economical physical		-y	having the quality of the thing mentioned	fatty rainy thirsty

Taken from *Oxford American Dictionary for learners of English*

XXII. Common Adverbs of Degree

absolutely	entirely	highly	quite	slightly	too*
almost	exactly*	more	rather	so	totally
awfully	extremely	nearly	real*	somewhat	utterly
completely	fairly	perfectly	really*	terribly	very*
definitely	fully	pretty*	relatively	thoroughly	

* common in conversation

12.3 Adverb Clauses of Reason (page 383)

	CORRECTION	EXPLANATION
D	**8** ✗ I was happy because learned something important. ✓ I was happy because I learned something important.	A clause needs both a **subject** and a verb.
	9 ✗ I'm proud of myself because now I **could** communicate with people in English. ✓ I'm proud of myself because now I **can** communicate with people in English. **10** ✗ I was sad because I **have to** leave soon. ✓ I'm sad because I have to leave soon. ✓ I was sad because I **had to** leave soon.	When the verb in the main clause and the verb in the adverb clause refer to a present time frame, we use present verb forms. When both verbs refer to a past time frame, we use past verb forms.
	11 ✗ We stayed at home. **Because** it was so hot. ✓ We stayed at home **because** it was so hot.	In writing, it's necessary to use an adverb clause in a sentence with a main clause. An adverb clause alone (*Because it was so hot.*) is an incomplete sentence.

Index

Class Audio Track List

ONLINE For these audio tracks and the audio scripts, go to the Online Practice.

Unit	Activity	Track File Name
Unit 8	Chart 8.6, p. 271	ELM2_U08_Track01_Chart8.6.mp3
	Activity 27, p. 272	ELM2_U08_Track02_Activity27.mp3
	Activity 28, p. 272	ELM2_U08_Track03_Activity28.mp3
Unit 9	Activity 1, p. 280	ELM2_U09_Track01_Activity01.mp3
	Activity 2, p. 280	ELM2_U09_Track02_Activity02.mp3
	Activity 34, p. 302	ELM2_U09_Track03_Activity34.mp3
	Activity 35, p. 302	ELM2_U09_Track04_Activity35.mp3
	Chart 9.10, p. 304	ELM2_U09_Track05_Chart9.10.mp3
Unit 10	Chart 10.9, p. 335	ELM2_U10_Track01_Chart10.9.mp3
	Activity 32, p. 335	ELM2_U10_Track02_Activity32.mp3
	Activity 33, p. 336	ELM2_U10_Track03_Activity33.mp3
	Activity 34, p. 337	ELM2_U10_Track04_Activity34.mp3
Unit 11	Chart 11.8, p. 366	ELM2_U11_Track01_Chart11.8.mp3
	Activity 35, p. 366	ELM2_U11_Track02_Activity35.mp3
Unit 12	Activity 17, p. 385	ELM2_U12_Track01_Activity17.mp3
	Activity 18, p. 385	ELM2_U12_Track02_Activity18.mp3
	Activity 24, p. 390	ELM2_U12_Track03_Activity24.mp3
	Chart 12.6, p. 394	ELM2_U12_Track04_Chart12.6.mp3
	Activity 29, p. 394	ELM2_U12_Track05_Activity29.mp3
	Activity 31, p. 396	ELM2_U12_Track06_Activity31.mp3
Unit 13	Activity 7, p. 407	ELM2_U13_Track01_Activity07.mp3
	Activity 25, p. 419	ELM2_U13_Track02_Activity25.mp3
	Chart 13.9, p. 428	ELM2_U13_Track03_Chart13.9.mp3
	Activity 39, p. 428	ELM2_U13_Track04_Activity39.mp3
	Activity 40, p. 429	ELM2_U13_Track05_Activity40.mp3
Unit 14	Activity 18, p. 451	ELM2_U14_Track01_Activity18.mp3
	Activity 19, p. 451	ELM2_U14_Track02_Activity19.mp3
	Chart 14.10, p. 463	ELM2_U14_Track03_Chart14.10.mp3
	Activity 36, p. 463	ELM2_U14_Track04_Activity36.mp3
	Activity 37, p. 464	ELM2_U14_Track05_Activity37.mp3
	Activity 39, p. 465	ELM2_U14_Track06_Activity39.mp3

OXFORD
UNIVERSITY PRESS

198 Madison Avenue
New York, NY 10016 USA

Great Clarendon Street, Oxford, OX2 6DP, United Kingdom

Oxford University Press is a department of the University of Oxford.
It furthers the University's objective of excellence in research, scholarship,
and education by publishing worldwide. Oxford is a registered trade
mark of Oxford University Press in the UK and in certain other countries.

Director, ELT New York: Laura Pearson
Head of Adult, ELT New York: Stephanie Karras
Publisher: Sharon Sargent
Senior Development Editor: Andrew Gitzy
Senior Development Editor: Rebecca Mostov
Development Editor: Eric Zuarino
Executive Art and Design Manager: Maj-Britt Hagsted
Content Production Manager: Julie Armstrong
Image Manager: Trisha Masterson
Image Editor: Liaht Pashayan
Production Artists: Elissa Santos, Julie Sussman-Perez
Production Coordinator: Brad Tucker

Special thanks to Electra Jablons and Rima Ibrahim for assistance with
language data research.

ISBN: 978 0 19 402825 7 Student Book 2B with Online Practice Pack
ISBN: 978 0 19 402844 8 Student Book 2B as pack component
ISBN: 978 0 19 402879 0 Online Practice website

Printed in China
This book is printed on paper from certified and well-managed sources.

ACKNOWLEDGEMENTS

*Although every effort has been made to trace and contact copyright holders before publication,
this has not been possible in some cases. We apologize for any apparent infringement of
copyright and if notified, the publisher will be pleased to rectify any errors or omissions at the
earliest opportunity.*

The authors and publisher are grateful to those who have given permission to reproduce the
following extracts and adaptations of copyright material: p. 31 definitions reproduced
by permission of Oxford University Press from *Oxford Basic American Dictionary*
© Oxford University Press 2011; p. 35 "Advice on Writing from the Poet Gwendolyn
Brooks," from "Gwendolyn Brooks," as appeared in *The Place My Words Are Looking For:
What Poets Say About and Through Their Work* by Paul B. Janeczko. Reprinted by Consent
of Brooks Permissions; p. 38 reprinted with the permission of Simon & Schuster
Publishing Group from *The Book of Answers* by Barbara Berliner with Melinda Corey
and George Ochoa. Copyright © 1990 by The New York Public Library and The
Stonesong Press, Inc. All rights reserved; p. 59 "How to Make an Origami Whale,"
The World Almanac for Kids, 2000, Elaine Israel, editor. Copyright © 1999 by PRIMEDIA
Reference Inc. Reprinted by permission of Infobase Publishing; p. 64 reproduced
by permission of Oxford University Press from *IE Transitions Student Book Level 2* by
Linda Lee © Oxford University Press 1999; p. 311 and p. 333 definitions reproduced
by permission of Oxford University Press from *Oxford Basic American Dictionary*
© Oxford University Press 2011.

Illustrations by: 5W Infographics: p. 55, 66, 74, 177, 221, 252, 256, 285. Mark Duffin:
p. 312 (top, 4 cars), 313. Dermot Flynn/Dutch Uncle: p. 73, 113, 335, 336, 469.
Jerome Mireault: p. 208. Kevin Rechin/Mendola: p. 116. Tablet Infographics: p. 22,
90, 114, 158. Joe Taylor/Mendola: p. 136, 226, 301, 353, 370, 415, 419, 467.

We would also like to thank the following for permission to reproduce the following photographs:
Cover: blinkblink/shutterstock; back cover: lvcandy/Getty Images; global: Rodin
Anton/shutterstock; p. 2 Giorgio Fochesato/istockphoto; p. 5 OUP/pdesign, OUP/
Graphi-Ogre; p. 6 Newton Daly/Getty Images, Simon Jarratt/Corbis, Gene Chutka/
istockphoto, Blend Images/SuperStock, Andres Rodriguez/Alamy, Image Source/
Alamy, Clerkenwell/Getty Images; p. 8 Paul Simcock/Blend Images/Corbis; p. 19
Brasil2/istockphoto, Bettmann/Corbis; p. 22 Blend Images/Alamy; p. 32 AP Photo/
Phil Klein, Dave M. Bennett/Getty Images, Walter McBride/Corbis; p. 35 AP Photo/

p. 39 Archer Street/Delux/Lion's Gate/Pathe/The Kobal Collection/BUITENDIJK, JAAP,
Tiger Moth/Miramax/The Kobal Collection; p. 42 Blend_Images/istockphoto;
p. 44 Visions of America/SuperStock; p. 46 Reuters/Corbis; p. 51 Gabriel Bouys/
AFP/Getty Images; p. 57 The Francis Frith Collection/Corbis, Caro/Alamy; p. 61
Prisma Archivo/Alamy; p. 62 Lordprice Collection/Alamy; p. 63 Grant Dixon/
Hedgehog House/Minden Pictures/Corbis; p. 64 Hulton Archive/Getty Images;
p. 66 kreego/shutterstock; p. 72 RW Photography/Masterfile, Lei Wang; p. 76
Angela Waye/shutterstock; p. 78 Jiri Hera/Alamy, Hans Laubel/istockphoto,
Bombaert Patrick/shutterstock, Karl Weatherly/Corbis, Hanka Steidle/shutterstock,
Worldgraphics/shutterstock; p. 79 Clint Hughes/Getty Images; p. 84 Atlaspix/
shutterstock, Pedro Ladeira/AFP/Getty Images; p. 96 ClassicStock/Masterfile; p. 105
Lauri Patterson/istockphoto; p. 118 Actionplus/AGE fotostock; p. 121 PhotoAlto/
Alamy, jump fotoagentur Susanne Treubel/Alamy; p. 127 OUP/Fuse; p. 139 OUP/
Photodisc, valzan/shutterstock; p. 143 Rich Wheater/All Canada Photos/SuperStock;
p. 156 Donato Sardella/WireImage/Getty Images; p. 157 Jurgen Frank/Corbis; p. 160
Paul Raftery/VIEW/Corbis; p. 164 Troy Wayrynen/NewSport/Corbis, Shannon Fagan/
Getty Images, David H. Lewis/istockphoto, Henrik Sorensen/Getty Images, Masterfile,
MM Productions/Corbis; p. 168 Jerry Dohnal/Getty Images; p. 170 Bettmann/Corbis,
Javier Pierini/Getty Images; p. 172 John Lund/Getty Images; p. 178 Aspen Photo/
Shutterstock.com; p. 184 Christopher Futcher/istockphoto; p. 188 KidStock/Blend
Images/Corbis; p. 191 BlueLela/shutterstock; p. 192 Cultura RM/Masterfile; p. 195
Phil Schermeister/Corbis; p. 198 Massimo Merlini/Getty Images; p. 200 Lucenet
Patrice/Oredia Eurl/SuperStock; p. 201 Mika/Corbis; p. 202 svetikd/Getty Images;
p. 206 Steve Debenport/Getty Images; p. 207 Kevin P. Casey/WireImage/Getty Images;
p. 212 Monalyn Gracia/Corbis; p. 216 ClarkandCompany/istockphoto, ThinkDeep/
istockphoto; p. 217 Kelvin Murray/Getty Images; p. 219 Russell Shively/shutterstock;
p. 223 Westend61/Getty Images; p. 226 AP Photo/NASA, Radharc Images/Alamy; p. 228
Ann Cutting/Getty Images; p. 231 Neustockimages/istockphoto; p. 232 Gelpi JM/
Shutterstock; p. 237 luciaserra/Shutterstock; p. 239 Jose Luis Pelaez, Inc./Blend
Images/Corbis; p. 240 Jerzyworks/Masterfile; p. 242 frytka/istockphoto; p. 243 Blaz
Kure/Shutterstock, Jochen Tack/imagebrok/AGE fotostock; p. 245 Aurora Photos/
Masterfile; p. 247 JGI/Getty Images, Klaus Tiedge/Getty Images, PhotosIndia/AGE
fotostock; p. 248 imagebroker.net/SuperStock, Stan Honda/AFP/Getty Images; p. 250
Panoramic Images/Getty Images; p. 253 STOCK4B-RF/Getty Images, Sollina Images/
Blend Images/Corbis; p. 254 MBI/Alamy, Blend Images/Alamy; p. 260 Eric Isselée/
istockphoto; p. 262 Gabe Palmer/Corbis; p. 264 PCN Photography/Alamy; p. 265
Jewel Samad/AFP/Getty Images, IOC Olympic Museum/Allsport/Getty Images; p. 266
Colin McPherson/Corbis; p. 268 AGE fotostock/SuperStock; p. 270 Niday Picture
Library/Alamy; p. 273 Hulton Archive/Getty Images; p. 274 Marc Brasz/Corbis; p. 278
khoa vu/Getty Images; p. 281 rusm/istockphoto, Leksele/shutterstock, hnijjar007/
istockphoto; p. 283 arek_malang/shutterstock; p. 287 Jose Luis Pelaez, Inc./Blend
Images/Corbis; p. 288 OUP/Jon Arnold Images, Ekkapon/shutterstock, Dimedrol68/
shutterstock; p. 289 GlobalStock/istockphoto; p. 291 Paul Prescott/shutterstock,
Andreas Rodriguez/istockphoto, Randy Faris/Corbis, Aping Vision/STS/Getty Images,
Andersen Ross/Blend Images/Corbis, Andrew Rich/Getty Images; p. 294 Annie Engel/
Corbis, LAURENT/GAELLE/BSIP/SuperStock; p. 297 AlaskaStock/Masterfile; p. 301
prochasson frederic/shutterstock; p. 305 JGI/Jamie Grill/AGE fotostock; p. 307
fotoVoyager/Getty Images, catwalker/Shutterstock.com; p. 308 Vanni Archive/
Corbis, Ellen Rooney/Robert Harding World Imagery/Corbis, Frank Fennema/
shutterstock, David Samuel Robbins/Corbis; p. 310 epicurean/istockphoto; p. 311
ZUMA Press, Inc./Alamy, Eye Ubiquitous/Alamy, Beverly Armstrong/Getty Images,
OUP/Ellen McKnight311, Ocean/Corbis, Eric Nguyen/Science Photo Library; p. 312
MS Bretherton/Alamy, Ralph Lauer/ZUMA Press/Corbis, CB2/ZOB WENN Photos/
Newscom, Alvey & Towers Picture Library/Alamy, Lisa S./shutterstock, XiXinXing/
Getty Images, Car Culture/Getty Images, Road & Track Magazine/Guy Spange/
Transtock/Corbis; p. 319 OUP/Photodisc; p. 322 Craig Joiner Photography/Alamy;
p. 325 Scott E Read/shutterstock, KidStock/Blend Images/Corbis, stocksolutionX/
Getty Images, Anne-Marie Palmer/Alamy; p. 327 Minden Pictures/Masterfile; p. 330
Norbert Wu/Science Faction/SuperStock; p. 331 OUP/Digital Vision; p. 332 Doug
Pearson/AGE fotostock, Sylvain Sonnet/Getty Images, Alan Schein Photography/
Corbis, Barry Lewis/Alamy, SeanPavonePhoto/Shutterstock.com, View Stock
Connection USA/Newscom, PjrTravel/Alamy, Iain Masterton/AGE fotostock; p. 333
Robert Eastman/shutterstock, Mikhail Melnikov/shutterstock, OUP/David Cook/
blueshiftstudios, Sirikorn Techatraibhop/shutterstock, Anan Kaewkhammul/
shutterstock, Lingbeek/istockphoto, ConstantinosZ/shutterstock, OUP/D. Hurst,
f9photos/shutterstock, wikanda/shutterstock, Gunnar Pippel/shutterstock, JM-Design/
shutterstock; p. 338 Armando Gallo/Retna Ltd./Corbis; p. 342 Charles Gullung/Getty
Images; p. 346 SGranitz/WireImage/Getty Images; p. 349 OUP/BLOOMimage; p. 351
Jon Hicks/Corbis; p. 358 Mark Poprocki/shutterstock; p. 365 Tetra Images/Corbis,
Martin Diebel/Getty Images; p. 368 Radius Images/Corbis; p. 371 OUP/BlueMoon
Stock; p. 372 Andrea Pattaro/AFP/Getty Images; p. 377 olaser/Getty Images, pdesign/
shutterstock, Artgraphixel.com/shutterstock; p. 378 OUP/Graphi-Ogre, Globe
Turner/shutterstock, Jessica Peterson/Tetra Images/Corbis; p. 379 wavebreakmedia/
shutterstock; p. 382 Lindsay & Gavin Fries, silentwings/shutterstock; p. 386
Lex Rayton/AGE fotostock; p. 388 Abel Mitja Varela/Getty Images; p. 393 Alija/
istockphoto; p. 398 pictafolio/istockphoto; p. 400 Jeffrey Coolidge/Getty Images;
p. 402 OJO Images Ltd/Alamy; p. 406 OUP/David Cook/www.blueshiftstudios.co.uk,
OUP/Dennis Kitchen Studio, Inc, anafcsousa/istockphoto; p. 407 Vl_K/Alamy,
karamysh/shutterstock; p. 410 Jo Ann Snover/shutterstock; p. 412 Blend Images/
Alamy; p. 417 B Calkins/shutterstock; p. 420 mathom/shutterstock, Mary Nguyen
NG/shutterstock; p. 424 James Morris/Axiom Photographic/Design Pics/SuperStock;
p. 426 BlueOrange Studio/shutterstock; p. 427 John Lund/Marc Romanelli/Getty
Images; p. 431 Zoonar GmbH/Alamy; p. 432 tarasov/shutterstock; p. 433 Junko
Chiba/Getty Images, Proehl Studios/Corbis, OUP/BananaStock, Wouter van Caspel/
Getty Images, Seokyong Lee/Bloomberg via Getty Images; p. 436 Album/Raga/Prisma/
Newscom, REUTERS/Tomas Bravo; p. 438 Chris Crisman/Corbis; p. 441 Keystone
Pictures USA/Alamy; p. 442 Tsuji/istockphoto; p. 444 Rich Legg/istockphoto; p. 446
Roy Ooms/Masterfile; p. 448 Sherrie Nickol/Citizen Stock; p. 449 Sigurgeir
Jonasson/Getty Images; p. 452 Bettmann/Corbis, Peter Yates/Corbis; p. 458 Richmatts/
istockphoto; p. 459 Corbis; p. 460 picturepartners/shutterstock, Denys Kurbatov/
shutterstock; p. 461 Naypong/shutterstock; p. 462 Ruy Barbosa Pinto/Getty Images,
Photo Researchers/Alamy; p. 464 Johner Images/Johnér Images/Corbis; p. 465
Jonathan Blair/Corbis; p. 468 Aspen Photo/Shutterstock.com, PhotoStock10/
Shutterstock.com, esting/Shutterstock.com, Justin Horrocks/istockphoto.